'A VERY GOOD BUSINESS'

One Hundred Years of
James Hardie Industries Limited
1888-1988

'A VERY GOOD BUSINESS'

One hundred years of
James Hardie Industries Limited
1888-1988

BRIAN CARROLL

ACKNOWLEDGEMENTS

Many people helped me put this book together.

The present Chairman, John Reid, and Managing Director, David Macfarlane, spent many hours with me, suggesting lines of enquiry to pursue, and commenting on my progress drafts. Bill Butterss spared time to see me on one of his flying visits from North America, and sent back useful comments on my drafts about aspects of company history that he knows well. Harry Hudson kept an eye on my progress drafts to make sure I did not stray from the facts in technical matters. None of them were the least bit heavy-handed in their approach, and none of them tried to give me writing lessons.

Annette Carter edited the drafts in her usual thorough style, helping the story to emerge more clearly. Christine Payne typed the many drafts we did as we tried to get it all right. Warren Penney took the whole accumulation of text and photographs and turned them into a visual delight.

Elaine Russell, Jane Fraser, Jennie Phillips and Claire Craig all put up with me with good cheer, helping the project along in all sorts of editorial and administrative ways.

My thanks to them all. They must all be glad we finally got it into print.

Brian Carroll

Melbourne
January 1988

Published by
James Hardie Industries Limited
65 York Street
Sydney NSW 2001

© 1987 James Hardie Industries Limited

First published 1987
National Library of Australia
Cataloguing in Publication Data

Carroll, Brian, 1930–
'A very good business': One hundred years of
James Hardie Industries Limited.

Includes index.
ISBN 0 9596775 5 0.

1. James Hardie Industries – History.
2. Business enterprises – Australia – History.
I. James Hardie Industries. II. Title.

338.7'67'0994

Edited by Annette Carter
Designed by Warren Penney, Snaps & Design
Typeset by Deblaere Typesetters, Dee Why, NSW
Colour Separations by Colour Scanners, Marrickville, NSW
Printed by Griffin Press, Adelaide
Printed in Australia

Previous page: Delivering Fibrolite in the 1920s.

FOREWORD

The opportunity to write the Foreword to this book, which chronicles the first one hundred years of James Hardie Industries Limited, is an accident of historical timing. I am fortunate that it fell to me to undertake the task.

'A Very Good Business' is intended primarily for the company's people – its present and former employees and its shareholders. Of course, we hope it will be of interest to those who do business with us and to those who are interested in learning more about Australia's past and the individuals and companies that have helped make it a nation.

The reminiscences of former employees, press cuttings, price lists, advertisements and other material were collected without any plan of the use to which they would be put. We are most grateful to all those who gave their time so freely.

Inevitably, a book such as this one will contain some compromises. We simply did not have the space to include all the interesting people and all the interesting events that have gone into our first hundred years. We are by no means unmindful of the role of the Company's many unsung heroes in its long record of progress.

The book deals only briefly with asbestos. The company-made products that contained asbestos, and as a result is involved in legal proceedings. We therefore believe it would not have been proper to discuss these matters, however seemingly unrelated.

In the past decade, the company has evolved from one that depended largely upon products using asbestos fibre as a raw material to one with three core businesses – building products, paper products distribution, and services and technology. Today, none of our products contain asbestos. We have substituted other raw materials such as kraft paper pulp, or we have, in the case of pipes, moved to new raw materials such as polyethylene or poly-vinyl chloride.

The development of asbestos-free technology and the transformation of fibre cement building products has been a long, expensive and difficult process – costing over $100 million. Now other international companies are seeking licences to use our asbestos-free technology and we have already received more than $1 million in royalties.

As well as thanking a large number of former and present employees, customers and families for their contribution, we also thank the many people who carried out the research which has been used in this book. Elaine Russell masterminded its production with cheerful enthusiasm and much attention to detail.

Brian Carroll, who is no stranger to the task, distilled the mountain of fact, folklore and anecdote into a book with great zeal and enthusiasm.

J. B. REID
Chairman
James Hardie Industries Limited

Sydney
January 1988

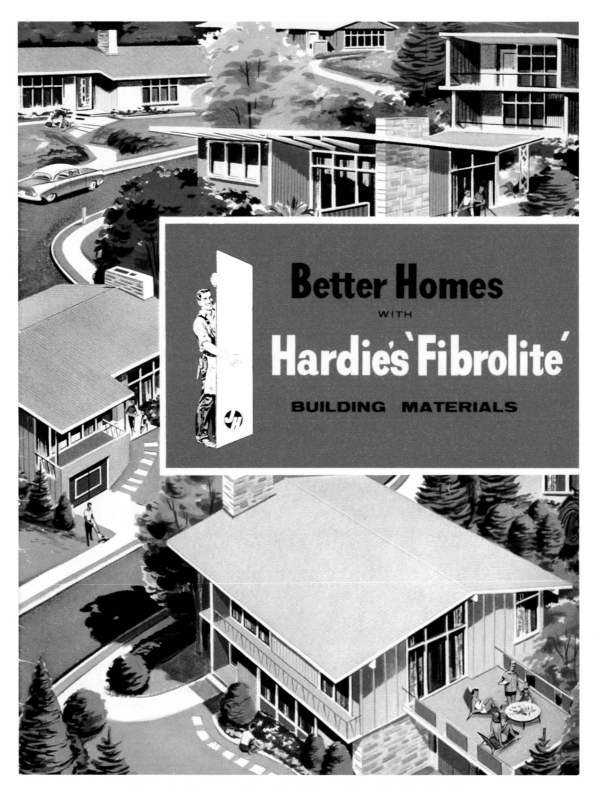

For much of its 100 year history, Hardies' prosperity was based on Fibrolite.

CONTENTS

Part Four: MARKETERS

Part Five: ENTREPRENEURS

Changing advertisements for changing times – Fibrolite in the 1920s, technology in the 1980s.

INTRODUCTION

Although James Hardie died in 1920, his name lives on in one of Australia's largest and most successful public companies. That it should have done so is one of the surprises of Australian business, for there has been no Hardie at the head of the firm since 1911.

In that year, the man James Hardie had taken in as a partner, Andrew Reid, became the sole proprietor. He led the business to growing prosperity and the status of a public company. Since his time, two of his sons and one of his grand-sons have led the firm, but they have never seen fit to displace the founder from pride of place in the company name.

James Hardie, a thirty-six-year-old bachelor not long out from Scotland, where he had worked in the family tannery at Linlithgow, started business in Melbourne in 1888 buying and selling consumable items for the tanners' and curriers' trades. He did well and was able to say he was 'working up what with care may develop into a very good business' when Andrew Reid, a family friend, wrote to ask about prospects in Australia.

Encouraged by Hardie's response, the twenty-five-year-old Reid arrived in Melbourne in 1892 and started work in the firm. The two men got on well, the business prospered, and in 1895 they formed a partnership. In 1903 Reid moved to Sydney to open an office there.

Another event in 1903 had a profound effect on the future fortunes of the business. While James Hardie was in London that year, his London agents gave him a package of samples of 'a new type of roofing and lining slate'. Made in France, it was known as 'fibro-ciment'. Hardie took on the Australian agency for the product, even though it was a little outside his usual range.

For a time, 'fibro-ciment' was no great success. It was in fact something of a loss-leader, owing to its high rate of breakage. At one stage, Hardie and Reid considered giving up the agency, but they decided to persist, and sales and profits from it grew steadily. Until, that is, the First World War made it all but impossible to import fibro-cement, as it had by then become known.

Andrew Reid had already been thinking of making fibro-cement in Australia. The problems caused by the war helped him make up his mind. He went to England and arranged for the supply of the necessary machinery and for a Swiss expert to come to Australia to help with it. The first sheets came off the production line at Camellia, near Parramatta, in May 1917.

From then on Fribrolite, as the Hardie product was called, began to play an ever-larger part in its business. In the 1920s and 1930s most of Hardies' more visible expansion was in Fibrolite, with new factories being set up in Perth,

Melbourne, Brisbane and Auckland and new products being developed, such as corrugated roofing, pipes and decorative board. In 1926, the business was divided in two, with one company to manage the Fibrolite side of the business, and one to continue trading in the wide range of agency lines that had been built up.

When Andrew Reid died, in 1939, his eldest son, Thyne, took control. An engineer by profession and personal inclination, he put the emphasis on technical excellence. His time at the helm, from 1939 to 1964, was one in which an Australian manufacturer could do this, for the economy was such that marketing and sales tended to take care of themselves. Thyne Reid brought the Fibrolite operations to a pitch of technical excellence that made the firm highly respected in fibro-cement circles around the world. Among the technical advances of his period were the autoclaving of Fibrolite sheets and pipes and the electrolytic extraction of mandrels from Fibrolite pipes. Both improved productivity and product quality markedly.

Thyne Reid's personal preference for engineering matters did not prevent him from seeing that marketing was becoming more important, too, and he ensured that good people were put in charge of it. By the time he died, in 1964, Fibrolite was being promoted not for sheeting entire houses and other buildings, but as the best product for particular purposes in composite construction. The quantity of Fibrolite used in individual houses might not be great, but by having some Fibrolite used in a large number of houses, total sales were steadily increased. Fibrolite pipes also sold extremely well, largely because of the vigorous promotional effort put into making their advantages widely known.

When Thyne Reid died, in 1964, his younger brother, John T. Reid, known to everybody as Jock, became Chairman of the Group. Jock had in fact been Chairman of Hardie Trading Limited for most of the time Thyne was Chairman of the fibre cement company. The two sides of the Hardie enterprise were only loosely linked, and had separate legal identities. By the time Jock took charge of the fibre cement operations, the sellers' market Australian manufacturers had enjoyed since the end of the Second World War had given way to one in which much more effort had to go into marketing and sales. Jock continued the established patterns of selling fibre cement building products for the uses they were best suited for, and promoting the advantages of fibre cement pipes. The strategy continued to work well, and the company continued to prosper.

The James Hardie Group was destined for great changes under Jock Reid's son, John B. Reid, who became Chairman in 1974 on his father's retirement. In 1977 the Group acquired the fibre cement business of Wunderlich Limited, which gave it control of almost all fibre cement manufacture in Australia. By then, although fibre cement still seemed to have a good future in Australia, its further growth was likely to be limited to about the rate of national growth. It was vulnerable to competition from other building products that served much the same purposes. It was also vulnerable to supply problems in that it depended on adequate supplies of asbestos, most of which were imported and hence much more expensive.

The clear solution was to diversify. But the problem was to find something that could offer comparable returns per share and be both compatible with the existing business and comparable in size. The solution came in 1978, when the giant international paper and publishing conglomerate Reed International decided to sell its Australian assets. In a $64 million deal, then the biggest takeover in Australian business history, James Hardie acquired those assets. Much of the Reed business was in building materials, which Hardie people knew well. Much was in paper and related fields, which within the next decade were to become major core businesses in the James Hardie Group.

After the Reed takeover, the Group set out on a series of further acquisitions, all designed to strengthen its position in markets it had entered with the takeover. In 1980 it acquired the remaining 77.4 per cent of Hardie Trading Limited, ending a separation of interests that dated from 1926. The pattern of acquisitions continued, albeit at a slower rate, to balance the Group's overall business.

In the mid-1980s James Hardie Industries Limited began to expand opportunities in North America. It bought into the paper and building materials industries there, began to export fibre cement building materials from Australia and New Zealand, and began preparations to start fibre cement manufacture there. It also began to invest, through an investment company, in high-tech industries that were in their early stages but seemed to have a promising future.

As the Hardie Group approached its second century, it had rationalised most of its operations by selling some at worthwhile profits, disposing of some with limited prospects at a loss, and closing down some whose prospects were even less promising. It had achieved its deliberate policy of eliminating asbestos from all its products, by replacing it with cellulose fibre where that was possible and finding substitute products where it was not.

The Group saw its future in three main areas: building products, paper merchanting and converting, and technology and services. It was still trading in raw materials and making fibre cement, but it was also involved in the design of computer chips. It also saw its future in world terms. It had joined that very select band, the small number of successful Australian-based trans-national companies.

PART ONE
MERCHANTS

JAMES HARDIE in the 1880s.

FIRST STEPS IN 'A VERY GOOD BUSINESS'

'I am working up what with care may develop into a very good business,' James Hardie wrote on 20 September 1891 to Andrew Reid, a fellow Scot who had asked about prospects in Australia.

Hardie was in his fifth year in Australia. He had opened for business in January 1888, at 523 Little Flinders Street West, in the burgeoning metropolis that saw itself as the Jewel of the British Empire, the Queen City of the South — the capital of Victoria. In the 'Marvellous Melbourne' of the 1880s, optimism seemed unbounded. Hardie was thirty-six when he opened for business there.

He traded solely on his own account and his letterhead said simply 'James Hardie'. He dealt in consumable and capital items for the tanners' and curriers' trades, both of which he knew well from long experience in his father's firm in Linlithgow, Scotland — Alexander Hardie & Sons, curriers and leather merchants.

Most items of luggage were made of 'solid leather' at the time James Hardie started his business.

Jim Hardie, as his Melbourne associates called him, had probably arranged the Australian agency for various suppliers before he left Scotland, either in person or by mail. He had certainly gone about his plans to emigrate quite methodically, and gathered an impressive range of references from Linlithgow people of note.

Hardie had been in Melbourne and had occupied the Little Flinders Street West premises for some months before he opened for business. His telephone, for instance, was connected late in November 1887. His telephone number, 923, he was to keep for some years, despite a shift from Flinders Lane (as Little Flinders Street West soon became) to Little Collins Street.

He had sailed cabin class from London on 7 July 1887 on the Pacific Steam Navigation Company's *Oroya*, an almost brand-new single-screw vessel which started her maiden run to Australia on 17 February of that year. She carried 126 first class passengers, 154 cabin class and 412 'China' class, and took about five weeks to reach Melbourne and Sydney. After a call at Plymouth to pick up more passengers, her route was most likely via Gibraltar, Naples, Port Said, Suez, Colombo, Albany, Adelaide and Melbourne to Sydney.

The ship arrived in Melbourne on 14 August 1887. We can imagine Hardie going into town to see what he could find out about the leather trade, and to look up people whose names he had been given as possible useful contacts. Then, although at least one of his references mentions his intention to settle in Melbourne, he rejoined the ship and went on to Sydney, where he arrived on 19 August 1887. His ticket probably included passage right through to Sydney, a fact that a canny Scot would no doubt have noted. He knew, too, he might be able to sell his wares in Sydney as well as Melbourne and thought he ought to look at the trade there. He spent some time there, then made his way back to Melbourne.

James Hardie began life at Linlithgow, West Lothian, Scotland, on 27 July 1851, the second child and first son of Alexander and Margaret Hardie. He also had two younger brothers and a younger sister. The Hardies were an old Linlithgow family, long established in the leather trade in one form or another. Margaret Hardie, James's mother, was the daughter of Walter Duncan, a thongmaker, and Janet Nelson, an orphan brought up in Hawick.

Alexander and Margaret Hardie were married on 17 August 1849 at Linlithgow East United Presbyterian Church by the Reverend George Sutton. They would doubtless have been married in Alexander's own church, the West United, at the other end of town, if it had not been without a minister at the time.

James Hardie grew to manhood in the family's substantial stone house in Royal Terrace, Linlithgow, a street that commanded views across the loch to farming land beyond it. He learned the leather trade in his father's tannery in the High Street, where he eventually took over the bookkeeping and office work. The Hardie tannery in Linlithgow carried on in the business until the 1960s.

In deciding to come to Australia, Hardie followed the same course as many a Scot before and since. He was one of three sons, and the family tannery could not support them all. He was the oldest, and probably the best businessman, the most likely to succeed in a new enterprise. He was born in the year of Australia's first gold discoveries, and Australia had been in the news all his life. Not being in robust health, he would have been attracted by the prospect of a kinder climate.

Hardie had certainly chosen what seemed like a good time and a good place to start his business. By 1888, Melbourne, barely fifty years old, was booming along at such a rate that many of its people, impressed by their own prosperity, had started

James Hardie made the voyage to Australia in the almost brand-new single-screw *Oroya*.

Employees of Alexander Hardie & Sons, curriers and leather merchants of Linlithgow, Scotland, taken not long before James Hardie left the firm in 1887 to start his own business in Australia.

to call it 'Marvellous Melbourne'. The prosperity was not to last, and it was not the whole truth about Melbourne, but it was what a businessman looking for opportunities would choose to see.

Melbourne's long period of prosperity had begun with the gold rushes of the early 1850s, and continued steadily through the decades since. The great influx of people who came in search of the precious yellow metal, and their offspring, eventually found jobs in the new manufacturing industries that grew up behind a protective tariff.

Melbourne, Anthony Trollope wrote in 1871, 'was the undoubted capital, not only of Victoria, but of all Australia'. There was 'perhaps no other town in the world in which an ordinary working man [could] do better for himself and his family with his work than... Melbourne'. True, the city's citizens were inclined to boast, a characteristic Trollope forgave them, since what they boasted about was 'certainly magnificent'.

All through the 1880s the rush to build an even greater Melbourne surged on. People streamed in. Between 1880 and 1890 the city's population rose from 290 000 to nearly 500 000. Industrial building went on apace and by 1890 there were 3000 factories, including many connected with the leather trade.

Melbourne began to boast, with some truth, that it had taller buildings than any city in Europe. It was the age of the Rialto and the Olderfleet. Only a few

Bourke Street, Melbourne, in 1888, the year James Hardie started in business. Much of the demand for leather was for harnesses for the horses that hauled goods and people around the booming city.

skyscrapers in New York and Chicago were higher than the lean, thirteen-storeyed Australian Building in Elizabeth Street. The new hydraulic lifts, of course, had helped make it all possible.

It was true that this great metropolis had nothing in the way of a sewerage system, and that Sydney people called it Smellbourne, but so far that did not seem to have deterred many in their headlong rush to be rich.

Former convict turned entrepreneur Simeon Lord is believed to have set up Australia's first tannery in Sydney in the early 1800s.

Australia's leather industry had developed along with its pastoral industries. Former convict turned entrepreneur Simeon Lord is believed to have started the first tannery, in Sydney, early in the 1800s. By the late 1880s tanneries were widespread.

In Melbourne, they tended to be concentrated where large volumes of water were readily available, such as in Footscray, beside the Maribyrnong River, and in Preston, beside the pipeline from the Yan Yean Reservoir.

The Aborigines knew the tanning properties of certain native tree barks, and white settlers soon found some wattle barks excellent for this purpose. Leather was in demand for many uses, such as harness and saddlery, drive-belts for machines, upholstery, boots and shoes. Melbourne had developed a substantial boot and shoe trade behind its tariffs, and a steady export trade in leather.

Although much tannery work was done by hand, it involved such devices as fleshing and splitting machines, and various chemical agents were used to produce the wide variety of finishes users wanted. It was in supplying such machines and chemicals that James Hardie saw his business opportunity in Melbourne.

The Master Tanners' and Curriers' Association, which had become inactive, showed new signs of life in November 1889. By March 1890 it was holding its meetings in Hardie's office, and in December 1890 he became its Honorary Secretary and Treasurer.

The first statement we have of James Hardie's assets is a balance sheet for 31 December 1890. Most of his total worth, £3469 1s 6d, was in machinery and chemicals imported for the leather trade. But he was not exempt from the speculative fever of the time, and bought land in the Melbourne suburbs of Surrey Hills and Essendon and at Drysdale (near Geelong). He had a half-share in a goldmine and money invested in a South Brighton brick company, which had probably done well during the building boom of the 1880s, but may have been faltering by the end of 1890.

Hardie's interest in land speculation may have been behind a trip he made to the Goulburn Valley, with a party of friends and acquaintances, on 1 January 1891. They were impressed by the Goulburn Weir, the irrigation systems it fed, and the plantings of peach, apricot and fig trees. 'In about four years time many of them can draw as much as £1000 profit from 10 acres of land,' he estimated, 'while those who go in for the wine manufacturing can even add to that; how long that may continue is impossible for me to say.' He obviously decided, however, to put most of his faith in the leather trade.

In September 1891 James Hardie's mail from abroad included a letter, dated 6 August 1891, from Andrew Reid, whom he had known in Linlithgow. Reid worked for Aitken Lilburn & Co., loading brokers, who handled Australia-bound

and other vessels out of Greenock. In his letter, Reid gave news of his family, mentioning the death of his younger sister, Jeannie. He also asked about conditions and prospects in Australia.

Hardie replied on 20 September 1891, warning Reid not to expect too much too soon. By then there were clear signs of the serious depression of the early 1890s. 'Anyone coming out from the old country has almost to begin life over again, by taking a situation at whatever he can get,' he wrote.

Some people who come out here are not content to wait... and, because they do not get a better thing than they left at home, at once take their passage back and give the place a bad name... Anyone who can get on at home will get on here, and in good times will make headway quicker here than in an old country. All that is wanted is patience and perseverance.

A meeting of the Master Tanners' and Curriers' Association. James Hardie is standing at the left. Squire Kennon, who was to become a close friend of Hardie's, is fourth from the left, seated at the table. Frank Luland, who was later to be a salesman for James Hardie in Sydney, is second from the right.

19

A MAN OF CHARACTER

James Hardie arrived in Australia with a sheaf of printed references, a fairly standard approach in those pre-typewriter, pre-photocopier days. They showed that he had a wide range of contacts in Linlithgow, and that they were willing to write of him in glowing terms. The dates, ranging from February to July 1887, suggest that he had gone about his preparations to emigrate in his usual unhurried fashion.

'I have very great pleasure in testifying that I have known Mr James Hardie... since he was a boy, and from that until now he has always conducted himself, either in public or private life, in a straightforward manner', wrote Archibald Mickel, who was Chairman of the Coal Gas Light Company, of which Hardie had been Treasurer.

To John Ferguson, Sheriff Clerk of Linlithgowshire and Town Clerk of Linlithgow, Hardie was a 'man of sterling character... universally respected [while] in his father's employment and latterly as a partner with him and his brothers of the well-known firm of Alexander Hardie & Sons, Curriers and Leather Merchants'.

George Dougal, Honorary Sherrif Substitute for the County of Linlithgow, was 'glad to be able to say that [Hardie was] a steady, sober, industrious and attentive young man, and ought to succeed in whatever he may engage'. James Walker, Rector of the Burgh School in Linlithgow, had in his dealings with Hardie as a fellow manager of the same church found him to be an 'upright, genial man of business in the best sense'.

John Thom, Solicitor and Procurator Fiscal, had 'the greatest pleasure in certifying that I have known Mr James Hardie, Leather Merchant of this Town, from boyhood upwards, and I know him to be the most diligent, industrious and capable in business, and obliging and agreeable in disposition'. A local magistrate, James McAlpine, had 'much pleasure in testifying to the good moral character he [had] always possessed, and to his practical and energetic mode of doing business'.

John L. Munro, of the West United Presbyterian Manse in Linlithgow, had 'found him to be a young man of great energy and activity, doing any work entrusted to him with promptness and devotion; of irreproachable behaviour; of spotless integrity; of thorough character'. He could 'commend him to any one who [wished] either a partner or a servant in business, as one sure to be faithful and upright'.

Now fully restored, this chair and bookcase, thought to have been used by James Hardie, were found in the old Hardie tannery in Linlithgow in the 1970s.

At present we are passing through a severe commercial crisis, and a good many clerks and tradesmen are out of situations, but these depressions in new colonies often pass over much quicker than they do at home; already some people say we are on the eve of a revival in trade, but so far I fail to see it.

There is no doubt that when railways are developed and irrigation schemes carried out there will be large farming industries carried on here including cheesemaking, butter, etc. ...Then there will yet be meat preserving stations built which will assume great proportions. ...The development of the mining industries again so far have been neglected except for gold [which is] now getting played out. ...Coal, iron, copper, tin [are] now being looked to and we may in many years see some large establishments in connection with these branches.

Hardie did not offer Reid a job in his own firm but said he would do what he could with the various shipping companies he knew. Reid's experience as a shipping clerk in Glasgow would stand him in good stead. 'A junior clerk gets £2 10s 0d, while some of the head ones may get as much as £6 or £10 a week,' Hardie wrote.

As to his own progress, he was '...working up what with care may develop into a very good business'.

JAMES HARDIE,
IMPORTER & LEATHER FACTOR,

James Hardie's early letterheads described
the firm simply as 'James Hardie'. He
started off as a sole trader.

ANDREW REID as a dapper young man.

CHAPTER TWO

A VOYAGE
TO AUSTRALIA

Andrew Reid had not had James Hardie's answer to his letter for long when he decided to take his chances in Australia. He had probably had the move in mind for some time, but he waited for the death of his sister Jeannie. She died on 24 July 1891, aged not quite nineteen, at the Reid family farm, Haining, at Haining Valley, finally succumbing to the pulmonary tuberculosis that had afflicted her for some years.

On 6 August 1891, only a few weeks after Jeannie's death, Reid wrote to James Hardie, as we have seen, asking about prospects in Australia. He was then twenty-four, a farmer's son just out of his articles with the Glasgow shipping company Aitken Lilburn & Co. He had no firm promise of a job in Australia.

On Saturday 28 November 1891 a group of well-wishers from the firm saw Andrew Reid off from Glasgow Central on the 1 p.m. train for Greenock, where he was to board the sailing ship *Loch Shiel* for his voyage to Melbourne. Even as the train left the station, he began to record his voyage in great detail, listing those who were there to bid him bon voyage, including his brother Charles.

His diary gives a matter-of-fact account of what must have been a tedious eleven weeks' voyage, without a single landfall between Britain and Australia. It got off to a bad start with weather that first prevented the ship from sailing for a week or so, and later blew the topmast staysail to ribbons, throwing Reid about the cabin, apparently 'to the amusement of other passengers'.

During this time, and the rest of the voyage, Reid spent much of his time studying shorthand, bookkeeping, arithmetic and logic, reading worthwhile books, and talking to passengers who had some knowledge of prospects in Australia.

He practised his shorthand by eavesdropping on the other passengers and taking down what they said. In this way he learned that one passenger, Ferguson, a 'toff in tone, style and appearance... owned land in New Zealand and Australia'. He took the opportunity of quizzing him on the prospects of a sheep run in Australia.

Among the books he read while waiting for the ship to sail were an account of Victoria from colonisation up to 1886 and a book by the Chaffey Brothers on the fruit industry in Mildura. 'If nothing tempting crop[ped] up in Melbourne', he could go there. He jotted down some calculations, working out that he could buy 10 acres at £20 per acre already planted with oranges, vines, apricots and other fruits. The trees would take three years to bear fruit, but during that time he could work on an adjoining estate for 6 shillings a day.

'A VOYAGE TO AUSTRALIA'

Sunday, 8 February 1892. All the passengers (myself the only exception, tho' I feel I would like to do it sometimes) seem to have completely succumbed to the habit of passing most of each afternoon in sleep. To me, the day seems too short as it is. I should prefer instead of killing it with sleep to have it lengthened rather to enable me to get thro' more work and reading.

HAINING VALLEY BOYHOOD

Andrew Reid, who was to do so much to make James Hardie what it is today, was born into a farming family at Haining, in Haining Valley, near Linlithgow, Scotland, on 23 January 1867.

His parents were Isabella Brown Reid (nee Grey), born on 12 July 1833, and Andrew Reid, born on 18 January 1829. They were married on 31 October 1855. Young Andrew was the seventh of their ten children, and the third-born of their four sons.

Andrew's early life probably followed the normal path of a farmer's son, and farming remained an interest throughout his life. At some stage he lost his right thumb, possibly in an accident with some piece of farm machinery. In true boyhood style, he buried the severed digit with some ceremony in the family plot at Muiravonside Church, recruiting the help of the household maidservant of the time for the occasion.

The loss of his right thumb probably accounts for a habit noted by many people in his business life. He wrote with his left hand, in a distinctively spiky style, using a pencil stub. He often asked office boys to collect short pencil stubs for him.

The Reid family had occupied Haining since the last years of the eighteenth century, but with the death of Andrew's father in 1896, the connection came to an end. The eldest son, Henry, had died in Cape Town in 1886, and the next eldest, Charles, had made his life in the United States. Their mother moved from the farm to Falkirk, to live in a house which was also called Haining. She died on 7 January 1906.

The Haining Valley farmhouse near Linlithgow, where Andrew Reid spent his boyhood.

Reid soon got into the swing of taking a cold salt-water bath every morning. He found it 'bracing and reducing'. He mentions his weight often enough in his diary to suggest that he was self-conscious about it. He missed his porridge for breakfast, and ate heartily at first. Seasickness soon put a stop to that on the day he took his last look at Scotland. It was 'a picture so exquisite as I can think would be unsurpassed for richness and grandeur on canvas or in any other land'. His heavy supper that night soon 'enriched the fishes'. He worked out his own cure for seasickness: stay on deck and take a little soup now and again. When he had to stay below, he lay on his bunk face down.

His comments on the people of Swansea, where the ship put in for repairs, give us a glimpse of what he regarded as important. They had 'no energy for business'.

Reid recorded his reaction to several books he read. Rider Haggard's *Witch's Head* he adjudged 'a fair story'. Kipling's *Light That Failed* was 'fairly interesting and strangely written'. Jerome K. Jerome's *Three Men in a Boat* was 'very funny, even excelling Mark Twain in some details'.

On Christmas Day 1891, eight days out from Swansea, Reid noted the weather as clear, the temperature in the sun 61 degrees Fahrenheit, the vessel's speed 8 knots. Ferguson, the landowner, made a pre-dinner cocktail of gin, orange bitters, sloe whisky and sugar, which Reid enjoyed with a cigar. Midday Christmas

Dinner included dumplings baked by Captain Radford's wife in Glasgow, which were judged excellent. He played deck quoits in the afternoon, saw two barques and a whale spouting, and played whist in the evening. Next morning, he took his cold bath at six, while enjoying a splendid sunrise and the sight of the horizon studded with eleven other ships.

He recorded the strained relations that developed among the passengers and between some of the passengers and the captain. At first he tried to keep clear of any entanglements, but then accepted a role as mediator. In the tropics he found the heat 'sightly above the degree of comfort'.

He took part in the dubious sport of hooking albatrosses and either killing them or letting them go after tying ribbons to their legs or pouring whisky down their throats. As the tedium continued, and he completed his bookkeeping lessons, he filled in time by making a fretwork penholder out of cigar-box wood.

At last, late on Friday 11 March 1892, Captain Radford spotted the Cape Otway light, and there was much hymn singing and inebriation on board. Next day at noon, the *Loch Shiel* passed through Port Phillip Heads.

When the first Melbourne newspapers came on board, Andrew Reid noted that Melbourne seemed to be bankrupt, many banks, companies and reputed men of wealth having failed.

None of this would have come as too great a surprise to a young man in the shipping business, who would have known that Melbourne's boom of the 1880s had run its course. But he could hardly have expected just how bad the coming bust would be.

He was soon at work with James Hardie, mainly as the outdoor representative. Within a few years he would establish good contacts for the firm, travelling widely to the other colonial capitals in Australia and to New Zealand. On 8 November 1893 he took on the additional role of auditor of the Melbourne Shipping Coy Ltd, at a fee of £2 a month. Their office was at the Shipping Exchange, 25 King Street, just around the corner from Hardies'.

Andrew Reid travelled from Scotland
to Australia on the sailing ship *Loch Shiel*.

CLARA BUNCLE, aged about eighteen.

CHAPTER THREE

THE FOUNDER
TAKES A BRIDE

On 11 January 1893, within a year of Andrew Reid's arrival, James Hardie, then forty-one, married twenty-seven-year-old Clara Buncle at her mother's house in West Brunswick.

Much of what we know about the Buncles comes from John Buncle's memoirs, *Experiences of a Victorian Manufacturer*. The family had been in Melbourne since 6 December 1852, when Buncle, his wife, Mary Ann, and their three daughters arrived there. (Clara was born in Melbourne fifteen years later.) They came from Crewe in Cheshire, where Buncle was a draftsman in the railway works. He left England disgruntled, having been passed over for promotion several times.

Melbourne in 1852 was a boom town, with people pouring in to search for gold or to ply their regular trade in the expanding gold-rush economy. Like many new arrivals, the Buncles had to begin their new life in a tent, so acute was Melbourne's housing shortage. They pitched theirs in Canvas Town, just across the Yarra River from the busy metropolis. They later moved to Bourke Street, and later still to a four-roomed cottage Buncle himself built in Byron Street, North Melbourne, during his first year in the colony. In time, they became prosperous enough to move to a fine house in West Brunswick.

A more mature James Hardie. He and Clara Buncle were married in 1893, when she was twenty-seven and he was forty-one.

Buncle was a competent jack-of-all-trades. He soon had a job in Melbourne as a millwright and pattern maker with Langland's Foundry. One task he did in his six months there was to install the first peal of bells in Victoria, at St James's Cathedral. When he lost his job at Langland's because he stayed away for two days to nurse his wife through a bad cold, he set up as a jobbing tradesman and soon began to prosper.

In gold-rush Melbourne labour was in such short supply that standards were rough and ready. John Buncle was enterprising enough to find as much work as he could handle. He painted his own sign on his North Melbourne house, and from then on was a signwriter. He had papered a room in his house in England and saw this as adequate experience to accept work as a paperhanger. His one golden rule was that every promise to a customer had to be kept.

To avoid having to go into town for hardware, he set up a hardware shop in the front room of his house. From this he moved into agricultural machinery and later started to manufacture it himself. As the years went by, the family came to be very comfortably off.

The Buncles had two more children in Melbourne a son and Clara Evelyn, who was to become James Hardie's wife. She was born at their North Melbourne cottage on 8 December 1865.

Economic conditions in
Melbourne in the 1890s had
become so bad that many
people depended on
handouts of food.

James Hardie and Clara Buncle were married in the ballroom of the bride's
mother's home, Milano, in West Brunswick. The ceremony was performed by the
Reverend J.W. Crisp of Geelong, and the bride was given away by her brother (her
father having died). The best man was Andrew Reid and the bridesmaid one of
Clara's sisters.

The newlyweds went to live at a house they named Lithca in Sydney Street,
Ascot Vale. This was the first of several houses they were to have of this name, a
well-known Scottish diminutive for Linlithgow. Here, on 21 March 1894, their
first child was born, Margaret (or Marguerita) Evelyn, usually known as Rita. She
died at Parkside on 26 March 1895, a few days after her first birthday.

Their next child, Vera Florence, was born at Flemington on 26 August 1895;
their next, Mary, on 16 November 1897, by which time the family was living in
the second Lithca, in Lisson Grove, Hawthorn. Their third child and only son,
Alexander James, was born in the same house on 3 June 1899.

At the time of his marriage, James Hardie must have felt some concern about
his business prospects. The Marvellous Melbourne of the 1880s had become the
Far-from-Marvellous Melbourne of the 1890s. In his role as Secretary and
Treasurer of the Master Tanners' and Curriers' Association, Hardie would have
been well aware of the depressed state of the Victorian economy, from which the
leather trade was by no means exempt.

'The finances are not in a flourishing condition,' the *Age* had said early in 1892.
Melbourne's prosperity in the 1880s was based not on its own productivity, or that

of its hinterland, but on a steady inflow of British capital. When interest rates rose in Britain, Victoria no longer seemed such an irresistible proposition. Moreover, wheat was at its lowest price for more than 100 years, silver had slumped badly, and merino wool was lower than it had ever been since Australia began riding on the sheep's back.

The first economic blows came early in 1891, three years after James Hardie opened for business. The building industry crumpled, unemployment grew, trade languished. People marched through Melbourne carrying placards demanding 'work or bread'. Where once there had been opulence, poverty stalked.

'Empty houses and shops were to be seen on all sides, a condition which is in marked contrast to that exhibited in 1888,' the National Bank manager at East Collingwood reported in September 1891. In Footscray, men loafed about the streets. Three firms there had ceased building railway carriages, while foundries and chemical works were far from fully employed. Northcote and Preston were now free from the pall of smoke that had previously come from Australia's busiest brickyards.

Banks began to close their doors, starting with the Mercantile Bank of Australia in March 1892, the one Andrew Reid read about even before he came ashore. The Mercantile had canvassed widely for deposits in Britain, from where 60 per cent of its funds had come. It was known to thousands of Scottish and Irish investors, so its failure was a considerable blow to British confidence in Melbourne. By then, more than twenty financial companies — investment banks, building societies, and savings banks — were unable to meet their depositors' demands.

> An adjourned meeting of the Master Tanners
> & Curriers Association called by circular was
> held in the Federal Coffee Palace on Thursday
> 27 Octr. 1892
> Present. Messrs Thomson. Vial. & Michaelis.
> Connelly, Westwood. Debney, Wally. Brearly
> & Secy.
> After minutes of last meeting were read and
> approved of. Mr Westwood who moved the
> adjournment. again introduced the subject
> of curtailing the out put; but owing to the smallness
> of the meeting it was arranged to let the Matter
> drop until we had a more representative gathering,
> Mr George Brearley & Secy were appointed to carry
> out the arrangements for the Smoke night.

James Hardie's role as Secretary of the Master Tanners' and Curriers' Association kept him in close contact with the industry.

Sole Agent in Colonies
/ — for —
Messrs. J. HALL & Co.'s
Machinery for the
Leather Trades

Tanners' Neutralizer

Messrs. SLACK & Co.'s
Celebrated
Evaporated Sod & Cod Oils

Messrs. HAY & Co.

Messrs. R. & J. DICK'S
Famous Balata Belting

Messrs. BUNTEN & Co.'s,
Valonia, Myrabs, Sumac,
Terra-Japonica, &c

Messrs. SANDS & CO.'S
Celebrated
Levant and Curriers' Ink.

Importer of
Best Newfoundland Cod Oil,
Setting Stones, Clearing
Stones, Sleekers, Knives,
&c., &c., &c., for
TANNERS and CURRIERS.

HON. SEC. & TREASURER
for
MASTER TANNERS
and
CURRIERS' ASSOCIATION.

The premises in Little Collins Street to which James Hardie moved in 1893.

When the Master Tanners' and Curriers' Association met on 20 October 1892, the members talked of the depressed state of the leather trade and how it might be improved. The meeting adjourned for a week, but owing to the small attendance at the resumed meeting it was postponed a second time.

The worst part of the economic crash came soon after James Hardie was married. Late in January 1893 the Federal Bank became the first of the Associated Banks to go under. The Commercial Bank of Australia closed on Easter Thursday and failed to open after the holidays. By the end of April, the English, Scottish and Australian Bank, the Australian Joint Stock Bank, the London Chartered Bank of Australia and the National Bank of Australia had all suspended payment. The Colonial Bank of Australia, the Bank of Victoria and the City of Melbourne Bank followed suit in May.

Opposite: This photograph, which shows the firm name as James Hardie & Co., was taken after Andrew Reid became a partner. Their partnership dated from 1 January 1896.

Some of the banks that closed had in fact been unsound. Others were simply the victims of rumour and panic. The fact of the matter was that Melbourne had lost confidence in itself, and it would be many years before it recovered.

To cope with the industry's economic problems, the Master Tanners' and Curriers' Association formed a 'sub-committee on the wages question'. It recommended at a meeting on 7 March 1893 that 'firms call their men together and suggest that a reduction of 10 per cent on wages be made at present, but when trade improves the wages be raised to the present standard again'.

In spite of the troubled times, James Hardie seems to have done well enough in business. In the year he married, he moved the business to a new address, 584 Little Collins Street West. In 1894 his letterhead described him as an importer and leather factor. He was the sole agent in the colonies for Hall's machinery for the leather trades, tanner's neutraliser, Slack's 'celebrated evaporated sod and cod oils', Dick's 'famous Balata belting', Sand's 'celebrated Levant and curriers' ink', and Bunten's valonia, myrabs, sumac and terra-japonica. He imported the best Newfoundland cod oil, setting stones, clearing stones, sleekers, knives and other items used by tanners and curriers.

By 1895 he felt prosperous enough to take Andrew Reid in as a full partner, and Reid was confident enough of the future to accept. The partnership dated from 1 January 1896, on which date the firm became James Hardie & Co.

The two men were a good combination. James Hardie was the office man, who by his own description was retiring and nervous. Nobody could have said that about Andrew Reid, who had a lot of Scottish charm and liked face-to-face contacts with people. Hardie had the capital the business needed, Reid the vigour to make it work.

Part of Andrew Reid's notes on his voyage to Europe and America in 1899. They recorded that he was 'Engaged 31st May, married 26th Oct 1899 to Peggy Thyne'.

CHAPTER FOUR

ANDREW REID ABROAD

Andrew Reid spent most of 1899 abroad, on the first of what were to be frequent overseas trips selling leather, finding new agencies and keeping up with industry trends. Soon after his return, the *Australian Leather Journal* ran a long interview with him. 'He is the sort of man who should take such trips,' the *Journal* said, 'because he can make use of the two very sensible eyes in his head, and the brain is a clear one.'

He told the *Journal* he had left Melbourne on 14 February 1899. Singapore he found 'one of the busiest of towns, but altogether Eastern — a regular crush of all races of men... a meeting place of the tribes'. While there, he had gone over the 'Gambier' country, 'for it was not pleasure that took him to Singapore'. Gambier (an oriental shrub, the extract of which is used in tanning) was a 'splendid little shrub' and had gone up to £28 a ton. The Americans thought a great deal of it for tanning ooze calf, with good reason, for the leather it produced was mellow and at the same time tough.

In India, where he visited Calcutta, Agra, Cawnpore and Bombay, Reid found only two tanneries with any pretence to be up-to-date, both in Cawnpore. In all the rest of India, the appliances were most primitive: tubs, in fact. When you could hire a man for two shillings a week, you did not trouble to put in machinery, the prime object of which was to save labour.

He had not been afraid to go to Bombay, even though bubonic plague was raging at the time of his visit, he told the *Journal*. Other Europeans were not scared, so why should he be? The plague 'attacked only the natives', he said, 'and they died like flies'.

Anyway, he had wanted to see the trade in myrobalan, an astringent, plum-like fruit used in dyeing and tanning. It was carried down from the jungle in bags and then sorted. The best were creamy coloured, but even the black were valuable, and were shipped to England to make extract. He visited all the godowns, as warehouses were called in Bombay. The trade done there was very large, and tanning had a big share in it. He thought his visit would not 'turn out altogether unprofitable'.

From India, Reid went on to Egypt, where he landed at Suez and took the train to Cairo and Alexandria. British rule had completely gained the confidence of the people, he decided, his conversation with at least one man in Cairo having fully borne out that view. He saw the pyramids and some of the great temples, and declared that Cairo, although an essentially Oriental city, was taking on a European look, thanks to the interference of the energetic west. In Athens, he wandered about the Acropolis and 'all the usual spots', as the *Journal* put it.

Margaret (Peggy) Reid, nee
Thyne. She and Andrew Reid
were married in Edinburgh on
26 October 1899.

WEDDING BELLS.— Mr. Andrew Reid, partner in the firm of Jas.
Hardie and Co., Melbourne, has married in Edinburgh Miss Peggy
Thyne. The reception was held at Roxburghe Hotel. Her brother,
Dr. George Thyne, gave away the bride. Mr. and Mrs. Reid left for
America to spend their honeymoon, and intended, after returning to
London, to leave for Australia.

The invitation card for the wedding was worded as follows :—

Dr. and Mrs. Thyne

request the pleasure of your Company at the Marriage of their Sister
Peggy, to Mr. Andrew Reid, in Free St. Bernard's Church, Henderson
Row, on Friday, 28th July, at 2.15 o'clock, and after that at the Rox-
burghe Hotel, Charlotte Square.

R.S.V.P.

2 Deans Terrace,
Edinburgh.   Carriages at 4.15.

After those two brief interludes as a tourist, Reid was back on the leather trail. He went to Smyrna, on the west coast of Asian Turkey, the home of valonia, a kind of oak whose acorn cups were used in tanning, dyeing and making ink. It was a very ornamental tree, maturing in less than twenty years, and Reid thought the government should encourage its cultivation in Victoria. From Smyrna he visited the ruins at Ephesus, including the remains of the Temple of Diana, the great goddess of the hunt.

Then it was on to Palermo, in Sicily, to see the trade in sumac, another shrub whose dried and ground leaves were used in tanning. It was often adulterated to give it a brighter look, but the Italian government had stepped in, and all packs had to be marked with the amount of adulteration. Anybody who bought the unadulterated article could be sure of the purity of his purchase, Reid told the *Journal*. That was one benefit of a somewhat autocratic government, he felt. It wouldn't stand any nonsense and imposed heavy penalties for evasion.

There was not much tanning done in Italy, but at Pompeii Reid had seen what was probably the oldest tannery in the world. It was in working order, but far from up-to-date. Any leather made there was used locally, but the surplus hides were exported to London, which had 'the knack of collecting everything to itself from all corners of the earth'.

In Paris Reid saw through several tanneries, but French tanners were very chary of giving hints, or even allowing visits. French calfskin had long had a high reputation, but it had been superseded in the open market of the world, no matter how steadily it might still hold its own at home. Paris was one of the loveliest cities in the world, Reid thought, and 'a man could spend a month there without bothering much about business'.

He was in the heart of business once he crossed the Channel, visiting all parts of Britain except the west. The largest tannery he saw was Martin and Miller of Glasgow, which handled 3000 skins a week. He also saw other big concerns such as William Paul and Co. (Limited) of Leeds, and Walker and Sons of Bolton.

English leather he thought to be 'simply the best in the world', especially the sole leather. John Bull did not hurry himself, as a rule, and took his time to do all things well. In the higher grades of sole, there was a solidity and finish about the English leather that people looked for in vain elsewhere.

In other grades, Australian leather compared very well indeed, as proved by the prices it commanded in the English market. Reid had to admit, however, that some leather imported from certain parts of Australia was retanned when it got to England. This may not have been on account of its inferiority, but with a view to selling it at a higher price as English.

The biggest of all the tanneries Reid saw were in America. The American Oak Leather Company, of Cincinnati, put through 1200 hides a day. The Pfister Vogel Co. of Milwaukee used up to 2400 hides and 4000 calfskins a week. A big combine amongst all the great tanneries there meant they were now making money. He did not think there was much chance of a combine in Australia, which had 'too many small men in business who must get rid of their stuff by hook or by crook'. People seemed to work more unanimously in America, Reid said. Their market was large and secure, and they indulged in little of the jealousy so rampant in other countries he could name.

Opposite: The *Australian Leather Journal* announced the date of Andrew and Peggy Reid's marriage incorrectly as 28 July 1899. They were in fact married on 26 October 1899, after Andrew had made a business trip to North America.

The trade was simply booming in America, even though it had been depressed enough a short time before. Wages were very high, with a man on a splitting machine earning from £8 to £10 a week, compared to about £3 in Australia. Still, 'our Yankee cousin' had to pay through the nose for everything, and workers there were not as well off as those in Britain and Australia.

The high price of labour compelled tanners in America to use machinery in every way ingenuity could discover. The Blumental tannery at Wilmington had 350 glazing machines in one room. Fleshing, unhairing, setting out and shaving, all done by hand in Australia, were done just as well in America by machines. Electricity was widely used, especially in beam houses, where the hides were moved about in pits of lime solution in preparation for removing the hair from them.

If British and Australian tanners were to keep up-to-date, they would need to go in for machinery, Reid told the *Journal*. It was unavoidable. When you could see 350 glazing machines, 80 staking machines, 60 pulling-out machines, 12 or 16 flicking machines, and sometimes 20 or 25 shaving machines under one roof, it was clear that there must be something saved by using them.

There were trusts in everything in America, and these grew into big monopolies, which took the gilt off high wages. The tanners could not combine in Australia, because there were too many of them, big and small, and they had to depend on an outside market. But a great deal could be done by working together to restrict the price of raw materials.

Reid did not know whether this could be brought about in Australia. But he did know that 'the Australian tanner who can afford to invest in the most recent machinery, and devote his attention to special lines of stock, will come off on top'.

The Justice leather-measuring machine was one of many products for which James Hardie & Co. became Australian agents.

A single man when he left Australia, Andrew Reid came back married. His bride was Margaret (usually known as Peggy) Thyne, daughter of John and Jane (nee Jackson) Thyne, who had farmed at Bonnytoun at Linlithgow. Both her parents were dead.

Andrew Reid and Peggy Thyne had known each other before he left Linlithgow, and they had kept up correspondence in the ensuing nine years. The *Journal* reported at first that the marriage was planned for 28 July 1899. It did not take place then, but on 26 October 1899, so it seems that Andrew and Peggy (or perhaps Andrew alone) had a change of mind about the date.

The postponement may have been related to Andrew's plans for travel in the United States, where the couple had intended to honeymoon on their way to Australia. Perhaps Peggy felt he should get business off his mind first, so he could give the honeymoon his full attention. From his point of view, if for some reason the proposed dates did not fit in with his commercial arrangements, his dedication to business might have dictated that it take precedence over domesticity. It always did in their future life together, with Peggy's apparent concurrence and understanding. Perhaps Andrew had a need to go to the United States earlier than expected, or to be in Britain later.

Peggy, however, was prepared to tolerate only one postponement. While Andrew was in New York he cabled her saying he had a great deal of business to do, and asked if they could delay the wedding for a week or two. Her reply has not survived, but he was back in Edinburgh by the day originally appointed. Apparently his 'business' included seeing New York's triumphal reception for Admiral Dewey, the hero of the Spanish-American War, who had led the United States fleet to victory over the Spanish fleet in Manila Harbour in the Philippines a few months earlier.

The wedding took place at Free St Bernard's Church, Henderson Row, Edinburgh. George Steven officiated, and the bride was given away by her twin brother, Dr George Thyne, who (with his wife Maria) issued the wedding invitations. The witnesses were Madge Thyne, the wife of the bride's elder brother, Thomas Jackson Thyne, and John Reid, the groom's younger brother. Andrew was thirty-two, Peggy thirty-one.

They left London on 15 November 1899 on the SS *Moravian*, bound via Teneriffe and Cape Town for Melbourne, where they arrived on Boxing Day, 26 December 1899.

180   THE AUSTRALIAN LEATHER JOURNAL.   JULY 15, 1901

CHAPTER FIVE

AN OFFICE IN SYDNEY

Soon after his return from abroad, Reid convinced Hardie the firm should have an office in Sydney, and in March 1900 he and Peggy went there to live. Reid was now the thrusting half of the partnership. James Hardie might have been happy to have the Melbourne business coast along, keeping within its financial resources. But not Andrew Reid. He was, according to the *Australian Leather Journal*, 'one of those very much alive and up-to-date business men who are always on the go'.

The firm needed to be in closer touch with its New South Wales and Queensland clients. There were plans to set up and manage a workshop in Sydney for Joseph Hall and Company, leather machinery makers of Leeds, for whom Hardies were the Australian agent.

The new office was in a small section of the office of J. Kennon and Son at 51 Pitt Street. Reid started there as a one-man band, selling and attending to such tasks as customs clearances by day, doing the books and mail at night. By June he had rented an office at 5 Macquarie Place, handy to the Circular Quay wharves.

Opposite: This advertisement from the *Australian Leather Journal* of 15 July 1901 lists the firm's second Sydney office, at 5 Macquarie Place. The first was a small section of the office of J. Kennon and Son at 51 Pitt Street.

George Street, Sydney, about the turn of the century, when Andrew Reid set up the firm's first Sydney office.

The Sydney office soon moved a few doors to larger premises, at 11 Macquarie Place.

In June 1900 Reid was back in Melbourne for a time while Hardie went to Adelaide, where he did good business selling Hall's tannery machines. When Reid went to New Zealand on a business trip, in July 1900, John Meighan came up from Melbourne to look after the Sydney office. Reid went to New Zealand fairly often and usually had a successful trip.

Reid soon began to develop a Sydney staff, and among those he appointed were two 'boys' destined to have a marked effect on the firm's destiny. George Rogers Sutton joined him in September 1900 as bookkeeper, shorthand writer and typist at 15 shillings ($1.50) a week, typing on a Blickensderfer that was even then a museum piece. He took over the not very onerous task of customs clearances in what was still the Free Trade colony of New South Wales. He also paid regular visits to the wharves to watch for goods consigned to the firm. In time, he would become Chairman of the Hardie holding company.

In June 1903 a bright, chubby-faced lad appeared at the counter and asked Sutton if there were any vacancies. There was one, and Stewart Walter D'Arrietta joined the firm as an office boy, at 5 shillings (50 cents) a week. In time, he would become Joint Managing Director.

Many of D'Arrietta's early tasks were related to the firm's Sydney agency for the Melbourne Steamship Company, which it had taken on in October 1901. This meant that more space was needed, and the firm moved a few doors to 11 Macquarie Place. It also had a store in Arbitration Street, which was also handy to Circular Quay. Hardies lost this business in 1904, when the Melbourne Steamship Company opened its own Sydney office, Andrew Reid being appointed Local Director, an appointment he held until the day he died.

James Hardie & Co.'s other trade continued to prosper, and in 1908 its offices and store were moved to the southern wing of the old Naval Stores Building at Circular Quay West, rented from the Sydney Harbour Trust. At first this seemed to offer far more space than the firm needed, but all floors were soon well stocked.

To service its valuable machinery agencies, in May 1902 the firm arranged for George Cropper, a 'competent workman' who had wide experience with tanning machinery, to be sent out from England by Joseph Hall and Company. In 1903, the Sydney Machine Company, a general engineering shop which specialised in tanning machinery repairs, was set up at 81 Hay Street, with Andrew Reid's brother John as Manager. John had been connected with the leather-dressing

In 1908, to cope with its growing business, the company rented space for offices and stores in the southern wing of the old Naval Stores building. All floors were soon well stocked.

A SALESMAN WITH EXPERIENCE

When Andrew Reid hired Frank Luland as a 'traveller' for the Sydney office, in 1904, he took on a man who knew the leather business well. Luland, then forty-seven, had been in the trade for more than thirty years.

In his memoirs, written in 1933, when he was seventy-six, Luland recalled that when he joined the firm its only employees in Sydney over twenty-one were himself and Andrew Reid. George Sutton and Stewart D'Arrietta, both later to become major forces, were known as 'the boys'. At that stage, the company was the Sydney agent for Melbourne tanners J. Kennon & Son. Its leather and tanning customers included Lukey & Nicklin, Farleigh Nettheim & Co. and J.C. Ludowici & Coy.

Luland was born on 3 February 1857 at Penfold's tobacconist shop in George Street. In those days, Sydney was still quiet enough for young Luland to play marbles in the street outside the shop. The family moved when his parents took over the Pembroke Castle Hotel in Surry Hills in 1865, and again when they built the Moore Park Hotel in 1868.

His first job was in 1870 at Russell's iron foundry in Bathurst Street, where he stayed eighteen months as timekeeper in the boilermaking shop at a wage of 9 shillings and fourpence (93 cents) for a 56 hour week. He lost that job when the plant closed down, virtually overnight, because of labour demands for a 48 hour week and two meal breaks a day. The owners, Peter and John Russell, were willing to concede a 48 hour week with one meal break, but having to close down the fires twice a day was more than the business could stand, they said.

Luland found a new job with T. W. Craven, a commission agent in Sussex Street, where his duties included sorting good eggs from bad, and potatoes from onions. It was 'too much for this kid', he wrote in his memoirs. He found another job, with Gibbs and Shallard, in Pitt Street, for two weeks.

Then came the leather trade. In 1872, when he was fifteen, his father took him to M. Alderson & Sons, who were tanners and japanners, as well as boot, saddlery and leather goods manufacturers, in Bourke Street, Surry Hills. They had been in business since the 1820s, and occupied about 4 hectares, from Bourke Street through to Dowling Street. He stayed there ten years, working 56 to 58 hours a week.

In 1880 he started his own tannery in Botany, where he lived for the next thirty-one years. He closed that business in 1904, and joined James Hardie & Co. at the Macquarie Place office as a traveller in the leather trades. 'Traveller' meant almost any outside salesman, even one who never left the metropolitan area and reported in at the office daily. His salary was £3 a week. Luland did, however, travel extensively, including trips to Melbourne, Adelaide and New Zealand.

Luland was a man of some consequence in the leather trade, both before and during his time with James Hardie. In 1904–05 he was President of the Master Tanners' Association of New South Wales, then Secretary of that body from 1905 until some years after the First World War. He was also the New South Wales delegate to the Federated Master Tanners' Association before and after the First World War.

He was a citizen of note in Botany, where he was an alderman from 1888 to 1911, mayor for five terms, and acting mayor for several years. He was at various times President of the Botany School of Arts, the Botany Literary Society, the Botany Protectionist Association, the Botany Borough Cricket Club and the Botany Sailing Club. His affiliations included the Masonic Lodge and the Manchester Unity Independent Order of Odd Fellows.

FRANK LULAND

business for some years in Scotland, and had lately travelled in America, where, according to the *Australian Leather Journal*, he had seen all the latest and most up-to-date machinery. John Reid died in 1907, and George Cropper became Manager. The Sydney Machine Company's works were later moved to Bullanaming (later Renwick) Street, Redfern, and finally to Botany Road, Waterloo, where they made tanning and laundry machinery for many years.

Andrew and Peggy Reid first lived at Randwick, in a house named Bonnytoun after the Linlithgow farm where Peggy had grown up. They were there for more than a decade, until 16 March 1912, when they moved to a new house, Neringah, at Wahroonga. Their three sons — Andrew (born on 20 December 1901), John (15 October 1903) and George (26 June 1908), each with Thyne as his middle name — were all born in Sydney.

Although Andrew Reid seems to have been in good health most of the time, he did have a bad period late in 1909. He was ill with 'lung trouble' for a month or so, and James Hardie came up from Melbourne to look after the Sydney operation. By the end of the year, Reid was well enough again to appear in the office for short periods.

Well Pleased.

Tanners who have had new Machines, or who have had alterations or repairs effected by us during the last two years, speak in the **Highest Terms** of the **Quality** and **Workmanship.**

The Manager of the Company, having recently worked in some of the principal tannery machine shops in England and America, has experience of all the latest ideas for the manufacture and supply of the most efficient and economical machinery for tanners.

Machines and Parts stocked. Correspondence solicited on all matters relating to the business.

SYDNEY MACHINE CO.

Works: 81 Hay Street
Office: 11 Macquarie Place **SYDNEY.**

In 1903 the firm set up the Sydney Machine Co.,
with Andrew Reid's brother John as Manager.

CHAPTER SIX

'ALL AT BEDROCK PRICES'

Melbourne tanner Squire Kennon. He and James Hardie became very good friends.

W hile Reid was developing the firm's business in Sydney, James Hardie was busy in Melbourne. In February 1902 the Melbourne office moved across Little Collins Street, to number 581–3, taking its telephone number, 923, with it. These premises were to serve the company for the next sixty years. Andrew Reid's grandson, John B. Reid, who became Chairman of the group in 1974, started work there.

Hardie had fitted these premises up at some expense 'for whitewashing and printing names'. 'You will no doubt say when you see it that it is worth all the money,' he told Andrew Reid in a letter. 'The offices are well fitted up. I thought it so much better to make a nice job when it is being done, as first impressions go a long way.'

The firm had long been short of room for its growing trade, Hardie told the *Australian Leather Journal*. The new premises had four times the floor area of those just vacated. Hardie's own office, the 'inner sanctum', was quite large, and would be used for Tanners' Association meetings.

On 27 February 1902 Hardie invited leather trade guests to inspect the new premises. The President of the Master Tanners' and Curriers' Association, Colonel Braithwaite, was unable to be there. He was busy as a military expert examining the saddles of the Victorian contingent to the Boer War, so Squire Kennon took the chair. Benjamin, as Vice-President, said he had been dealing with Hardie for fourteen years, and he had great pleasure in seeing the firm move into larger premises. His experience of Hardie was that for honesty of purpose and straight dealing he could not be surpassed. He was practically the father of the Master Tanners' and Curriers' Association.

Proposing a toast to Hardie, Squire Kennon noted that it was only a few years since Mr Hardie started in the very humblest way, and he had built up a very large business. Hardie, he went on, 'certainly possessed the social qualities which greatly help a man in his business'.

Edward Hallenstein said that without Hardie, the Association would have been dead long ago. Now his growing business meant he had to give up being Secretary, but he would still be on the committee. Feehan, of Dalgety's, on behalf of the auctioneers, said the handsome premises 'were worthy of the man, and the man worthy of the premises'.

Meanwhile, Hardie had initiated an interstate conference of tanners, who met at the Federal Coffee Palace in Melbourne. Edmund Barton's Protectionist Party had won the first federal election, and there was much talk of Protection. Hardie suggested 15 per cent as an appropriate tariff on imported leather, in terms of both revenue and protection, and the conference agreed to propose this to the Federal government.

Hardie was less enthusiastic about a tariff on tanning machinery. Andrew Reid wrote to the *Australian Leather Journal* that it was a mistaken notion that up-to-date machinery could be made in Australia. 'We are quite six years in arrear,' he said, 'and yet our legislators, in almost the same breath, talk about encouraging the industries of the country and put 20 per cent on the tools to do it with.' The whole leather trade, he said, was threatened by a minority of 'a dozen or two' workmen who made machinery. The benefit of tariff protection was all very well for them, but it increased the tanning industry's costs.

In August 1902 Hardie visited Adelaide, where he found trade 'dull', owing partly to drought, partly to all three Broken Hill mines being on strike. To Andrew Reid, he wrote: 'My hurried trip to Adelaide was only fairly successful. Things are very quiet with the South Australians. There are twenty curriers walking round Hindmarsh out of work. Such a thing has not been known for many years.' He was glad to know that Reid was 'doing well and getting good orders'.

Later that month, Hardie became quite ill, first with influenza, then pleurisy, then typhoid fever. He was in bed at his Hawthorn home for seven weeks, with an at times alarming temperature. By mid-October he was allowed up, but it was to be six weeks before he could go back to work. His condition had caused great concern among his friends, the *Australian Leather Journal* observed. It was a sign of how well he was regarded in the trade that so many people asked: 'How's Jim Hardie?' A steady stream of enquiries about his health also arrived by telegram and letter.

While James Hardie was in the United States in 1903, he arranged the sole agency for the Whitney fleshing and unhairing machine.

Hardie (second from left) took part in tanners' and curriers' social functions, such as their annual picnics.

By November he was able to spend an hour or two at the office each day, and by mid-December he had made a complete recovery. Albert Zwar and James Munday, both leading tanners, invited him to recuperate at their country homes.

On his doctor's advice, Hardie now decided on an overseas trip. In what amounted to a surprise party at Scott's Hotel in Melbourne, the day before he left, his leather trade friends wished him bon voyage. He thanked them all for their good wishes, and assured the tanners he would keep his eyes open for anything that might interest them in their business. If he could be of service to any of them while away from Australia, he would gladly do anything that lay in his power. Good humour prevailed and many a bottle of Heidsieck's dry monopole champagne was emptied. The day was an exceeding warm one, the *Australian Leather Journal* noted, and, as everybody knew, tanners were a dry and thirsty lot.

James and Clara sailed from Melbourne on 3 March 1903. They left the ship at Naples, and travelled overland via Roma, Lucerne, Marseilles and Paris to London. Then they went to various English and Scottish provincial towns, looking up contacts and watching for new developments in leather.

Naturally, Hardie had plans to go to Linlithgow, mainly to see his mother, who was now eighty-four. Quite by chance, he was to be at her bedside when she died, at 7.45 p.m. on 14 May 1903, eight days after she suffered a stroke. Hardie signed the entry of his mother's death at Linlithgow Registry the next day.

Hardie carried on with his travels, meeting in London, no doubt by prior arrangement, his good friends Squire Kennon and Herbert Burgess. The three were entertained in June 1903 by a group of Scottish tanners. A special train took them to Loch Lomond, where a splendid dinner waited. They steamed across the placid waters of the loch, then 'took train' to Glasgow for supper at St Enoch's hotel, where there was further speech-making and geniality.

Hardie and Kennon went to the United States and Canada, visiting New York, Boston, Philadelphia, Niagara Falls, Montreal and Toronto. They arrived back in Melbourne on 7 October 1903 in RMS *Oratava*, and Hardie's account of his trip soon appeared in the *Australian Leather Journal*, complete with plugs for the new agencies he had secured.

He had won the sole agency for the famous Perfection leather-measuring machines made by Nightingale and Company, of Danvers, Massachusetts, and also the agency for the Turner Tanning Machinery Company, of Boston, whose pulling-out machines he described to the *Journal* as 'marvels of ingenuity and mechanical skill'.

He had also signed up as the sole agent for Whitney fleshing and unhairing machines, and won agencies for the Sirocco Manufacturing Company (for their revolving fans), the British Electric Plant Company, Sapon soap powder, and other specialties suitable for the Australian market, including 'a new type of roofing and lining slate'. Hardie people were to hear a lot more of that.

The firm had its London agents, W.A. Sparrow & Co., of St Mary's Axe, buy and ship to both Melbourne and Sydney large supplies of tanning materials from Calder & Mersey of Liverpool, gum tragasol from another Lancashire firm, and chemicals and dyestuffs from various parts of Britain and Germany.

Sparrows also arranged large shipments of sumac leaves, mainly from C. Cracolici & Cie, of Palermo, in Sicily. These were dried and press-packed into bales to be shipped, and would then be soaked to make a tanning extract.

At one time, Sparrows were asked to supply sumac samples from other sources. This led to a large order, but as soon as the first shipment arrived, Sparrows had a cable to cancel all further orders with the new supplier. The bales were full of warehouse sweepings, and the sumac was useless. When the Italian consul came to inspect the goods and supported the complaint, the supplier offered to replace the shipment. Hardie declined this and succeeded in getting not only his money back promptly but also all the shipping expenses.

While Hardie was away, the business continued to prosper. As the *Cyclopaedia of Victoria* put it in 1903, 'the firm have a high reputation for keeping the best goods available... all at bedrock prices'.

PRESENT AT THE 'SHOP WARMING'

The list of those present at James Hardie's 'shop warming' of 27 February 1902 reads like a 'who's who' of the Melbourne leather trade of the time. It included Squire Kennon, Thomas Broadhurst, William Zwar, Edward Hallenstein, Andrew Walker, W.S. Stephenson, Joshua Pitt, P. Hardenack, Thomas Watson, T. Connelly, T. C. Plante, L. R. Lloyd, J. Totton, J. Feehan, H. Burgess, W. Akehurst, Harry Brearley, M. Benjamin, E. Michaelis, T. Scorse, R. Reid, T. Debney, R. McComas, A. Appleton, S. McLean, T. Cooper, C. Woolf, J. Zander, P. Reynolds, F. Kitson, H. J. M. Campbell, George Campbell, A. Glasgow, A. E. Kane, George Brearley and Alfred Lawrence.

CHAPTER SEVEN

A 'NEW TYPE OF ROOFING AND LINING SLATE'

The 'new type of roofing and lining slate' James Hardie arranged to sell in Australia on his visit to Britain in 1903 was fibro-ciment, made by the Fibro-Ciment Company of Poissy, in France. In time, fibro-cement (as it became known) was to become very closely linked with the Hardie name.

Company folklore has it that fibro-cement was passed off on Hardie almost as a joke, if not a minor confidence trick, by William Bolton, Sparrows' youthful shipping manager. A package of fibro-cement samples, used as a doorstop, had been gathering dust for a year or so in Sparrows' office when Hardie called. 'Let's get rid of these,' said Bolton. 'Let's give them to Hardies.'

If the story is true, Sparrow people must have been amazed when Hardie gave them a trial order for about £100 worth of the strange new product on the spot. Bolton seems to have been an opportunist, and he may have sensed that foisting the samples on Hardie was worth a try.

Fibro-cement was quite new. Various people in Europe had been trying for ten years or so to find a process to marry fibrous material and cement in a building sheet, with varying success. Only three years or so before Hardie bought the first trial shipment, an Austrian, Ludwig Hatschek, had used a strawboard-making machine to produce a sheet made up of thin, paper-like laminations. This was the process the Fibro-Ciment Company used. Roofing slates were then thought to be the product with most potential.

The original two crates ordered were sent to Melbourne and sold to the Victorian Railways for linesmen's huts. A report came back that fibro-cement was too brittle and 'no good'. Despite this report to Sparrows, the firm sent an order for a further four crates. An order for eight crates came later, and the business grew steadily.

People were at first reluctant to accept that fibro-cement sheets could be used safely outside. To get a small order for a verandah front for the Turkish Baths in Elizabeth Street, Sydney, Hardies had to give a written guarantee that the sheeting would stand the weather. Reid thought it worth the risk. Only a few pounds were involved, and if the material stood the test, its use might be greatly extended. It was a business risk destined to prove well worth the taking.

Fibro-cement proved to be a losing line, however, mainly because of breakage. To help overcome this problem, Reid and Sutton decided to make it a special department in Sydney, with young D'Arrietta in charge and Norman Turnbull as traveller. In time, they developed into the Builders' Supplies Sales Department. That was a further landmark in Hardies' growth, for builders' supplies were to become their main business.

Ludwig Hatschek, an Austrian, who developed the process for making fibro-cement only a few years before James Hardie brought samples of it to Australia.

Opposite: Fibro-cement, destined to become the core of the firm's business, took third billing in this James Hardie promotion.

This suburban house in Sydney was built in 1906 with a fibro-cement slate roof (left), seen here (above) 49 years later.

One of the first big orders for fibro-cement was for the old Bondi Surf Shed, forerunner of the larger concrete structure. An early Melbourne order was for a new 'temporary' Spencer Street Railway Station, which was to last until the 1960s.

An article in the *Australian Leather Journal* of 1906 reported an exhibition stand by Hardies, which included fibro-cement. The report noted that 'James Hardie & Co. are making a specialty of their fibro-cement slates and sheets. A house built of this material is thoroughly fireproof, cool in summer, and comfortable in winter... Melbourne University has some rooms finished with fibro-ciment; the sanitoria at Broadmeadows and at Mitcham are built with it. For butter factories, dairies, chemical works, deed boxes and such like it is unsurpassed.'

Fibro-cement became popular enough for firms in England to start making it, and Hardies began to draw from there. The firm continued to import all its fibro-cement needs until the First World War made this all but impossible. In 1915 Andrew Reid would go to Europe and arrange to import the machinery and expertise needed to start making it in Australia.

By 1909, 'fibro-ciment'
it was still at the
bottom of the product list.

Dear Andrew

Your letters dated 15ᵗʰ & 21ˢᵗ to hand. The o/d drafts coming due, and current accounts coming due certainly caused me a worry and made night hideous for want of sleep. As the o/d mounts up to £2800 & not know what o/d you [...] could not send [...] uneasiness. [...] [...]ount for shares by [...] of John M Reid [...] we could do. Even [...] ted, otherwise they [...] Another matte[r] [...] was that John Reid [...] [...], ha[d] we not paid up [...] have been prompted [...] have paid Campbell [...] is we could do with [...] it. I may tell you [...] [...]sking if he could offer any [...] could offer was [...] 10 Tons at £8-15/- this we had to take and sell to a client at £9. We have to keep all this from Campbell as he would naturally kick at the low price we paid him. It was not so much the debit against you that

CHAPTER EIGHT

'DEAR ANDREW'

J ames Hardie seems to have kept up a regular and chatty flow of letters to Andrew Reid, if we are to judge from a bundle of them that have survived. They give us a fairly gloomy picture of the business in the first decade of the new century, with much of the emphasis on the poor state of trade and the alarming state of the overdraft.

'What worries me is the balance of valonia and other goods that may be detained in London again, and the payments come one on top of the other as they have the last few months,' Hardie wrote on 16 February 1901. 'Next month should see a large amount of money coming in but, as the bank balances at the end of this month, I am doing all I can to have a small balance to our credit at that time. After that I will try and get a holiday, hoping that the tension will be past by that time.'

By the end of that month, he was even more worried. 'A letter came from R. & J. Dick saying they have been on the point several times of writing and asking us why we were not sending returns, so you see I had good grounds for fearing that they might take some action,' he wrote on 1 March 1901. 'I want to cable another £2,000 as soon as possible and will strain every nerve to do it at an early date. Money may be a little easier in about a month when the Lark shipment of bark returns begin to come. It has been an anxious time with me, with the strains of meeting the heavy payments. I think the anxious times will now be past, after this month at least, and I think we will get on all right.'

But the bad news continued. 'Business is getting very quiet in Victoria, in almost every branch, but the tanning is suffering thro' this obnoxious Factories Act...,' Andrew Reid read in his partner's letter of 26 March 1901. 'I fear we are in for a quiet time now, as everything is being upset in anticipation of the Royal Visit, combined with what I fear may be a big drop in leather. Things point that way at present, so with dear hides and dear bark the outlook for the tanners is not bright.'

The quiet state of business showed up in the accounts. 'I am sorry to say that [the balance sheet] is not so good this last half year, although our turnover was £5,000 more than the preceding half year,' Hardie wrote on 5 February 1902. 'We have had to pay £160 for exchange and cabling Dick money. Advertising instead of showing a profit has exceeded its share by £49... Salaries are higher, while £200 has been written off for bad debts... The expenses this half year will be heavy, owing to putting up new offices, white washing, painting names &c.'

A month later, on 3 March 1902, Hardie wrote that the firm had 'not sent Dick any money this year yet [and] must cable some soon'.

On 3 July 1902: 'Our expenses this half year will however be very heavy, what between the offices, extra hands, removing and extra travellers. I fear the balance

Opposite: James Hardie at his desk.

will not be a large one, thus our reason for being careful about the one %'s &c. The Tasmanian traveller has not so far been a success. He has been away two months and has not sent a single order.'

The debt to R. & J. Dick continued to worry Hardie. 'We had to discount bills for the third time this year and cable £1,000, which means a loss of £33 in exchange and cabling,' he wrote on 3 July 1902. 'Against this we have of course had the use of the money. We must however cable another £1,000 at an early date. Our balance at the Bank is £24 today even after discounting £1,100 worth of bills. The bark to be shipped by S.S. *Perth* will have to be paid for early next week.'

One of James Hardie's letters to Andrew Reid.

Some years later, finance was still a problem. 'The overdraft coming due and current accounts coming due certainly caused me to worry and made night hideous for want of sleep,' Hardie wrote on 24 March 1908. 'As the overdraft mounted up to £2,800 and not knowing what overdraft you had as well, and your assurance that you could not send anything did not help allay my uneasiness. Then Dick cabled out for us to remit amount for shares by cable, which we had to do on the face of John M. Reid going home.'

On 18 April 1909: 'Business is very quiet here at present… The house you arranged to roof at Hampton here is likely to lead to a loss, as you seem to have omitted allowing for eaves and valleys. The measurement should have been 25 squares, not 19 squares as quoted… We have lost a good many orders lately through B.K. Morton cutting the price of Lincona down almost under our landed cost of our belting, so that the outlook for us is getting very gloomy… I saw the Bank Manager about a private advance on Bolton Park. He said he would give it to me at 5½%. I thought I could easily have got money say from the Savings Bank at 4% or 4½%, but I am told they only advance money against rent producing property, so fear I must get the money from our Bank for a few months… If I can draw the amount from the business to clear the property, the titles for land as well as my house can be lodged with the Bank for any overdraft we may require. We will be overdrawn about £1,000. As you have lately had about £500 of bark from us, you might send us a cheque for that amount. As you know, we had to pay Campbell cash for it within the week. The amount against Sydney in our books is about £10,000, so you might send us something. Money is very tight here.'

On 31 May 1909: 'Business is fearfully dull in Victoria… Had it not been for the high prices obtained for wheat and wool I am afraid there would have been a regular slump in general business… Belting is moving very slowly… As for Newfoundland cod oil the bottom has almost entirely fallen out of this for the time being… Money very scarce. Several boot manufacturers have suspended payment… They had a private meeting of creditors and arranged for extension of time. We are in for £4. They say we may be able to get it within 12 months… Have enquiries for some of the land at Bolton Park, but have arranged to allow the Golf Club the use of it for three years on condition that they pay 4½% on £2,500. I wanted 5% but they do not think they could arrange for any more members to play on the ground…'

Business no doubt was a struggle, but we may wonder if Hardie was not being just a little too dourly Scottish. It would be interesting to see Reid's letters, to see to what extent they shared Hardie's pessimism. He probably thought it prudent not to reply to most of them.

In spite of their troubles, both men and their families seemed to enjoy a fairly affluent lifestyle by the standards of the time. Even as he wrote, Hardie was moving to what could be regarded as a grand house in a highly desirable suburb: Lithca, within a property he called Bolton Park, at Brighton. Reid was making plans for his own dream home at Wahroonga, which he built in 1912.

CHAPTER NINE

SENTIMENTAL JOURNEY

In 1910 James Hardie made a journey home to Scotland, after the usual round of farewells. At midday on 24 February 1910 he entertained a few friends at the Federal Coffee Palace in Collins Street. Councillor Carnegie, ex-Mayor of Kew, on behalf of those present, presented him with a handsome travelling rug, and Hardie responded with a 'neat speech'.

That evening, at Scott's Hotel, a large gathering of tanners and people from related trades farewelled seven men from the industry about to leave for London, Hardie among them. The others were Thomas Burgess of the Hawthorn Tannery, Preston tanner Thomas Broadhurst, A. E. Pizzey, Bayer agent R. Weir, Perth tanner and leather merchant B. Rosenstann, and 'Bert' Brearley.

'It has been whispered,' said Captain A. E. Kane, President of the Master Tanners' Association, who was in the chair, 'that some of the shoe manufacturers have commissioned Mr Hardie to travel throughout the British Isles and pick out 1000 suitable young ladies to bring to Australia to work the machines in the boot factories.' If this were a fact, he congratulated Mr Hardie and wished him success in his mission.

When Hardie's turn to speak came, he stood up amidst loud applause. He said that the voyagers were true patriots all, for 'be it understood, they were leaving their country for their country's good'. They would all try to induce migration to Australia. He would visit his native land, 'of brown heath and shaggy wood', and do all in his power to further the best interests of the Australian leather trade.

Hardie and Clara left Melbourne for London on the *Malwa* on 1 March 1910, Andrew Reid coming down from Sydney to see them off.

On 6 July 1910 Hardie was at Edinburgh's Waverley Station to meet the Burgesses, who had come up from Leeds. After lunch, they went by taxi to the home of Hardie's youngest sister, Margaret (Peggy) Greenhorn, who greeted them with typical Scottish hospitality, ready to join them on their travels. By six that night, the party was installed at Fisher's Hotel at Pitlochry.

They made their way by steamer up Loch Ness and the Caledonian Canal, stopping at Spean Bridge for a time. Then they went on to Fort William, where they stayed for some days, preparing for their planned ascent of Ben Nevis.

All three ladies 'pooh-poohed the idea of being left out', Burgess wrote in his account of their travels, which appeared in the *Australian Leather Journal* on their return. They 'acquitted themselves that day in a way that left... no... doubt about their being fitted for the franchise'. After ten and a half hours climbing up and down the mountain, they finished up as fresh as the two men.

Burgess had to remonstrate with Hardie on the way up. He turned so often to admire the view that Burgess became suspicious, and caught him taking 'medicine'. Burgess tried it himself, as it seemed to be doing Hardie a lot of good. He then 'took the precaution of carrying it, especially as... the doctor had said it was only to be taken between meals or sandwiches, or something of that sort'. He let Hardie have a little when he found a nice ice-cold stream, where he could follow the prescription's instruction to 'dilute with aqua pura', something not all Scots would approve doing to whisky. Another day trip they took was to Mallaig, via Glencoe, Arisaig and Loch Finnan.

Hardie was amazed at the growth of Glasgow, which was 'almost incomprehensible to old residents when they [were] told of new suburbs and new names unknown 20 or 30 years [before]'.

During this trip, the Hardies travelled not only in Britain but also on the continent and in America.

James Hardie on top of Ben Nevis, with Mrs Burgess, his wife (Clara) and his sister (Peggy Greenhorn).

JAMES HARDIE with his son, ALEX, about 1920.

FAREWELL
TO THE FOUNDER

In 1912 James Hardie was sixty. His health had never been robust, and he decided to retire. No doubt he and Reid had talked about that prospect and how they would handle it.

So on 10 May 1912 they signed a dissolution of partnership retrospectively as from 30 June 1911, and lodged the papers required under the Registration of Firms Act. Reid agreed to pay Hardie £17 000 for his share of the firm, £5000 of it in cash, the balance over ten years at 6 per cent interest.

The *Australian Leather Journal* reported on 15 June 1912 that James Hardie & Co. was 'now trading under the new proprietary of Mr Andrew Reid, who succeeds his old friend and partner, Mr James Hardie, who retires after long and faithful service to the tanning and leather trades of Australia and New Zealand'.

Wishing Reid all future success, the *Journal* noted that he was well supported by a courteous and genial business staff — Sutton and Luland in Sydney, Marsden and James in Melbourne — all of whom had long been associated with the firm. Marsden would have the help of George Gregson, lately manager of Dalgety's produce department in Brisbane.

Marsden found the going a little tough. On 16 September 1912 the *Journal* reported that he had been 'confined to his home for several days last month'. Since Hardie had retired, a large portion of the work he had done had fallen on Marsden, and he had become 'run down'. But he was soon back at work again.

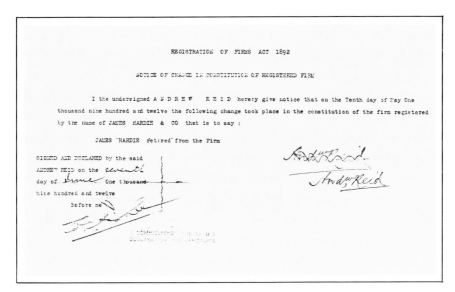

Notice announcing that Andrew Reid had become the sole owner of James Hardie & Co.

James Hardie with a group of children at one of his daughter Vera's parties at Bolton Park, his Brighton home. Vera 'was always ill with excitement' before her parties.

On 6 February 1913 the Master Tanners' and Leather Manufacturers Association unanimously elected Hardie a life member, 'for past valuable services'.

Hardie devoted the rest of his life to community work and his family. By now they were living at the house in Bolton Avenue, Brighton Beach. Hardie Street still marks the site of his Bolton Park.

The whole family were involved in local bodies, James with St Leonard's Church and the Progress Association (of which he was President for a year), Clara and the girls with the Red Cross during the First World War. A surviving newspaper cutting gives an account of a 'garden fete and croquet gymkhana' held at Bolton Park on 11 November, probably in 1915, when the Hardies' daughter Vera was twenty, Mary eighteen and Alex sixteen. The two Hardie 'young ladies' helped organise the occasion and had charge of the Christmas novelty, sweets stalls and tulip bed, while Alex, with the help of Bruce Mair, manned the penny ice-cream stall. This kind of money-raising work probably says something about the image the Hardies had of themselves, a highly respected and highly respectable middle class family with a strong sense of community and civic responsibility.

Alex Hardie (above) in uniform. He joined the Army as soon as he was eighteen, but did not see active service. He died in 1924, aged twenty-four, after surgery for a mastoid condition. Vera Hardie (right), at the age of thirty, taken in 1925.

When James Hardie was sixty-six, the family moved once again, this time to the corner of Burke Road and Beaver Street, East Malvern, close to the Ewing Memorial Church. This house, also called Lithca, had a croquet lawn alongside it, and on this they built another house.

At some time during the First World War, Hardie's son, Alex, expressed an interest in farming as a career, so the family bought a property at North Poowong in Gippsland. Alex joined the army in 1918, almost as soon as he was old enough, but the war was over before he saw active service.

James Hardie, then sixty-nine, was visiting Alex at North Poowong when he died, on 20 November 1920. The death certificate, attested by Dr A. Cowell, gives the cause of death as arteriosclerosis and heart failure and says he had been suffering from it for three years. He was buried in the Presbyterian section of Brighton Cemetery, the first in what was to become a Hardie family grave.

Alexander James, Hardie's only son, died tragically young, at twenty-four. He developed a mastoid condition and, on the advice of three doctors, had surgery at a private hospital in Melbourne on 3 April 1924. Two days later he was dead.

James Hardie's two daughters, VERA (left) and MARY.

Clara Evelyn Hardie, James's wife, died at her home, 65 Burke Road, East Malvern, on 3 November 1948, a month short of her eighty-third birthday. Five years before she died, she had seen her second daughter, Mary, then forty-five, wed Ernest Edward Davies, a widower with a son. They were married at the family home, but Davies died only sixteen months later. Mary herself died of cancer on 12 December 1951.

Vera Florence, the last Hardie survivor, lived an active and useful life. She was at work for the 'Save the Children' Fund when, on 21 January 1969, she died, aged seventy-four, as the result of a car accident.

None of the Hardie children had offspring, and the Australian branch of the family died out with them.

James Hardie's wife, Clara, survived him by almost twenty-eight years. She died in 1948, aged almost eighty-three.

PART TWO
MANUFACTURERS

CHAPTER ELEVEN

FIRST MOVES INTO MANUFACTURING

On 7 May 1915 a German submarine sank the Cunard liner *Lusitania* within sight of land off Kinsale Head on the Irish coast. Andrew Reid, his wife, Peggy, and their youngest son, George, then aged six, might well have been among the 1150-odd passengers and crew who died as the ship went down. They had been booked on it from New York, but something made them change to another vessel.

The Reids had left Australia in March, bound for America, Britain and Switzerland. The First World War had begun to interfere severely with supplies of fibro-cement, by now a major part of Hardies' trade. Demand for it in Europe had soared, shipping space was scarce, and exports had ceased. Andrew Reid decided to go to Europe to look into making it in Australia.

Reid had been talking of local manufacture for some time, for on 22 August 1913 Charles Gass, a Brussels machinery agent, wrote to him: 'My friends have informed me that you are interested in a plant for making asbestos sheets.' He did not pursue the matter too vigorously, until the wartime shortage made it urgent.

It may seem strange to modern readers that Reid should take his wife and child on such a voyage in time of war. But we must remember that in early 1915 the worst horrors of all-out war were still in the future. When Reid saw war conditions in Europe, he all but abandoned the entire scheme. The firm that originally supplied French-made fibro-cement now had its own works in Kent and refused to consider the idea that Hardies should make it in Australia.

Still, he was able to arrange for Felber Jucker & Company Ltd, of Manchester, to supply the machinery from a Swiss firm, the Societé Suisse des Usines Eternit, of Niederurnen, and send a Swiss expert on fibro-cement technology, Ernest Witzig, along with it. The agreement, signed on 10 November 1915, provided that Hardies would pay a penny a square yard royalty on flat sheets, and twopence a square yard on corrugated, these being the only products to be made in the early stages. The machinery came to Australia, sixty-five crates of it, on the SS *Clan MacCorquodale*, which was torpedoed and sunk on its return trip.

Reid set up a company, the Asbestos Slate & Sheet Manufacturing Company Ltd, to make fibro-cement products. It was incorporated on 31 May 1916, with a capital of 50 000 £1 shares, of which 29 420 were issued. Andrew Reid was Chairman, the other Directors being George Sutton, Stewart D'Arrietta and William Williamson, a leading Sydney building contractor and former President of the Master Builders' Association, with Donald Chisholm Cameron as Secretary. Andrew Reid was issued with 500 shares, fully paid up, to cover his out-of-pocket

The front page of prospectus of original Hardie company formed in 1916 to make fibro-cement slate and sheet.

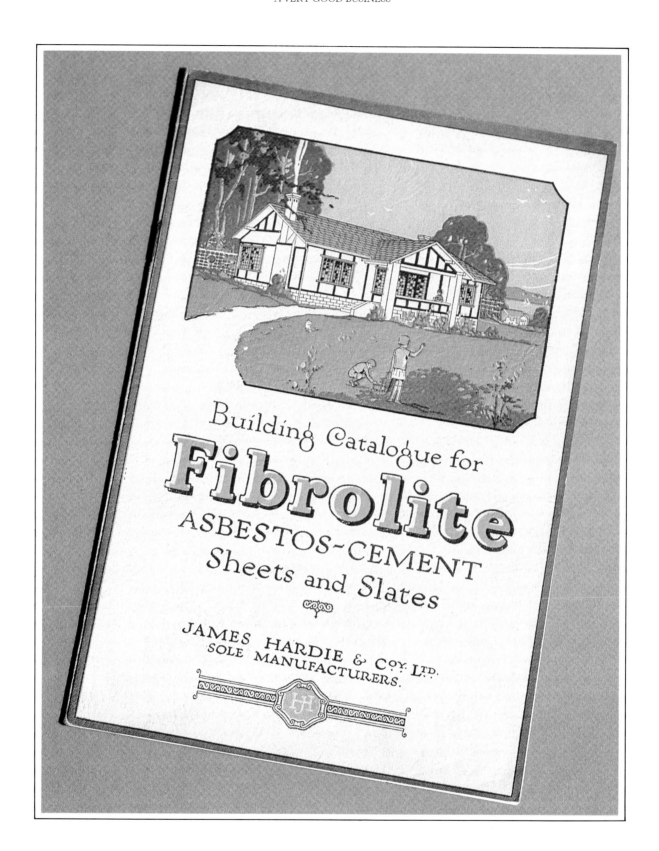

expenses in the United States, Canada, England and Europe and other expenses and work he undertook in setting up the company.

Marketing was left in the hands of the established James Hardie firms in Sydney and Melbourne, to preserve the goodwill built up with the imported product since 1903. Before the war, over £100 000 worth of such goods as the company proposed to manufacture had been imported annually into New South Wales and Victoria. The demand was likely to increase as time went on.

The initial plant would be able to turn out at least £30 000 worth of fibro-cement a year. The factory would be built in such a way that more machinery could be added without much extra outlay, and each added unit would reduce the cost of manufacture. The plant included several innovations that would increase the range of fibro-cement products that could be made, and this in turn would expand the market created by imported fibro-cement products.

Good cement was readily available locally. The only raw material of value that would have to be imported was asbestos, but the company had hopes that it might later be provided from within Australia. If this did not eventuate, it would be little worse off than the various British and European factories, then working so successfully, which also had to import their asbestos supplies.

In June 1916 the new company bought a site on the Parramatta River at Camellia from a syndicate consisting of Andrew Reid, Stewart D'Arrietta, George Sutton and Chisholm Cameron. The site had both shipping and rail connections, and local labour was available. On 29 July 1916 the directors met there to decide the position and layout of the factory, a task in which they had the help of Cyprian Truman, who oversaw the building of the first factory and then became its first manager.

Cyprian Truman, who oversaw the construction of the Camellia plant and then managed it.

Opposite: Although Hardies saw themselves as manu-facturers, they soon began to use such marketing aids as brightly coloured catalogues to inform potential users about their products.

The Swiss expert, Ernest Witzig, arrived from Europe soon after to set up the machinery and see it through its pilot run. Drawings for the factory showed a neat, steel-framed building, but in fact it was built with telephone pole uprights and timber trusses.

The first sheets came off the Camellia production line in May 1917. The local product was well received by those who had previously used the imported sheets and was soon being sold as Fibrolite, the name registered on 8 August 1917. The first Fibrolite show home was built at the Royal Agricultural Show Ground in Sydney in 1917. In October 1918 the company bought another 4 hectares of land beside the Camellia factory site, almost doubling its size.

Reid was soon looking at setting up another plant in Victoria. But cement was scarce, and Victoria had to wait until 1927 for its Fibrolite factory.

Although it was to have by far the most profound effects on the company's future, making fibro-cement was not Hardies' only move into manufacturing brought about by the First World War.

In Melbourne, the company set up a leather belting factory in Ferrars Street, South Melbourne, to replace the Balata belting it could no longer get from R. & J. Dick & Company of Glasgow. In the same building, it also started making simple tannery equipment and chemicals for the leather trade.

The company had found itself unable to get supplies of the collodion solutions tanners used in making patent leather, which it had for many years imported from

the United States. One of the raw materials for collodion was nitrocellulose, which was also the basis of cordite, then very much in demand for making ammunition.

But Australian ladies still wanted their shiny patent leather handbags, Australian gentlemen their shiny patent leather shoes. So in 1917 Hardies began to make nitrocellulose, using scrap photographic film as a raw material. That was the start of the Spartan operation, because nitrocellulose was then also one of the materials used in making car lacquers. It turned out to be no simple step, but it did lead in time to the manufacture of a wide range of surface coatings, for automotive, industrial, marine and domestic building use.

From that start, it was a short step to selling general industrial chemicals. An agency deal with the British United Alkali Company was arranged in 1915 in spite of the war. It began with sulphide of sodium, which tanners used to remove the hairs from hides. The company did so well with this that United Alkali later gave it the agency for their whole range of alkalis, including soda ash, caustic soda and bicarbonate of soda.

These chemicals were amongst those that became very hard to get because of the war, and their prices had soared. Caustic soda rose from £12 10s 0d a ton before the war to £80, bicarbonate of soda from £7 10s 0d to £60. When bichromate of potash became impossible to get, users switched to bichromate of soda, which rose from 3d a pound to 2/6d.

In their struggles to keep supplies flowing, Hardies at times did some odd deals,

The original fibro-cement factory at Camellia, taken about 1920.

as supply and demand (and prices) changed rapidly. At one stage they sold 1200 tons of bark in Japan, then bought it back in Durban. They sold 70 tons of caustic soda in Java, then bought it back in New York. Another time, to get £35 000 worth of leather to South Africa, they shipped it in a Japanese steamer to Japan, where it was to be transhipped to South Africa at the then amazing freight cost of £40 a ton. While it was on a wharf in Japan, it was damaged by a tidal wave.

Business did, however, carry on. In 1916 the company opened an Adelaide office. It had planned this before the war, but had put it off until the position became clearer. In September 1917, to release office space at the Circular Quay premises for storage, the company bought and modernised office premises at the corner of York and Wynyard Streets, later occupied by Westpac.

In 1918 the Sydney and Melbourne trading businesses were incorporated as separate entities, Sydney on 4 April as James Hardie & Coy Ltd, Melbourne on 23 April as James Hardie & Co. Ltd. Of the 70 000 original shares, Andrew Reid had 40 800, his wife, Peggy, and their three sons (Andrew Thyne Reid, John Thyne Reid and George Thyne Reid) 5000 each, George Sutton 6000, Stewart D'Arrietta 2700 and Donald Chisholm Cameron 500. Reid and Sutton were the two Directors, Cameron Secretary. D'Arrietta became a Director in 1920. Melbourne had Reid as a major shareholder, but no other links with the Sydney company. It had Adelaide as a branch.

During the postwar boom, rumour had it that leather would be so scarce that

ERNEST WITZIG: THE SWISS CONNECTION

Ernest Witzig, the Swiss engineer who came to Australia in 1916 to set up the original fibro-cement plant and see it through its trial run, intended to stay twelve months. But he settled in Australia, married an Australian, became an Australian citizen and stayed the rest of his life, taking on various roles within the developing Hardie fibro-cement business.

Witzig often protested when people called him an engineer, which he said he was not. He became known for his serious manner and his habit of making apparently fussy adjustments to the machines. He was known to those who worked for him as tough but fair. He was 'a wizard at figures'.

Witzig was born at Kesswil, in the Canton of Thurgovie in Switzerland, on 14 February 1893, and was only twenty-three when he came to Camellia. He had studied industrial chemistry at the university in Zurich, which he came to regard as his home town. His original contact with Hardies was through his uncle, who worked at the Societé Suisse des Usines Eternit, the Niederurnen firm that made the original equipment Hardies ordered through Felber, Jucker & Company Ltd in Britain, and with which Hardies still have an association.

If Witzig and Andrew Reid ever met before he came to Australia, their conversation would have been limited. Witzig spoke French and German, with a preference for French, and Reid spoke only English. Witzig took an English course soon after he arrived in Australia, but he seems to have had a definite language problem in his early years at Camellia. For some strange reason, the only person he could really understand was Andrew Reid, who never lost his strong Scottish burr.

When the company set up its second fibro-cement plant, in Perth, Witzig went there as Works Manager in 1921. He lived in a boarding house at Rivervale, near the works, and there he met the owner's niece, Gladys Veronica Byrne — usually known as Bobby, after the Scottish poet, whose surname was near enough to hers for those who give nicknames. He moved again, in 1926, to Melbourne, when the company established a third plant there. But he was soon back in Perth briefly to marry Bobby Byrne. By then he was thirty-four; she was twenty-two.

The couple settled happily in Melbourne and were not exactly pleased when Ernest was transferred back to Perth in April 1933 as Branch Manager, particularly as that plant was not operating at all well. He was made a Branch Director in May 1938, in an effort to make him happier about being in Perth rather than Melbourne. He had found Melbourne's climate more to his liking than that of either Sydney or Perth.

Ernest Witzig was a James Hardie man through and through. He was not a talkative person, his wife recalled in 1981, but when he did talk he usually had only one topic, James Hardie, 'breakfast, dinner and tea'. His major outside interest was betting on racehorses, but he was also keen on gardening and live theatre, two interests he shared closely with his wife.

He was still in Perth in March 1949 when ill-health forced his retirement. The Witzigs moved back to Melbourne to live in the house they had built on the seafront at Williamstown. Ernest died in Williamstown Hospital in August 1961, at the age of sixty-eight.

Ernest Witzig, the Swiss fibro-cement expert who came to Australia in 1910.

many people would have to go without shoes, and buyers were paying £18 a dozen for Indian goatskins. Grundy, a partner in T. & H. Wilks of London, for whom the company acted as buying agents on commission, came to Australia and bought large quantities of upper leathers. Some of his purchases were so expensive that they cost about the same per ounce as silver and travelled to Britain in the ship's specie room. By the time they got to London, their price had collapsed, and the deal nearly ruined Grundy's firm.

Some other trades boomed along after the leather business collapsed, and this enabled Hardies to cover losses on imported stocks. The company was proud that all through the war and the postwar boom and collapse it never had to force completion of contracts by legal means, and was never in legal dispute with its suppliers.

Early in 1919, just after the war, the company had problems getting enough asbestos for making Fibrolite and began to search for local deposits. The best of those it found seemed to be at Barraba, near Tamworth, in northern New South Wales. It set up a crushing plant and began production in July 1919, but the asbestos there was very short in staple and yielded a low percentage in relation to the volume of rock that had to be processed, which made it very costly to produce. The plant closed down in June 1923 after producing only a few hundred tons.

Andrew Reid spent most of 1919 overseas. He left for America, Britain and Switzerland on the *Niagara* on 21 January and arrived back, on the same ship, on 24 December.

The certificate of incorporation of the Melbourne company issued seven years later on 22 May 1925.

Early Hardie salesmen travelled by motor cycle and sidecar.

CHAPTER TWELVE

FIBROLITE-BASED EXPANSION

In the 1920s and 1930s most of Hardies' more visible expansion was in Fibro-lite, with new factories in Perth, Melbourne, Brisbane and Auckland, and new products, such as Fibrolite pipes, Super-Six roofing (so called because it was 6 inches from ridge to ridge), and Tilux decorative board.

In March 1920, when a shortage of cement in the eastern states coincided with the opening of the first cement works in Perth, the Board decided that the time was ripe to start making Fibrolite there. It bought 2 hectares next to the West Australian Cement Co. Ltd at Rivervale, and work on building a plant was soon under way. Production began in September 1921, and flat sheet was soon being shipped to Victoria.

Ernest Witzig moved from Sydney to become Works Manager. Perth builder Robert Law, who was Chairman of the local cement company, became a Director of the Asbestos Slate & Sheet Manufacturing Company Ltd, with responsibility for the local Fibrolite operation. He resigned from the Board in March 1929, but stayed on as a Local Director for Western Australia.

Fibrolite store at the corner of City Road and Clarendon Street, South Melbourne.

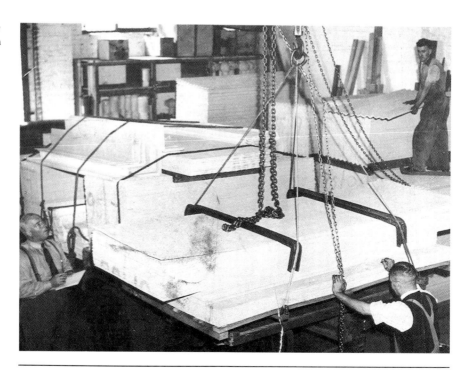

In July 1920 the Board looked at the prospect of starting a Fibrolite plant in Brisbane, but decided to shelve the idea. A plant was not built there until 1934.

In June 1920 the Asbestos Slate & Sheet Manufacturing Company Ltd was reconstructed by selling all the assets of its manufacturing operations to a new company of the same name, with an authorised capital of £250 000. The Directors of the new company, Andrew Reid, George Sutton, Stewart D'Arrietta, William Williamson and Robert Law, were the same as for the former one. At the same time, James Hardie & Coy Ltd, the Sydney company, was reconstructed, and a new company, with the same name and an authorised capital of £250 000, took over its assets.

So far, Fibrolite had been made under a royalty agreement with Felber Jucker & Co. Ltd. This still had five years to run when George Sutton, on his first trip to Britain, in November 1921, negotiated Australian rights to the process for a lump sum of £30 000.

More significant in development terms, however, was Andrew Reid's trip to Europe in 1922, for while in Italy he saw asbestos cement pipes being made. In 1923 the company started to experiment with ways of making them, and in May 1925 it had success with a process George Sutton originated. Commercial operation began in 1926 at Camellia and in 1929 at Rivervale.

In the Sutton process, which the company patented in Australia and many other countries, flat sheets of Fibrolite were wrapped while still 'green' (moist and pliable) over a collapsible mandrel (tube) and covered with calico. Wire rope under tension was then wound round the body of the pipe so formed. After initial setting, the wire rope and calico were removed, then the mandrel was collapsed

The Only Asbestos Cement Sheet
Manufactured in W.A.

ASBESTOS CEMENT SHEET

Fibrolite

PRICE LIST

1st September 1929

All Previous Lists Cancelled

JAMES HARDIE & CO. LTD.
Manufacturers
RIVERVALE, W.A.   Phone B 1636

In this 1929 price list, James Hardie describe themselves as 'Manufacturers'.

Corrugated Fibrolite sheets at Camellia.

Laying Fibrolite pipes, in central NSW, in the late 1920s. Fibrolite pipes became an important part of the Hardie business in the late 1920s and the 1930s.

and removed. The process was based on one Sutton had seen in use for making rubber hose at the Colonial Rubber Company Limited.

The pipes, each 11 feet long, and still bearing the imprint of the wire rope, were immersed in water tanks for fourteen days for curing, then air dried for another fourteen days. A lot of space was needed for the water tanks and air drying, but this method was the one used until 1953, when it was replaced by steam curing.

The Sutton process gave a low-density pipe, with a limited life expectancy. These pipes proved to be unsuccessful, and the company continued to be associated with them, especially in Western Australia, even after better methods of making pipes had been devised.

Joints were made at first by a cast-iron bolted gland. But from 1934 an improved spigot-and-socket joint with a round-section O-ring was used. By the end of 1935 this was in use at all the company's pipe plants and had been accepted by water bodies.

Other products were added to the Fibrolite range from time to time. Production of Super-Six corrugated sheet began at Camellia in 1926. The first major structure roofed with it was the Roxy Theatre at Parramatta. Moulded asbestos brake linings and 85 per cent magnesia for insulation were first made at Camellia in 1930. Conduit piping to carry electrical cables joined the product range in 1937, in 6 foot lengths. Products specially made for the New South Wales Railways included moulded cable ducts and station name signs.

In June 1926 the company bought land at Brooklyn, on the outskirts of Footscray, an industrial suburb in Melbourne's west, and began building a new Fibrolite plant there in September. Ernest Witzig came back from Perth to manage it, and John Henderson moved to Perth to take charge there. The manufacturing company took over distribution of Fibrolite products in Victoria from the trading company, paying it for the goodwill it had built up in the market.

The first flat sheets of Fibrolite came off the Brooklyn production line on 6 June 1927, the first standard corrugated sheets a year later, and the first Sutton pipes in 1933. The Melbourne and Metropolitan Board of Works had encouraged the company to make them, so that it could supply parts of Melbourne with water earlier and more economically than would otherwise have been the case. Andrew Reid's second son, Jock, moved to Melbourne in 1932 as Manager of the Fibrolite operation, responsible to George Gregson, who was a Director of both the manufacturing and trading companies. One early order of note in Victoria was for the roof of the Ford factory at Geelong.

The Melbourne plant won its largest roofing order to date in 1936, when General Motors-Holden's Pty Ltd decided to use Fibrolite for much of its new factory at Fisherman's Bend. To meet this order, the plant had to expand its moulding department. Various General Motors-Holden's and Ford plants around Australia were at the time built largely of Fibrolite, including mouldings, such as cover strips. In October 1936 the company bought more land at Brooklyn to allow for future expansion.

In April 1933 Witzig went back to Perth as Sales and Factory Manager, and Henderson moved to Melbourne as Manager. After three years in Melbourne,

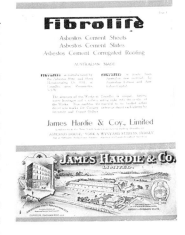

Modern marketers might see little merit in showing a picture of the factory in a product brochure, but Hardies thought it important enough to include in this early brochure.

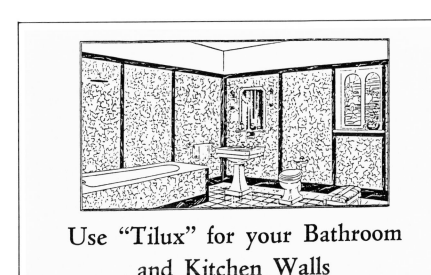

An early advertisement for Tilux, first made at Camellia in 1929.

Fibro-cement, used by New South Wales Railways (above), has also been used for the walls and ceilings of this bedroom (right).

Henderson went to Sydney as understudy to D'Arrietta. In November of the same year Noel Hill joined the company as its first technologist and was put in charge of developmental work at the newly set-up Laboratory and Research Department at Camellia.

In January 1934 the Board decided to go ahead with building a Fibrolite plant in Brisbane, an idea it had shelved in 1920. Land was bought at Newstead, and building began right away. Campbell MacDougall, from Camellia, became Works Manager there, with Ashby Hooper from Brooklyn as Deputy. Cyprian Truman, who had been associated with Fibrolite production almost from its beginning, retired as Works Manager in Sydney in April 1937, but stayed on as a Director.

In August 1935 the company bought the patent rights for Australia to a pipe-making machine from Italian engineer Adolfo Mazza. Frank Page, who joined the company as General Engineer on 12 April 1937, was soon busy setting up Mazza pipe machines at Camellia and Brooklyn. Production began at Camellia at the end of 1937, and at Brooklyn at the end of 1938, and a second machine was installed at Camellia soon after.

During yet another overseas trip, in September 1938, Andrew Reid bought Australian and New Zealand rights to make pipes by the Magnani process, which required less capital and was therefore more suitable for smaller markets. Page travelled to New Zealand to install a Magnani pipe machine for the Auckland company.

Adelaide did not get a Fibrolite plant until the Second World War, when transport problems disrupted supplies from Sydney and Melbourne. John T. Reid, George Sutton and Ashby Hooper went there in September 1940 to look at the prospects, decided they were favourable, and agreed to set up a jointly owned company with Australia's other major manufacturer of asbestos cement products, Wunderlich Limited.

Norman Thorpe, for many years a Fibrolite salesman in Victoria, ready for the road.

Sutton process pipe-making machine, as first used at Camellia in 1925.

FIBROLITE FOR TALKIE PICTURES

'The introduction of the Talkie Picture has opened a new field for Corrugated Fibrolite,' Stewart D'Arrietta wrote to Hardie sales people and agents in 1929. 'A large percentage of the Picture Houses are roofed with Corrugated Galvanised Iron and during heavy rain it is practically impossible to hear the voices..., and if continued, people will refrain from attending Talkie Pictures during wet weather.

'We have roofed a number of Picture Theatres in Sydney with Corrugated Fibrolite, and from a sound point of view during a rain storm the results have been very satisfactory.

'In addition to any new Picture Theatre that may be erected, we feel sure that in the course of time something will have to be done with the roofs of the existing Theatres covered with iron.' D'Arrietta suggested to interstate managers that they should arrange for their representatives to interview all picture show proprietors, both in the suburbs and in country areas, and introduce them to Corrugated Fibrolite.

'The coolness of a building roofed with this material and the freeness from condensation are other advantages not possessed by galvanised iron,' he went on. 'The temperature of a Picture Show is a very important factor, as most of the more expensive seats are in the gallery, which is closer to the roof than the other seats, and consequently more subject to the heat than the cheaper seats. A difference of only a few degrees should be a big consideration when considering the roof of a building of this description.'

The manufacturing company, Asbestos Cement Pty Ltd, with authorised capital of £45 000, was managed by Hardies, with D'Arrietta as Chairman, John T. Reid and George Sutton as Directors, and Chisholm Cameron as Secretary. The Board of Asbestolite Pty Ltd, the selling operation, had two nominees each from Hardie and Wunderlich.

While so much of Hardies' development in the 1920s and 1930s was based on Fibrolite, the company had also been moving steadily into other building products. In 1919 the Melbourne company started a fibrous plaster works in Barwise Street, North Melbourne, which operated until 1929. Quite independently, the Sydney company started a fibrous plaster works at Redfern in the same year. In January 1920 it moved to Mandible Street, Alexandria, and continued there until it closed in 1941, during the Second World War.

In September 1923 James Hardie began to make Samson wire gates and fencing in a small factory it had built also in Alexandria in September 1921, where it had experimented with making book matches. The match project had not been commercially viable, but the wire-gate and fencing project was. It operated until mid-1941 when, due to wartime shortages of materials and the lack of new housing construction to provide a market, the company closed it down.

At the end of 1936 the company decided to make terracotta tiles in Brisbane. It bought just over 20 hectares at Bulimba, on the lower Brisbane River, for £1770, and in April 1937 formed Hardie Tile Works Pty Ltd, with capital of £25 000. Production started in August 1937.

In 1938 James Hardie took its first step in manufacturing outside Australia when it began to make Fibrolite in New Zealand. Australian-made Fibrolite had established a good market in New Zealand. In 1925, Pipitea Wharf, one of the most exposed buildings in Wellington, was roofed by Hardies' own fixers, sent over from Sydney. In 1929, Jack Knutson, who had been with the company in Melbourne since 1919, moved to New Zealand to represent all Hardie interests there, including Hardie Trading Pty Ltd as well as Fibrolite.

By 1936 the New Zealand trade in Fibrolite was good enough to encourage D'Arrietta to go there to look at the prospects of starting a local plant. Given the task of finding a suitable site, Knutson chose one in the Auckland suburb of Morningside, only to have it taken over as a school site by the Education Department. This proved to be a blessing, because he found a much bigger site at Penrose with adjoining land available for expansion.

The Bureau of Industry, then the sole authority for approving or rejecting proposals for setting up new plants, granted a licence. Two competitors objected, but the Appeal Authority, Sir Francis Frazer, upheld the decision. The New Zealand company was registered on 7 July 1937, with the original capital of £50 000 all subscribed from Australia by Hardie Asbestos Cement Pty Limited. Campbell McDougall, who was Works Manager at Brisbane, moved to Auckland in 1938 to supervise building work and the installation and commissioning of plant. From site preparation to production took only three months, and the plant made its first sheet on 8 July 1938. The original plant at Penrose had only one sheet machine, which made both flat and corrugated sheet. Pipes were made by the Sutton process from flat sheets.

The Centennial Building at the 1940 New Zealand Centennial Exhibition, was sheeted with Fibrolite.

The first major contract for the New Zealand plant was in 1940, for the exterior walls of the impressive New Zealand Centennial Exhibition buildings in Wellington. The first pipes were made for the initial water supply in a small town south of Auckland.

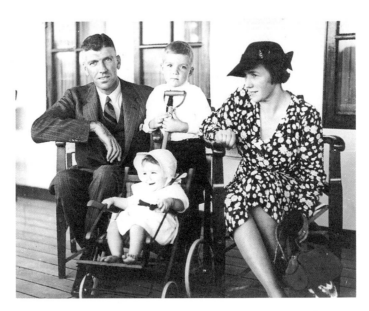

Campbell McDougall and his family on board ship, bound for New Zealand, where he would manage the new Hardie plant.

CHAPTER THIRTEEN

SEPARATE WAYS

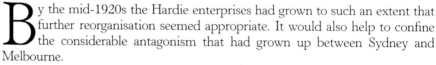

By the mid-1920s the Hardie enterprises had grown to such an extent that further reorganisation seemed appropriate. It would also help to confine the considerable antagonism that had grown up between Sydney and Melbourne.

In Sydney, the top executives, which meant George Sutton, Stewart D'Arrietta and Chisholm Cameron, got on well together. They had a common adversary in George Gregson, who managed Melbourne. They did not trust him, and the feeling was mutual, apparently for no better reason than that he was 'Melbourne' and they were 'Sydney'. All took great delight in cross-border raids to pick up orders in the other's territory. What they could not purloin, they would thwart.

All this soon became clear to anybody who had to deal with both companies. When John Adamson arrived in Australia in the early 1930s to take up a job at the Hardie Rubber Company, and told Gregson in Melbourne he would be seeing Sutton, D'Arrietta and Cameron in Sydney, he was warned to beware of them, as they were 'crooks'. When he told the Sydney threesome Gregson had met him in Melbourne, they gave a similar opinion of him.

Sutton, D'Arrietta, Cameron and Gregson were all dedicated men of business, fiercely loyal to *their* company (whichever it was), and committed to ensuring its commercial success. They worked hard and unswervingly to achieve its objectives. The cut and thrust between Sydney and Melbourne were subordinated and directed to those ends.

Andrew Reid did nothing to foment the Sydney – Melbourne division, but he did not bother to oil the troubled waters either. With Gregson and the others barely on speaking terms, he never had to worry about them joining forces to bring about any change in the company that might lessen his role as its driving force.

Gregson was sensitive about any intrusions into what he regarded as his territory, not the least reason being that he shared in the profits. His sensitivity even applied to Andrew Reid taking steps that affected him without prior consultation. When Reid said 'We've just bought the Parbury Henty building,' Gregson corrected him. 'No, Andrew,' he said, '*You've* just bought the Parbury Henty building.'

When the building was sold at a profit and Gregson said, 'We did well on the deal,' Andrew Reid was quick to correct him. 'No, George,' he said, '*I* did well on that deal.'

Gregson had been in charge in Melbourne since 1913, having come there as Joint Manager in 1911 at Andrew Reid's persuasion. He had been with Dalgetys in Brisbane until then. The other Joint Manager was A. A. Marsden, who became Manager on James Hardie's retirement. Marsden retired in 1913.

George Sutton joined the firm as a bookkeeper in Sydney soon after Andrew Reid set up an office there. He rose to become Chairman of the holding company while Andrew Reid's eldest son, Thyne, was away at the Second World War.

George Gregson managed the Melbourne operation from 1913 until he retired in 1952. This is how he appeared in *500 Victorians* in 1934.

To separate the various activities, the company's accountants, Davey Garcia & Company, put 'A Case for Opinion' to Andrew Reid. They suggested a holding company to be called Jas Hardie's Property & Investment Co. Ltd, a national fibro-cement manufacturing company to be called Hardie's Building & Asbestos Manufacturing Co. Ltd, and Sydney and Melbourne companies, each to be called Hardie's Trading Company Limited. Andrew Reid chose not to accept any of these names. The first was not in keeping with the ideas of the founder, who had never been known to contract his name to 'Jas'. The second was too cumbersome. The latter name almost made it, for the Melbourne trading company.

Reid, in his characteristically spiky pencil notes, crossed out the Davey Garcia names and inserted others. He wanted to keep the existing name as intact as possible, and had to decide which part of the company would have it. Tradition said the trading activities, being closest to the original business, should. But

A Helping Hand For Burnside Homes

During a trip to London in August 1922, this time with his second son, Jock, Andrew Reid read one morning in the *Times* of a boys' orphanage in Connemara, Ireland, that had been burned out.

The fire had been started by the Sinn Fein because the boys' fathers had fought for Britain in the First World War. Fearing that they could come to further harm, the British Government sent a destroyer to Ireland to bring them to England, where they would be safer. But there still remained the problem of housing them. An advertisement in the *Times* asked: 'Will someone lend a house large enough to accommodate 33 boys and staff?'

Andrew Reid had for some years been a Director of the Burnside Homes for orphans at Carlingford, near Parramatta. It happened that Sir James Burns, who had established the Homes, was also in London. He was in hospital, but still saw Reid. They talked about the prospect of taking 'the Connemara boys' at the Burnside Homes, but did not have enough space.

One more home would solve the problem, so Reid left the hospital and sent a telegram to D'Arrietta telling him to build a home for thirty children at Burnside Homes and to have it ready within six months. Then he offered, on behalf of the Burnside Homes, to house and educate the children and settle them into life in Australia.

Reid heard from James Murdoch, Acting President of the Burnside Orphan Homes Board, that there seemed 'to be some little perturbation in Anglican Church quarters [in Sydney] in connection with the fact that the Presbyterians [had] stepped in and clinched matters in this important movement, and certain folks in high places [had] been inquiring whether, even though the boys are put in Burnside, they would be allowed to have them confirmed into the Church of England'.

The Presbyterians responded by giving the Anglicans 'to understand quite clearly that when the boys go there they become Presbyterians and will be trained as such, and that no other authority, whether Church or State, can be allowed to interfere'.

commerce said that fibro-cement, by now the rising star, the major profit earner, should. D'Arrietta certainly pushed this view. He had spent more than twenty years building up the fibro-cement business in association with the name James Hardie and he did not want to lose the goodwill associated with it. Andrew Reid saw the merit of this view, and agreed that the name James Hardie & Coy Limited should go to the fibro-cement side of the business.

To give effect to this, in September 1926 the Asbestos Slate & Sheet Manufacturing Company Ltd bought up the building materials departments and distribution organisations in all states from the Sydney and Melbourne companies, changed its name to that of its parent, and increased its authorised capital from £250 000 to £500 000. The original company, now in effect the holding company, became Hardie Investments Limited.

Two new companies were formed to hive off the 'general merchandise' sections: Hardie Trading Pty Ltd in Melbourne, with paid-up capital of £80 000, and James Hardie Trading Co. Pty Ltd in Sydney, with paid-up capital of £33 468.

Hardie Trading Pty Ltd was incorporated in Melbourne on 2 December 1926 and held its first board meeting on 16 December. Andrew Reid was Chairman, and George Gregson Managing Director. The other two Directors were G. A. Woinarski and N. D. Bailey, with R. J. Coles as Secretary. The company took over all the departments and manufacturing interests of James Hardie and Company Limited except for Fibrolite and other building materials. Its trading territory was to be Victoria, South Australia, Western Australia and Tasmania.

Hardie Trading Managing
Director George Gregson
(right) with Andrew (centre)
and Jock Reid at a company
function in Melbourne.

The original directors of the Sydney trading company, James Hardie Trading Co. Pty Ltd, were Andrew Reid, George Sutton, Stewart D'Arrietta, Arthur Sparks, Thomas Cook and William White, with Chisholm Cameron as Secretary. Its territory was to be New South Wales and Queensland, and it established its Sydney headquarters at the warehouse at 378 Kent Street.

At the time of the reorganisation, the general merchant sections of the two companies each had six departments. The Tanning Departments supplied tannery needs, including locally made and imported machinery. The Laundry Departments dealt in clothing supplies and general commercial laundry equipment. The Dye Departments, the smallest and least profitable, sold dyestuffs and mill sundries to the textile trade. The Engineering Supplies Departments sold pulleys and leather belts (both imported from R. & J. Dick and locally made) to drive them. The Chemical Departments were agents for lines from the British United Alkali Company and other overseas principals. The Rubber Departments sold solid vehicle tyres, retreading compounds and components for milking machines.

As things turned out, the separation of activities was more formal than real. For the first two years, George Gregson ran not only the Melbourne trading company but also the Melbourne business of the manufacturing company, which included the task of building the new Fibrolite plant at Brooklyn and getting it into production. He was appointed a Director of the Victorian manufacturing company in July 1928. Sutton, D'Arrietta and Cameron did not much like visiting

William Williamson, the only 'outside' director of the original fibro-cement manufacturing company, the Asbestos Slate & Sheet Manufacturing Company Limited. He was a leading Sydney building contractor and a former President of the Master Builders Association.

Melbourne, and the only continuing contact was through Andrew Reid.

Gregson operated from the premises at 581–583 Little Collins Street, to which James Hardie had moved in 1902. They had been bought from the former landlord, Mrs Peacock, in 1913 and were now owned by the Reid Trust and leased to Hardie Trading Pty Ltd, who sublet the ground floor to James Hardie and Company Limited for its Melbourne Fibrolite business. Melbourne activities came to be known as 'upstairs' for trading matters, and 'downstairs' for Fibrolite and related matters.

For the first couple of years after the separation, Gregson was still sufficiently preoccupied with Fibrolite matters to leave much of the trading work to Woinarski and Bailey. But this did not prove to be entirely satisfactory, and when Woinarski retired, in 1928, Gregson suggested that a Sales Manager be appointed to sell Fibrolite under his supervision, so that he could return to more active control of the trading activities, which he much preferred.

Stewart D'Arrietta. At one stage the firm thought of abandoning fibro-cement because of the losses caused by breakages. Instead, Andrew Reid put the fibro-cement in the young D'Arrietta's hands. It became the mainstay of the James Hardie business.

CHAPTER FOURTEEN

A CORPORATE HOME

About the same time as the companies were being restructured, moves were afoot that gave the group a new permanent head office address in Sydney. Early in 1926 the New South Wales government announced that it would in time acquire the company's main office, at the corner of York and Wynyard Streets, for Sydney's underground railway. An opportunity to acquire a nearby property came up in May 1926, when a warehouse at the corner of York and Barrack Streets, occupied by Petersen, Boesen and Company, was burned out. The company bought it at auction for £95 000.

The first idea was to make good the existing building, but this soon gave way to a plan to rebuild it completely. The company had surplus cash and — with the example of Germany's runaway inflation to help it make up its mind — decided its reserves would be safer in bricks and mortar than in fixed-value securities. The contract for the first section of Asbestos House, as the planned new twelve-storey structure was to be called, was let on 12 December 1927 to Hutcheson Brothers. The architects were Robertson & Marks in conjunction with John Reid and Son (no relation), with Charles Reed as construction engineer.

The first building to be known as Asbestos House was at the corner of York and Wynyard Streets, Sydney.

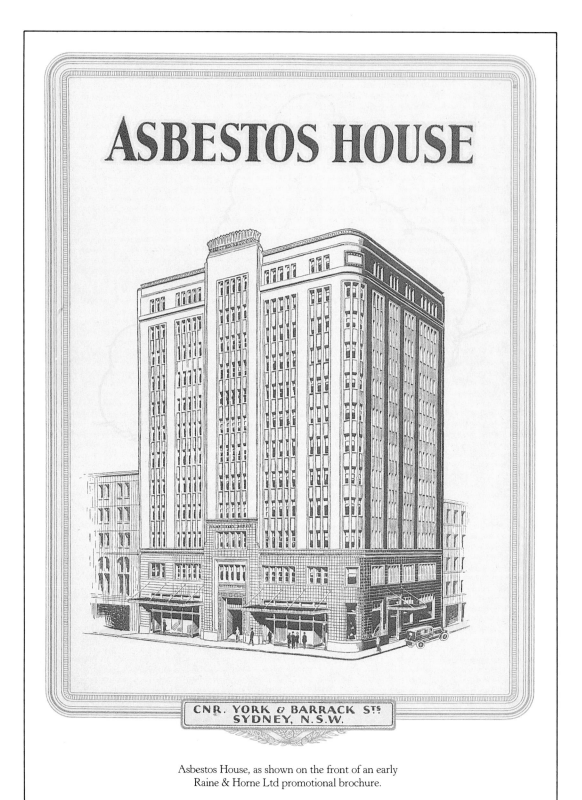

ASBESTOS HOUSE

CNR. YORK & BARRACK STS
SYDNEY, N.S.W.

Asbestos House, as shown on the front of an early
Raine & Horne Ltd promotional brochure.

Temporary office arrangements had to be made. To ease pressure on the York and Wynyard Street premises, the office staff of the Sydney trading company moved to 378 Kent Street at the time of the separation. In October 1927, the date set for moving out of the York and Wynyard Street property, the company was lucky enough to get temporary office space in Alcock's Building, on the corner of York and Barrack Street, diagonally opposite Asbestos House, which was by then under construction.

An artist's impression of the Hope Tavern, the first building on the site of the company's new corporate headquarters.

The first staff moved into Asbestos House on 14 August 1929. The move across York Street into the new building was made on a Saturday afternoon, to avoid losing half a day of work. People simply picked up their desks and office paraphernalia and carried them across York Street. Most of them were less than pleased at missing out on their normal Saturday afternoon activities, but nobody complained too volubly.

Hardie people by no means filled even the half-finished building, and an advertising brochure was prepared by Raine & Horne (who are still managing the building in 1987) to extol its virtues to potential tenants. It occupied 'a dominating position right in the very heart of the business centre of Sydney'.

'Situated at the corner of York and Barrack Streets, and looking into George Street and Martin Place,' the brochure said, 'it is in the heart of the wholesale commercial portion of the City, being in close proximity to the principal houses trading in softgoods, machinery, general engineering, hardware, chemicals, dyes, paper and stationery, electrical goods and appliances, wireless, jewellery, building materials, footwear, general rubber goods and tyres, foodstuffs, etc., etc., etc.

'From every viewpoint, the location is an ideal one for both business and professional men, being within 100 yards of the General Post Office, the Wynyard Square Railway Station, leading banking houses, and within two or three minutes walk of most of the leading insurance companies, shipping companies, cable companies, the Supreme Court, daily newspapers, and the retail shopping centre of the City. Many well-known solicitors, accountants, and professional men are also located in buildings in the immediate vicinity.

'Asbestos House is eminently suitable in every respect for general occupancy by both commercial and professional men, offering as it does every desirable feature of a modern office building.

'The incessant demand for maximum daylight in office buildings has been fully provided for, every floor being so flooded with brilliant daylight that all floors may be sub-divided to obtain perfect lighting from outside, practically eliminating the necessity of using artificial light during ordinary business hours. This is a feature that should appeal to prospective tenants, more especially those to whom maximum daylight is essential — such as architects, civil engineers, surveyors, and commercial artists.

'It is interesting to note that at the present time a proposal is under consideration by the authorities to widen York Street on the opposite side to Asbestos House, to a width of about 100 feet. If this scheme eventuates, the increased width of York Street will extend from the North Shore Bridge to the Town Hall, thence via Park Street to the Eastern Suburbs, making it one of the finest thoroughfares in the State. Whilst nothing definite has been done in this direction, the Railway Commissioners have already purchased the land on the Eastern side of York Street from the new Wynyard Square Railway Station to Barrack Street.' (This proposal never got past being just that — a proposal.)

'Although occupying the most central business site in Sydney, Asbestos House is free from the irritating noises of trams and heavy traffic.

'A portion of Asbestos House will be occupied by the owners, James Hardie and Company Limited, whilst the remaining offices will be made available for letting to approved tenants. The Lower Ground Floor is an excellent one, and, having good height, light, and ventilation, is eminently suitable for a showroom or coffee room. All floors throughout will be covered, where required, with a high-grade linoleum by the owners, and offices will be sub-divided to suit tenants on the usual basis.'

Early tenants included Lintas (the advertising agency for Unilever), Mercantile Credits Limited and Hardie Rubber Co. Limited. Some stayed for decades and moved only because no space was available for expansion.

The contract for the second section of Asbestos House was signed on 9 January 1935, and work was completed in March 1936. Its name was changed to James Hardie House in 1979. The group sold the building in 1987 but retained a long lease and naming rights. A 1986 brochure issued by Raine & Horne once again praised the building effusively.

Illustration of the main entrance vestibule
in an early Raine & Horne Ltd
promotional brochure, 'showing the
massive and artistic design'.

CHAPTER FIFTEEN

A START FOR SPARTAN

Paint manufacture, first started to fill a gap in supplies caused by the First World War, went on to become a major Hardie operation. One of the early processes was critical enough for the recipe to be kept in a sealed envelope in case the one man who knew it, a Mr Lloyd, should expire unexpectedly and take his secret with him. It was the method of making white lead by carbonising metallic lead in chambers filled with horse manure.

After acting for some years as sales agents for an American manufacturer, R.N. Nason & Company, of San Francisco, in the late 1920s the company began full scale manufacture of paints under technical licence from Nason, in a relationship that lasted until the 1960s.

This came about as the result of the company's experiments with nitrocellulose lacquers at its premises in Ferrars Street, South Melbourne, in an attempt to go into production locally without the need to pay licensing fees. George Gregson tried some on his own car, and the results, in his words, were 'one hell of a mess'. He told Andrew Reid: 'If we really want to understand this, we should send Hesketh to America.' Reid took one look at the car and agreed.

Hesketh, the Chief Chemist, was on the next boat, and his trip led to a deal with Nason for technical advice. A small factory was built at West Footscray, partly because the Ferrars Street factory had been burned down, partly because the day was foreseen when the site there would not be able to accommodate the growing paint business.

The agreement provided that Hardies would pay Nason 5 cents for every imperial gallon of nitrocellulose lacquer they made for automobile, furniture, interior decorating or similar trades, for ten years. Nason would furnish the necessary formulas and give instructions for making the various lacquers. They also undertook not to make a similar agreement with any other lacquer manufacturer in Australia.

In 1932 Hardie Trading Pty Ltd, which ran the Spartan factory, set up its first subsidiary, Spartan Lacquers Pty Ltd, to market Spartan products in New South Wales. Until then, they had been sold through James Hardie Trading Co. Pty Ltd, the Sydney trading house.

In 1933, after Gregson had been to San Francisco to negotiate an arrangement for Nason brand products to be made at the Spartan factory at West Footscray, a second subsidiary of the Melbourne company, R.N. Nason & Coy Pty Ltd, was set up to market them. Spartan products were by then being well received, particularly the automotive finishes. Extensions to the new factory were opened in 1934 by the then forty-year-old Robert Gordon Menzies. The future Prime

MORRIS

SPARTAN
COLOUR
SELECTIONS
for
1937

Manufactured by
HARDIE TRADING PTY. LTD
West Footscray, Vic.

Bodies built by
RUSKIN MOTOR BODIES Pty. Ltd.
Melbourne, Vic.

Spartan developed a good share of the automotive finish market.

Minister had recently become Commonwealth Attorney-General in the Lyons Government, after a period in the Victorian Parliament, where he had been Attorney-General and Deputy Premier.

In 1938 Spartan Lacquers Pty Ltd began to manufacture some lines at Botany, in Sydney, including clear lacquers, floor finishes, soldering fluids and rot-proofing compounds. The Botany plant was later used to make metal hangers for drycleaners, polyvinyl chloride for gramophone records, dry-cleaning soaps, and other chemical products.

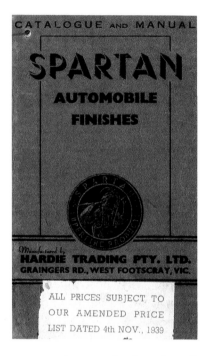 

In an age when fewer Australians owned cars, and we made rather than imported cycles, Spartan wooed the cycle enamel market (left). Spartan followed the Hardie Trading lead in selling direct to industrial users (right).

CHAPTER SIXTEEN

THINGS COULD HAVE
BEEN WORSE

If Andrew Reid was worried about the state of the Australian economy in 1928, he did his worrying from afar. He spent much of the year overseas, and not always on business, with Peggy and his second son, John, usually known as Jock.

One of the few of his letters that have survived tells us that on 18 September 1928 he was at the Ugadale Arms Hotel at Machrihanish, in the Canadian maritime province of New Brunswick, and that for the 'past fortnight' he had been 'playing golf mostly and seeing the country'. He had been 'so much on the move lately' that he had had little time to write except for special letters about urgent matters. Jock was more intent on business, and was at the machinery show at Olympia, in London.

Still, Andrew Reid could not get away from business entirely. George Gregson kept up a steady stream of letters from Melbourne, mostly about how hard business was, and what a rotten deal he was getting from the Hardie men in Sydney. The letter from New Brunswick was a reply to Gregson's letter of 30 July 1928, which has not survived, but which was clearly only one of several about tough times in Melbourne.

'No doubt some economies are necessary if things are as depressed as you have indicated in previous letters,' Reid said.

'It is very disagreeable to pass out good old servants like Fardell [and] we should not do so until possibly finding him another job. If you put him upstairs, you should possibly curtail in other directions because I cannot see the trading company doing much good for a year or two, until lacquers develop better.

'I was hoping for a progressive policy, with Woinarski's young activities upstairs in lines like lacquers and paints, but evidently we cannot look for much rapid progress. Rather you would have to be ultra-conservative and probably cut out more than otherwise. However, you will soon get a grip of the conditions upstairs and act accordingly.'

(In Melbourne, 'upstairs' was shorthand for the trading activities.)

Another of Reid's letters to Gregson was written in Edinburgh on 27 September 1928. He had arrived there to find two letters from Gregson, dated 14 and 16 August. One of them had brought the good news that 'the balance [was] on the right side' in the trading company's accounts. Reid reported that the weather in Edinburgh was good, that he was having some shooting and golfing, and that life was agreeable. He had been to the Mull of Kintyre. He would be in Edinburgh

Laying Fibrolite pipes,
Perth (WA), in the early
1930s.

until 15 October, when he would head for the south of France, there to await news
of some pipe patents from America before he set sail for Australia.

Gregson answered on 7 November 1928 with five pages of close typing.
Although much of the depression was passing, he did not think the economic
position was very healthy in Australia, which relied too much on wool. He noted
that Courtaulds had cut their prices for artificial silk and that some authorities
were 'not keen on the textile outlook'. Still, the season had improved greatly in
most of Australia.

The company had seen an improvement in general trade, owing largely, he
thought, to the recruitment of trained men. Fibrolite was 'progressing pretty well'.
He had made temporary arrangements for Fardell, but would tell him that they
were only temporary and advise him to look out for another job.

Within the next few years, the Hardie enterprises, like most others in Australia
and all over the world, would come to appreciate just how right Gregson had been
when he said he did not think the economic position was very healthy.

Some of the day-to-day detail of how the company fared in the Depression has come down to us in a file of letters from Perth. On 3 April 1930 the local manager, John Henderson, reported that building in Perth and suburbs was 'practically at a standstill'. Sales for flat sheets in town had suffered, but country business was keeping up well and seemed likely to continue to do so for some time.

The country business had been helped out by big orders from Cuming Smith and Mt Lyell Farmers' Fertilizers Ltd for corrugated sheet for their plant at Bunbury. Beyond that, White, the traveller who covered the country areas, did not share Henderson's enthusiasm about the prospects there. He wrote from Bunbury in April 1931 that 'so far the only good thing is the weather'. Along the track, people all seemed to be waiting on a few pounds from the next potato crop to hold them up. Even then, the price would probably be 'rotten'. The trivia White thought worth reporting gives us an idea of just how hard it was to get an order; even then, the problem of getting paid lingered on.

He did have a few prospects, which he ran through in his letter. A farmer named Pigott, who was 'sound enough', would order in about a month. He was busy top-dressing, but would be lining the walls and ceiling of a couple of rooms. White had 'put in a spoke' about silos wherever he called. He expected to run out of leaflets for them before he reached Manjimup and asked if more could be posted to him there. If the silos at Manjimup were a success, they ought to go right through the south. Bowles of Yarloop, who was a corrugated prospect, had done his job with iron, and would not be ordering Fibrolite.

Johnson would be ready for 'the butter factory stuff' on White's return trip. He would settle his account at the end of the month. Brearly of Waroona was in town and said he 'was calling our way to settle'. Weller was 'going for his life and [had] some more prospects', and had given White a cheque for £25. White spent a lot of time on that trip looking for Marriott, a customer from whom he hoped to extract some money on account. When he was eventually tracked down, 'out in the bush', Marriott 'said he was broke, others had done him in for cash, etc., etc. He offered all the silver he had in his pocket [about 8 shillings].' White gave him until his return trip through the area 'to build on that amount'.

White planned to stay the next day, Thursday, in Bunbury, then to go on via Boyanup, Capel and Busselton to Margaret River. He thought one night in Busselton would be enough, and on Saturday he would go back to Bunbury, where he would spend Sunday. On Monday he would go to Donnybrook, then head 'right down to Manjimup', then work back via Bridgetown, Boyupbrook, Dinnieup and Wilga to Collie. He thought that would 'cover the lot or near enough for this trip'.

The car was 'going good', White reported. This car had caused Stewart D'Arrietta, back in Sydney, some concern. He had suggested to Henderson that White should be able to do the country by train. On being told that this was difficult, he had asked, 'as the cost of running a car is rather a big item, do you think it would be possible to arrange with some other firm not in competition with us or any of our clients, to share the expense of running the car? It would be a decided advantage if this could be arranged.' Nothing seems to have come of the suggestion.

White had better news from Busselton. He had actually got an order for two

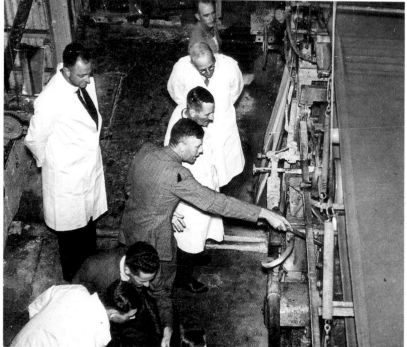

Left: Queensland Premier Forgan Smith (with glasses) inspects the new Hardie plant at Newstead, Brisbane, in the 1930s. The factory (above) was built in 1934.

sheets of Fibrolite, which he phoned through to Perth. He had been in the local agent's office when the customer had phoned. They had had no stock, but he had seized the opportunity and arranged for the sheets to be railed from Perth that very day.

Then he got back to the bad news about Bunbury. It was very quiet. Millars had two places going up, labour-only jobs and another just started. The latter would be Fibrolite on the outside walls. Fowler was going to do the job and would place the order the next week, when he had given them the exact sizes. He had fixed a bit of Tilux for another bathroom job coming through Millars, who had not ordered any 'Dura' (Durabestos, the fibro-cement sheet made by the opposition, Wunderlich) since last August and did not intend to do so, but were just going to pick up their needs locally.

Wunderlich's man was also on the track. White, who had met him in Bunbury, reported that he was a 'young man from inside', who had 'got nothing'. White had managed to switch two small accounts from Wunderlichs. He had persuaded the Narrogin Trading and Agency Co. to order through him, even though he gave them only 10 per cent commission, compared with the 15 per cent they had been getting from Wunderlich. The local undertaker, who also did some building, had been buying from Wunderlich, but would 'come our way in future'. Local builders had 'nothing on', except Hough, who was 'using a few sheets but has them on hand'.

White's letter goes on to report his efforts to get people along the track to pay something off their accounts, an enterprise in which he had not had much success. Power was 'not at home'. His wife said 'he may be in tomorrow', and White would 'wait on him'. Lockwood 'hadn't a bob', and any money he did manage to get would go to pay the overdue instalment on his truck. He would pay Hardies 'something next month'. White had had a 'hell of an argument with Blacksmith'. Still, Blacksmith had cooled off towards the end, and White thought he 'may get him down a bit yet'.

One possible way to keep the Fibrolite factory equipment and employees in work of some kind was to find alternative products they could make. Firms in the fibro-cement business overseas made clutch facings and brake linings. Perhaps the Fibrolite factories could do likewise.

By about 1930 Thyne Reid had begun to experiment with moulding or forming various mixtures of asbestos, bitumen and other substances into clutch plates and brake shoes. In this work he recruited the help of Jim Goldie, who was in charge of electrical maintenance at Camellia. His ideas for the various mixtures came from a chemist named Scott at Hardie Rubber, a long-established operation which had been added to the company's interests in the 1920s.

The first experiments were done in the laboratory, using various mixtures made in beakers and then spread out to dry. Goldie's role at first was to make electrically heated formers for drying the material and curing it under pressure. He also made a water-cooled drum for use in measuring the coefficient of friction of various compounds.

Once a particular mixture began to look promising, they would prepare a larger batch, in a kerosene tin, and make sheets of varying thicknesses on one of the idle machines that in better times had made Fibrolite.

Later they built rollers to compress the sheets and large electrical ovens to dry them. Since each sheet was 10 feet long and 3 feet wide, these ovens had to be substantial.

On one occasion Thyne Reid drew on a tablecloth over dinner the production layout for a brake-lining machine. It was about two storeys high and used cast 'lunettes' (crescent moon-shaped moulds) to form the cut sections of brake lining. The linings stayed in the lunettes to cure as they passed alongside gas heaters on their upward path on the conveyor.

All of this had to be done at minimum cost, for nobody really knew if the plant could make brake linings that would compete with the opposition product. But in time they were able to turn out passable brake linings, cut to width on a bandsaw and to length by hand. They adapted their techniques to make linings in production quantities, and Hardibestos brake linings were ready for the market. George Kimber, to whom D'Arrietta allocated the task of selling the new product, managed to borrow pre-drilled sets of rival brands of brake linings so that Goldie could make templates for correctly placing the drill holes. The new products sold well enough to encourage the plant to continue making them.

When George Kimber put the first catalogue together, he fell into the classic trap of thinking of it from his own point of view rather than from the customer's. Linings were listed according to type, followed by the name of the cars each type fitted. What people in the trade wanted to do, of course, was look up the car from an alphabetical list to find out what type of lining they needed. The whole concept of the catalogue had to be revised.

In time, brake linings were to become a major Hardie interest, notably during the Second World War and in later years.

CHAPTER SEVENTEEN

'A CHARM WHICH EMBRACED YOU'

Andrew Reid was one of those rare people who made all who had dealings with him feel that they, as individuals, were important. In an age before formal management techniques had developed to any extent in Australian business, he had the knack of getting things done through people.

One of the best descriptions we have of him came from a British source, Stan Crabb, who joined Sparrows, Hardies' London agents, in 1920 as a bill-of-lading boy and stayed on to become Chairman. He had many dealings with Andrew Reid during his various London visits.

He recalled in an interview in 1979 that Andrew Reid had a 'charm which embraced you, and... stood apart from you... He was always the boss, but the boss in the nicest sense. And no matter whether he was talking to the chairman or the office boy, he was always the same — his attitude was the same... very gentle, very homely...'

He was 'over six feet, when he stood upright' and 'inclined to be bow-legged'. He 'always wore tweedy sort of clothes'. He always went straight to Sparrows' office after he landed, and his suit was 'always dreadfully creased — from being badly packed... slung into a bag'. He was slender and fresh complexioned, 'not a robust man', with white hair that had been auburn.

He was as canny as Scots are supposed to be when it came to shaving prices. One particular item that became almost a running joke was the price of the penknives Hardies used as promotional giveaways.

'You bought half a gross of these for me last time I was here,' he would say when he was in Sparrows' office. 'I paid one and threepence-ha'penny for them. If you could get them for one and threepence-farthing, I'd take a whole gross.'

Crabb would look up the last purchase and find that Reid had indeed paid one and threepence-ha'penny, but that he had bought a full gross. When told of this, Reid would order half a gross and wait to see if the supplier, George Wostenholme of Sheffield, would weaken. By the time he left Britain, he would have given in and ordered the full gross as usual. He always had a penknife or two in his pocket, ready to give to a good customer or useful contact.

The association with Sparrows developed into such a close one that the firm had a photograph of Andrew Reid hanging in its boardroom beside one of James Hardie. The original version showed a young Andrew Reid, probably taken some time in the 1890s. In the 1930s he said it was time to replace it with something more realistic, and had a new picture taken in London.

Stan Strachan, who worked in Hardie offices for fifty years, remembered his first encounter with Andrew Reid one day in 1918, when he was still an office boy. 'You're new,' Reid said. 'Do you like your job?' The brash young Strachan

Andrew Reid was 'slender and fresh complexioned', with white hair that had been auburn.

Andrew Reid extolling the virtues of a Fibrolite moulded rainwater pipe bend to two factory visitors.

answered quite truthfully that he did not. 'All right,' said Reid, 'just keep your head down and you'll get along all right.' Within the next year or two, Stan Strachan often had to take cheques to the Chairman to be signed. Reid always asked how he was getting on.

Frank Page, who joined the company as a general engineer in 1937, when he was about twenty-three and a recent university graduate, recalled from his couple of brief meetings with Andrew Reid that he was 'a gruff but friendly man, who was interested in what we were doing and asked a series of questions'. He knew who Page was without being introduced, knew what work he was doing, how it was going and what sort of troubles he and his workmates were having.

At Christmas he would do the rounds, handing out a modest Christmas bonus. He usually told the recipients to spend the money wisely, often to 'put it in a good company'. Whenever he went on one of his many trips abroad, the Chairman would go around the office, saying goodbye to everybody.

He often took members of his family on his business trips, which always included a considerable element of getting far enough away from the business to be able to think about it clearly. On one occasion he pointed out the letters 'SPQR' engraved on part of the ruins in the Forum in Rome to his second son, Jock. They conveyed a useful business message, he said: 'Small Profits, Quick Returns.'

Andrew Reid continued the family interest in farming. At one time he owned Balfron, on the south coast of New South Wales, where he had a Jersey dairy herd. His major interest, however, was Narrangullen, a fine merino property on the south side of Burrunjuck Dam, near Yass.

He set up an Aberdeen Angus stud there, starting with bulls and cows he bought on one of his journeys to Scotland. Family folklore has it that he bought two bulls and that for some reason he gave Clifford Minter (of Minter Simpson) first choice. Minter took what proved to be the better of the two and started the highly successful Kahlua Stud near Scone.

Royal Agricultural Society records show that Andrew Reid was a major force in the Aberdeen Angus industry, and he often gave trophies for Aberdeen Angus cattle at Sydney's Royal Easter Show. At one time, 'Graceful and her calf' adorned his postcards. The mainstay of the property, however, continued to be merinos, with never more than a few hundred head of Aberdeen Angus. The Reid's third son, George, managed it until he was killed in the Second World War.

On the long road trips to Narrangullen, Andrew Reid seems to have been something of a speedster. Given his busy life, he no doubt resented the time it took, particularly in those days of primitive roads, most of them dirt except for short sealed sections through the towns. Peggy contrived to have his powerful Bentley replaced by a somewhat less speedy Morris. The mechanics at Camellia often had the job of replacing its burned-out exhaust valves.

The Morris was one of fifty or so Sparrows bought for the company over the years, before Morris had any system of export to Australia. Sparrows bought Morris Oxfords and bullnosed Morris Cowleys from a staff member's brother, who had the Morris franchise in Brentwood, Essex. At first they went to Melbourne, later to Sydney. Hardie representatives used them to 'reach the suburbs and outer districts around Melbourne and Sydney [and] to trot around the countryside', as one Hardie old-timer put it.

Andrew Reid's desire to get around in a hurry led him into thinking he would buy an aeroplane. His second son, John (Jock), was to be his pilot. But Peggy got to hear of the plan, and the aeroplane scheme never got off the ground.

Peggy Reid was well known to many company people. Stan Strachan remembered that in his days as an office boy he was given the job every Friday morning of taking the 'house money' to her at Neringah. He would push the sealed envelope well down in his pocket, then put a handkerchief on top of it, so it would not come out. He would walk down to Circular Quay, take a ferry across to Milsons Point, and catch a train there for Wahroonga. The Reid house was near the station, so he would soon be knocking on the front door. Mrs Reid always told the maid to give him something to eat and drink while she checked the money.

Peggy Reid was firmly of the opinion that people needed looking after. One of her ways of doing this was to keep soup always ready on the stove, so that anybody arriving at the house could be given a bowl to refresh them — even on Sydney's hottest days.

Peggy Reid in Scotland in the early 1930s.

This portrait of Andrew Reid, taken in May 1938, is the last known photograph of him.

Andrew Reid (right), with Arthur Sparks, a company salesman. Reid had a reputation as a fast driver. His wife, Peggy, cramped his style to some extent by having his Bentley replaced by a Morris.

On her many visits to the office, she brought violets for all the girls there. She did them all up in individual posies, then carried them in a large basket. Thyne, Jock and Doddy (George) all had to get up early in the morning to pick them. This went on even after the boys were of working age, for Jock sometimes let it slip that the female office staff could expect violets later in the day.

She found it hard to keep track of money. On her overseas travels with Andrew, he would often give her a sum of local currency early in the day, only to ask for it back a bit at a time as the need arose. At the end of the day, she would have no idea where it had all gone, or even that he had taken it all back. In Sydney, each time they drove over Sydney Harbour Bridge, Andrew would automatically put out his hand in her direction, and she would just as automatically put the toll money into it.

After Peggy died, in 1934, Andrew lived on at Wahroonga, with Farrell, one of the Connemara boys, as his housekeeper. Those who knew Farrell say he was no expert at the job, but the two men got by.

Andrew continued his philanthropic ways after Peggy's death, giving various gifts in her memory. He built the Margaret Reid Home for Crippled Children at St Ives at a cost of £9500, and donated another £10 000 towards an endowment fund for working expenses. He also gave donations to Knox Grammar School,

'FATHER OF THE FAIRBRIDGE MOVEMENT'

Andrew Reid became known as the 'Father of the Fairbridge Movement' in New South Wales for his role in helping it become established there.

The Fairbridge plan for caring for child migrants from Britain originated with Kingsley Fairbridge, a Rhodes Scholar from Rhodesia. Appalled at the plight of the underprivileged children of Britain, with no future but poverty and probably degradation, he wanted to transfer them to the wide open spaces of the colonies. With help from well-wishers at Oxford and elsewhere, he founded the first Fairbridge Farm School at Pinjarra in Western Australia in 1912.

In 1935 a group of Rhodes Scholars in New South Wales decided to set up a similar farm school in their state. One of them, N. H. McNeill, Principal of Knox Grammar School, persuaded Andrew Reid, who was closely involved with the school, to become chairman of a committee formed to back the plan. Reid and R. W. Gillespie, another member of the committee, guaranteed the £20 000 estimated to be needed. Reid had been to Pinjarra and was familiar with the scheme.

A subscription list opened in the *Sydney Morning Herald* in February 1938 soon passed its target of £50 000, and, on the committee's behalf Andrew Reid bought Narragoon, a property of about 700 hectares, 6 kilometres from Molong, in the Lachlan Valley.

The first party of twenty-eight migrant children arrived in March 1938, a second party of twenty-eight in June. By the time Andrew died, early in 1939, the Fairbridge Farm School at Molong was a going concern.

After the Second World War, the British Government banned the migration of children without their parents. The Fairbridge Society began a scheme by which families (including one-parent families) were encouraged to migrate to Australia, the children being cared for by Fairbridge until the parents had established a home for them. This had its problems, because the children (in Molong) were too far from their parents (usually in Sydney).

In an attempt to keep the Farm School going, the Fairbridge Council began to accommodate Australian children, but public financial support was not adequate. In 1973 the Farm School was closed and the property sold. The Fairbridge Council reorganised the Society as the Fairbridge Foundation and Trust, which passes on its income to institutions concerned mainly with the welfare of children.

where the trade school and memorial gates were erected in Peggy's memory, and contributed £6500 towards setting up the New South Wales Fairbridge Farm School, to encourage young people to migrate to Australia to work on the land.

He went overseas again in 1938, and came back ill. He died on 6 January 1939, of heart failure, after an attack of pleurisy, followed by pneumonia. He was cremated at a private funeral.

As well as his directorships within the James Hardie Group, Andrew Reid was a director of Nepean Sand and Gravel Co. Ltd, Wallarah Coal Co. Ltd, Mercantile Credits Pty Ltd, and the Melbourne Steamship Co. Ltd, whose ships and offices flew their flags half-mast when he died. News of his death was reported at length in both the *Scotsman* in Edinburgh and the *Herald* in Glasgow. Only a week or so before he died, his cheque for £50 had reached Provost McKay of Linlithgow, for coal to be distributed to the poor of the town. He had, said the *Scotsman*, since 1930 been a generous giver to the needy people of Linlithgow.

PART THREE

ENGINEERS

CHAPTER EIGHTEEN

JAMES HARDIE AT WAR

On 11 January 1939, within a week of Andrew Reid's death, his eldest son, Andrew Thyne, usually known as Thyne, was appointed Chairman of James Hardie & Coy Pty Ltd, the manufacturing and marketing company for fibro-cement, brake linings and similar products.

Sutton, D'Arrietta and Truman continued as Directors, and two new members joined the Board: Donald Chisholm Cameron (who had been Accountant since its formation in 1913, and Secretary since 1916) and John Henderson (who had joined the company in 1926, managed the Perth and Melbourne Fibrolite operations and been moved to Sydney to assist D'Arrietta).

Two weeks later, on 26 January 1939, in a business-as-usual approach to his new role, Thyne Reid went abroad. He had probably sensed, as many people had, that the time was fast coming when business would be anything but 'as usual'. Talk of war was in the air, and this might well be the last overseas trip anybody from Hardies could make for some years.

The tradition of overseas travel, of keeping in touch, had been strong in the company almost since its formation. Andrew Reid had been overseas shortly before his death, and had almost surely come back with a more sharply focused view of attitudes in Europe, a view he had probably conveyed to Thyne and the other Hardie Directors.

Thyne was back in Australia when the Second World War actually did start, on 3 September 1939. But not for long. He was one of the 400 or so Hardie employees who joined the armed forces before the company was declared a protected industry, vital to the war effort.

A man of adventurous spirit, Thyne Reid had always regretted that he had not been involved in the First World War. He was about thirteen when it started, and seventeen when it ended, and must have been stirred by the many tales of derring-do that were part of the propaganda of the time. His interest was sustained by the stories of those who came back and recounted the stirring events they had taken part in. His widow recalled in 1979 that 'he rather worshipped these older men', who preferred to remember only their good experiences. He was by nature inclined to prefer the company of older men and he had a special regard for returned servicemen, whom he believed to be particularly hard workers.

So, when the Second World War began, he was determined not to miss it, even though at thirty-eight he was well over the age at which he would be expected to volunteer automatically, and his role in industry would have been regarded as more important. He rushed in his application to join the services, but 'he had the good sense not to go in as a private'. He contrived to join the regular army for one

One of James Hardie's advertisements during the Second World War. Fibrolite sheets and pipes also found their way to North Africa, where they were used to build army huts and to carry the water supply in besieged Tobruk.

day as a sergeant, so he could go into the 2nd AIF with a commission. The Board granted him leave of absence – a mere formality – and George Sutton took over as Chairman.

Reid had toyed with the idea of joining the Royal Australian Air Force, for he had useful experience as a pilot. But he saw that at his age he would not be allowed to fly but would be kept in a ground job, which had little appeal for him. So he opted for the army, which would be more likely to put his engineering training and experience to use.

This proved to be so, and he was attached to a Light Aid Detachment, a sort of casualty clearing station for vehicles. He and several engineers like him were sent to Melbourne for about three months to be trained. Their wives went too, and they all passed the time fairly pleasantly. He was soon promoted from Lieutenant to Major, skipping the rank of Captain, then to Lieutenant-Colonel.

He was in charge of the First Field Workshop, which was on its way to France, under the overall command of General Morshead, when the British Army evacuated from Dunkirk. The Australians went to Britain instead. Morshead gave them all leave, and they scattered all over Britain, to any place they had friends or relations. There was only a handful of them, but they were spread so far and wide that there seemed to be a lot more. Thyne's wife, Katharine, had a letter from her sister which said: 'Oh, we feel so much happier, much safer now that the Australians have come.'

Thyne Reid first saw action in North Africa in 1940, in the initial push into Libya, then an Italian colony. The British forces, including the Australians, forced the Italians right back to Benghazi. Then German Panzer divisions under Erwin Rommel arrived and reversed the process.

Reid showed his pragmatic approach to life in the retreat from Benghazi, where he was one of the group left behind to blow up supplies that had to be abandoned. When he finally thought the Germans were just about on them and announced it was time to go, his driver found he had put water instead of petrol in the fuel tank. While driver and batman got on with clearing the fuel system as fast as they could, Reid took photographs.

On the retreat from Benghazi, he found himself besieged, one of the original Rats of Tobruk. Making the best of the situation, he took up residence in an abandoned Italian caravan and found an Italian cook who could do wonders with bully beef and herrings. Whenever he managed to get some liquor he shared it with others, and whenever they had some he helped them drink it.

Still, Reid took the war seriously. He had learnt to tell from the sound of a shell just how close it was coming, and often importuned his repair crews to keep at work instead of repeatedly rushing to the trenches when there was no real need. His comments at such times earned him the nickname Mocker Reid among some of the troops.

One bomb did, however, come very close. Now living in a brick building, he had got up in the middle of the night and was outside when it hit, bringing a brick wall down on his bed. It killed a lot of his troops, including his batman, whose loss really saddened him. Even so, he managed to see the funny side when, next day, at the funeral service, the padres took refuge from approaching Stukas in the newly dug graves.

An independent thinker like Thyne Reid was not really meant for the army,

This wartime advertisement had a patriotic slant, but it was also a solid piece of marketing. It asked Queenslanders to use a non-metallic product made in their own state for roofing. This would help conserve the metals essential for a decisive victory.

Opposite: Although he was thirty-eight when the Second World War started, Thyne Reid was determined not to miss it and was quick to join the 2nd AIF.

Corrugated Fibrolite huts in a prisoner-of-war camp, 'somewhere in Victoria'.

however – even less after he came back to Australia and was posted to Victoria Barracks in Melbourne. Company folklore has it that he was rather forthright in a report he wrote on the 25-pounder guns then being made with some pride of achievement in Australia. They might be all very well in the Western Desert and in Europe, but the Australian Army could expect to do much of its fighting in New Guinea, where it would have to haul its guns up mountains. The best approach to the 25-pounder gun was to stop making it, he said.

He also fell out with those in higher ranks when he was appointed Inspector of Workshops and was again rather too forthright in his comments. In mid-1943 the Army decided Thyne Reid should be 'recalled to industry', and the feeling seems to have been mutual. He came back to the company, but did not resume his role as Chairman. He was content to leave George Sutton in that job, while he took the title of Supervising Engineer.

Those he left behind had certainly been busy while he was away, both in Australia and New Zealand. In the early days of the Second World War, many Hardie people volunteered for the armed services, and more continued to do so until the company was declared a protected industry, effectively preventing those who were left from enlisting.

They had worked hard in Hardie plants, supplying flat sheets, roofing and pipes for army camps and hospitals, and for munitions factories and stores. Fibrolite sheets and pipes even found their way to North Africa and were used for army huts and to carry the water supply in besieged Tobruk.

As transport by sea became more difficult, supplies for the South Australian market, until then shipped from Camellia, became almost impossible to sustain. Major armament projects were growing up there, so, in an attempt to provide for

People still at work in
Hardie plants and offices
became accustomed to
seeing photographs of
former colleagues in the war
zones. Noel Brabant (second
from right) sent this one.
Hardie people were stopped
from enlisting when the
company was declared a
protected industry, essential
to the war effort.

them, shipments by rail started from Brooklyn. But the demand could not be met
properly, owing both to problems of transport and the need to supply equally vital
projects in Victoria.

In September 1940, George Sutton, Jock Reid and Ashby Hooper went to
Adelaide to look into the prospect of building a plant there. They found a site at
Birkenhead and, in association with Wunderlich Ltd, Hardies formed two
companies, Asbestos Cement Pty Ltd, to make the product, and Asbestolite Pty
Ltd, to distribute and sell it. The brand name was Asbestolite. The total capital
for the project, £50 000, was subscribed equally by Hardie and Wunderlich.

Hardies managed and controlled the manufacturing company, whose directors
were George Sutton, Jock Reid, Stewart D'Arrietta and Chisholm Cameron.
Brooklyn people were given the task of organising and erecting the plant, and of
providing key people to run it. The eight sent included a Manager, Nelson
'Rowley' Hudson, who had been Assistant Manager at Brooklyn, as well as an
accountant, a senior foreman and picked men from the fitters' and carpenters'
shops. The South Australian works began production in 1941. Hardie and
Wunderlich shared the management of the selling company, Hardies providing
two of the directors. Chisholm Cameron became Secretary of both companies.

To manage the selling company, which owned the manufacturing company,
Hardies and Wunderlichs at first had hopes of recruiting an 'impartial' manager.
When advertisements failed to find anybody with appropriate experience, they
agreed to give the task to Alan Woodford, who had for many years been one of
Hardies' country and metropolitan travellers in Victoria. He had to handle the
sensitive issue of allocating scarce product between distributors, some of whom
could be classified as Hardie oriented, some Wunderlich oriented.

The need to make fibro-cement in South Australia during the Second World War led to the setting up of a joint Hardie-Wunderlich plant which made Asbesto-lite fibro-cement sheets. The name survived until the 1960s, when Hardies bought out the Wunderlich interest. The different name in South Australia was a constant marketing problem, which prevented the use of national advertising media. Brochures, such as this one from the late 1950s, had to be produced in two versions, one for Fibrolite and one for Asbestolite.

One early casualty of the war was the Alexandria plaster board factory, which had operated there since 1920. With housing construction all but at a standstill, there was little demand for fibrous plaster, so the plant was closed.

Like many other Australians, James Hardie employees helped finance the war by buying war savings certificates. The company helped in this with a scheme, started in August 1940, by which it put up 80 per cent of the cost of the certificates and allowed employees to pay them off in monthly instalments.

Japan's entry into the war, on 8 December 1941, led to a major camp building program, to house both Australian and Allied troops, and the demands on Hardies' factory and fixing people became even greater. In 1944 a McDougall Corrugator was installed at Brooklyn, and this produced standard corrugated sheeting automatically and much faster than the previous method.

The brake linings division, the only moulded brake-lining maker in Australia, also became much busier. At first the demand was simply for brake linings for motor vehicles for the armed forces, but it soon developed to include trailer mounted guns, Bren gun carriers, tanks and aircraft. Hardies supplied brake linings for Australia's wartime output of 3500 military aircraft, including Wirraways, Beaufort bombers and Beaufighters. The plant at Camellia worked three shifts and employed about 400 people.

When Japan came into the war and cut off supplies of natural rubber from Malaya, Ian Archibald devised synthetic resin substitutes for use in brake linings. Japan's entry into the war also meant that the United States Army became a customer for Hardibestos brake linings. They found them very suited to the hard conditions in the Pacific islands, where beaches were used as roads, and brake linings had to withstand salt and sand impregnation. Linings sold to the forces for replacements all had to be in tropic-proof packaging, which often meant dipping the parcels in wax. Hardie experts were called upon to help the services solve various braking problems not directly related to linings, such as the steering of Bren gun carriers and chrome plating of aircraft brake drums.

Towards the end of the war the Canadian Army showed some interest in buying brake linings from Hardies. The war ended before a deal could be completed, but the Canadian Department of National Defense wrote to say that they had tested the samples sent and that if the war had gone on Hardies would have been a source of supply for replacement brake linings for all Canadian army vehicles.

A major Hardie Trading contribution to the war effort was through Spartan, which made vast quantities of aircraft and munitions finishes and rust-proofing compounds. The trading company itself, both in Australia and New Zealand, imported and distributed a huge variety of materials for munitions and other essential purposes, and was declared a protected industry in both countries because of its vital role in the war effort.

Andrew Reid's youngest son, George, died in the war. He had not worked for Hardies but had taken over the pastoral property at Yass. He joined the army early in the war, built up a reputation as a front line infantryman, and served at Tobruk. He was killed at Lae in New Guinea in 1943, as a Company Commander with the rank of Captain. His elder son, Alexander Thyne Reid, became a Director of James Hardie Industries Limited in 1973.

More than 400 Hardie employees enlisted in the armed services during the Second World War, and at least fifteen of them did not come back.

Queensland Branch Manager George Kimber with his wife and serviceman son. Many Hardie employees had sons, friends and other relatives in the armed services.

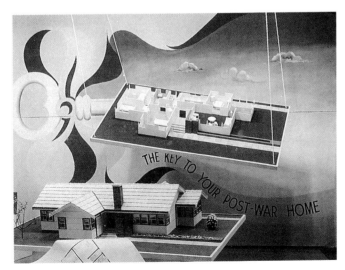

Hardies kept up Fibrolite promotion during the war,
with an eye on the postwar housing market.

CHAPTER NINETEEN

AN ENGINEERING 'GENIUS' AT THE HELM

Thyne Reid as a young man in his twenties.

'Thyne, I think, was as close to being a bloody genius as any bloke I've struck.' So said Frank Page, a fellow engineer who worked with Thyne Reid at Hardies from 1937 until Reid died, in 1964. Other people who worked closely with him had much the same view.

Thyne Reid, like his father, was a constant traveller. He had the same restless spirit, but his interests were different. Where Andrew Reid had gone off in search of another agency, another deal, Thyne went in search of engineering ideas, of better ways to make what the company already made. He was an engineer through and through, and the period during which he led the James Hardie enterprises was one in which engineers had their greatest influence.

His love of engineering was reflected in the fact that when he came back to the company after his four-year encounter with the Second World War, he did not resume the role of Chairman but became instead Supervising Engineer. Only when George Sutton chose to leave the role of Chairman, in 1953, did Thyne Reid resume it.

When Reid became convinced, in 1947, that pressurised steam curing offered the best prospects for full development of the fibro-cement market in Australia, he went on a technical survey of American methods with Ted Heath, of the Research Section at Camellia. In later years, he sent Heath and other Hardie people on several prolonged trips to the United States to research such topics as pipe-making techniques, machine design and asbestos substitutes.

Using personal contacts made during this period, Ted Heath and Frank Page, the Group's Technical Director, did a technical survey in 1950 of all the major fibro-cement makers in the western world, in association with the Water Research Foundation. Their visits led to agreements to exchange technical data with leading British and American firms, who acknowledged that James Hardie had made major contributions to the industry's pool of knowledge.

Thyne Reid was born on 20 December 1901, when his parents were living at Bonnytoun, in Randwick. He was christened Andrew Thyne, and as a child was usually known as Andrew. That led to increasing confusion between him and his father as he grew older. His mother found that when she called out 'Andrew!', her problem was not that both of them came, but that neither of them did. She began calling him Thyne, and it stuck.

He decided at an early age, when he was at Shore, that he would be an engineer, an idea his father seems to have embraced readily enough, even if a little stintingly for Thyne's liking. When Andrew said to him, during his last year at school: 'We

had better put your name down for the tech,' Thyne replied: 'I don't want to go to the tech, I want to go to the university.' Although he had many academics amongst his friends, Andrew Reid had little time for universities. He had more faith in on-the-job training in the office, which to him meant beginning with such basic tasks as putting stamps on envelopes, and working your way up. All three of his sons did such stints, but Thyne prevailed upon his father to let him do something he saw as more useful.

He spent a great part of his university days at St Andrew's College at the University of Sydney, when his parents were overseas. At the university, he made many lifetime friends, including some who came to work with him at Hardies. These included Campbell MacDougall and Ashby Hooper, both returned soldiers from the First World War who were getting on with their education. He was fresh from school and considerably younger, but they impressed him, just as they awed him. He did nothing brilliant as a student, just enough to get through his exams. One story has it that he was out rowing on the Parramatta River the day before his finals.

After he graduated, he went to Sheffield, in England, where he worked as an engineer for a small firm in a job almost surely arranged by his father. He had no great love for Sheffield. His wife, Katharine, observed after his death that 'Thyne wouldn't have gone to hell, he'd have gone to Sheffield'. While he was there he had some kind of falling out with Andrew, and for a time insisted on living on the fifty

Thyne Reid (fifth from left) in his rowing eight. He is said to have spent the day before his final engineering examinations rowing on the Parramatta River.

shillings a week he earned. He lived in a little boarding house, where the landlady had the habit of putting the teapot spout in her mouth and blowing into it to clear away blockages of tea-leaves. One of his party tricks was to imitate her. He bathed at the YMCA.

The differences between Thyne and Andrew seem to have been short-lived, and normal family relationships, and no doubt allowances, were soon restored. His more spectacular clashes were with his mother, whose fiery temper was well known, as was her instant remorse. Thyne himself was known to have had his temperamental moments.

While he was in England, Thyne went to Cambridge to look up a childhood acquaintance, Katharine Wilson. His parents and hers had often been visitors to each other's houses when the Reids lived in Randwick and the Wilsons in Woollahra. Katharine's Scottish father, a man of great medical eminence, had come to Sydney as a lecturer in anatomy at the University of Sydney and had become the first professor of anatomy as a separate chair. She and Thyne had seen each other now and again in later years, when the Wilsons went up to the Reid house at Wahroonga, and on outings such as days at the zoo. But when her father was offered a chair at Cambridge, in 1920, she and the rest of the Wilson family went with him. The renewed friendship between Thyne Reid and Katharine Wilson blossomed, and on 31 December 1926 they were married. He was twenty-five, she was twenty-two.

In May 1927 Thyne joined James Hardie as an engineer. Not surprisingly, he made fairly rapid progress, and in November 1930 he became a Director. He developed a reputation for unconventional – even eccentric – behaviour.

One of his major fascinations was machinery, and how to make it work better. He had the ability to think changes right through in his head, without the need to put anything down on paper, a habit Katharine at times found annoying, for he would lie in bed through the night, wide awake, plotting modifications that might make this machine or that work just a little better.

Thyne Reid with his Stutz car, in the mid-1920s.

Opposite: Products such as Tilux helped extend the range of uses of fibro-cement.

Katharine was not the only person these nocturnal thinking sessions annoyed. Thyne had a reputation for leaping out of bed in the small hours, driving to the Camellia plant, taking machines apart, and not having them back together when the production operators arrived. This played havoc with production schedules, and the Board formally resolved that not even the Chairman's son was entitled to take machines apart on a sudden whim.

Once a little discipline had been established, many of Thyne's ideas proved to be quite useful. On hearing of a problem, he would suggest a solution, and the people concerned would try it out at the first reasonable opportunity. More often than not it seemed to work. If a drawing was needed, he was just as likely to sketch it on the back of an old envelope as to have it done formally in the drawing office.

Thyne's ability to think things through in his head meant he was not tied to a desk, or even to an office. A lot of his thinking, even when he was Chairman, was apparently done on Bondi Beach, where, he maintained, he could do it without petty interruptions. He had, according to Katharine, 'a wonderful clam-like secretary', Miss Davis, who on being asked if he could be found on Bondi Beach would simply let out a little giggle. Reid's habit of retreating to Bondi Beach led to some exaggerated stories that he ran the company from there, with a system of runners whose task it was to ferry instructions to various James Hardie people.

Those who were in the company at the time say this is stretching the truth a little too far.

Thyne Reid was the 'hands on' type of engineer, with little time for chains of command. He wanted to be on the job himself, at the coal face, at least talking to those who would actually do the work, but he was just as likely to take off his coat and help them. One example of this occurred in 1951, when a new Magnani pipe machine was being set up at the new Perth plant at Welshpool. The official opening and all the promotional work had been organised and the dates set. With deadlines bearing down on them, those who had the task of getting the machine into production simply could not get it to work properly. Reid, one of the few people in the company who had actually seen a Magnani working, flew to Perth and spent a week there getting it up and running. Then, in a fairly typical action which showed both his shyness and his impatience with ceremony and protocol, he flew back to Sydney without waiting for the official opening.

Like his father, Thyne Reid usually managed to include a measure of pleasure as well as business in his travels. He had promised Katharine that he would take her back to see her parents within two years. As things turned out, it was five, for they did not make the trip until 1932.

On one trip, when he went to see Adolfo Mazza and his son-in-law in Italy about pipe making machines, Katharine, who was his interpreter, could not fathom one Italian expression, even though she was reasonably fluent in Italian; it turned out to mean ball bearings. After that the men took up their pencils and talked on paper. Thyne had further business looking at a plant in Yugoslavia, but after that he and Katharine motored on, south to Dubrovnik and north to Budapest, before resuming business in Vienna, where they met D'Arrietta.

On his travels, Thyne was made welcome by industry people all over the world. They believed, quite correctly, that his ambitions for James Hardie lay only in Australia, and they came to trust him with information they would not have given to many people. He had something to offer them, too, because James Hardie, isolated in Australia, had developed a reputation for innovations in technology. It also had a reputation for innovative marketing, with one of the highest sales to population ratios in the world.

The only time Thyne Reid spoke seriously of overseas expansion was when Turner & Newall seemed to be thinking of setting up a plant in Australia. They sent two men on an exploration mission, followed by their Chairman, Bill Shepherd. Reid let it be known that if Turner & Newall made any move towards any involvement in the Australian market Hardies would set up in opposition to them in Britain. He knew that James Hardie had enough technical knowledge and experience to hold its own in Britain. Turner & Newall seem to have dropped any interest they may have had in Australia.

Thyne was under no illusions about how far the Company's friendly relations with Turner & Newall would extend once they had designs on Hardies. 'You cannot take the word of the so-called English gentlemen,' he once said. Shepherd was known among Thyne Reid, Jonah Adamson and Frank Page as 'Bloody Bill'.

On the trip he made in 1932, Thyne learned to fly, in England. His special interest was in the autogyro, which he had read about. He had a flight in one, and came back to Australia enthusing about it. The following year, when Andrew was in England, he bought one for Thyne and had it sent out to him. The possibility

Thyne and Katharine Reid. They knew each other as children in Sydney, but were married in England, where Katharine had moved with her parents.

Opposite: Magnani pipe machines in the factory at Welshpool, Western Australia, 1954.

of commercial development, or an easier way of getting about Australia, we can speculate, was just as much in Andrew's mind as paternal generosity. He was well known to be an impatient driver of vehicles that were limited to the ground.

Thyne had more or less to teach himself to fly the autogyro, which caused him some grief, because he did not realise at first just how sensitive it was to wind. When it tipped over on one side and broke its rotor, he had a long wait until a spare arrived. Katharine Reid recalled forty years later that they 'had lots of fun in it, because you could fly to places you never would have done in ordinary planes... over the Barrington Tops and that sort of thing'. The Army took it over during the Second World War, and it eventually passed into the hands of the Power House Museum in Sydney.

An autogyro differed from a helicopter in that it got only its lift from the unpowered rotor (really a rotating wing), and depended on a propeller, similar to that on a winged aircraft, for its forward motion. It had to run along the ground, like a winged aircraft, to get the rotor turning, before it could lift off. It could not hover like a helicopter, but it could go quite slowly.

After the war, Thyne's interest switched to fixed-wing aircraft. He bought a De Havilland Dragon, in which he and Katharine, in company with various friends, flew to many parts of the outback, enjoying themselves immensely, camping out beside the aircraft each night. Later he bought a De Havilland Drover, which he still owned when he died.

Katharine Reid 'navigating' for Thyne. They often took trips together in the planes they owned at various times.

This L-shaped fibro-cement home was typical of those shown in Hardie promotional material of the late 1950s and early 1960s. Such designs helped live down the image of the 'fibro-box'.

CHAPTER TWENTY

A NEW APPROACH
TO MANAGEMENT

On his many trips overseas, both before and after the Second World War, Thyne Reid took a special interest in how industrial management was developing in the United States. He saw that management was becoming a separate skill, with more emphasis on planning, delegation and control, and with functional management replacing personalities. He was a foundation member of the Australian Institute of Management.

His ability as an engineer may have been matched by his ability as an administrator, but he chose to devote most of his talents to the engineering side of the business and to delegate much of the administration. Although he left George Sutton as Chairman on his return from the war in 1943, he began to feel that the established management trio – Sutton, D'Arrietta, Cameron – for all its good qualities, might not be comfortable in the new era which Hardies now had to enter. It was a time for Young Turks.

In January 1947, therefore, Thyne Reid appointed his kinsman John Thyne Adamson as his Personal Assistant, to look into applying modern management techniques to the various James Hardie enterprises.

Adamson developed a plan to reorganise Hardies that could be put in place in stages. It left the Board intact, but gave power over most decisions to an Executive Committee. Thyne Reid and the Board approved the plan in principle in November 1948 and appointed Adamson Chief Executive Officer of the company, which left Sutton as Chairman and D'Arrietta as Managing Director. Nobody who was there at the time recalled them as being pleased about the new arrangement, but it was certainly a gentlemanly way of dealing with the changing circumstances.

The reorganisation started with the technical functions, which were at the time the most critical, for demand still far exceeded supply.

When the economic climate changed suddenly, in 1952, Reid felt the time had come to put the whole plan into effect. A long period of inflation and a flood of imports had brought Australia to one of its periodical balance of payments crises. The government's stern remedial measures, including import and credit restrictions, led to a major drop in building activity, which soon cut the demand for Hardie products.

Stewart D'Arrietta retired as Managing Director but stayed on the Board. John T. (Jonah) Adamson took over as Managing Director and Chairman of the Executive Committee. Chisholm Cameron retired as Secretary and became Director of Finance.

Members of the Committee, as well as Adamson, were John T. (Jock) Reid (in

George Sutton, one of the 'Old Guard', stayed on briefly as Chairman of the holding company after he retired as a Director of the operating company.

Stewart D'Arrietta, one of the 'Old Guard', stayed on the Board after Adamson took over as Managing Director.

his role as Victorian Branch Manager), Frank Page (as Chief Plant Engineer, the technical member), Jim Rhys-Jones (production), Jack Knutson (sales), Tom Tidey (personnel), Alan Bennett (finance and secretarial) and Gordon Hayman (engineering). Tidey, first appointed in September 1951, was the group's first Personnel Manager, and one of the few at work in Australian-owned companies at the time. Bennett, who replaced Cameron as Secretary, had been Assistant Secretary.

George Sutton retired as a Director of the operating company but stayed on briefly as Chairman of the holding company. He retired from that role in July 1953, on his own initiative, and was succeeded by Thyne Reid.

By then, James Hardie had gone public. An Extraordinary Meeting of Hardie Asbestos Cement Ltd agreed on 12 November 1951 to change its name to James Hardie Asbestos Limited. It had a nominal capital of £2 000 000, of which £1 150 000 was paid up. The Sydney Stock Exchange listed the company in December 1951, Melbourne in July 1953. In September 1954, Reid Investments Pty Ltd, the family company Andrew Reid had formed, bought all the shares in

John (Jonah) Adamson, whom Thyne Reid appointed first as his Personal Assistant then as Managing Director of James Hardie & Coy Pty Limited.

Many Hardie executives were sceptical about the value of budgeting when it was first introduced. The New Zealand office showed its views in this cartoon. From left to right are John King, sales manager, Campbell McDougall, who was in charge of Hardie operations in New Zealand, and Ken Haydon, assistant secretary.

Hardie Investments Pty Ltd. In May 1954 a new public company, Hardie Holdings Limited, bought all shares in Reid Investments Pty Ltd, and was itself listed on the Stock Exchange.

Sutton stayed on as a Director until 27 June 1962, when he finally retired from all roles with the Hardie Group. Stewart D'Arrietta retired on the same day. Cameron retired from the Board of James Hardie Asbestos Limited in June 1964, but stayed on that of James Hardie & Coy Pty Ltd.

In a 1962 Investment Review of James Hardie Asbestos Limited, Melbourne stockbrokers Davies and Dalziel said that although the company was a 'family' company, 'it suffers from none of the disadvantages inherent in many companies falling into this category. Management at Board level is first class and has a history of excellent achievements behind it... Management of the Company has considerable depth and there are plenty of capable men to call upon when the time comes for the present Board members to retire'

Chisholm Cameron, also one of the 'Old Guard', retired as Secretary and became Director of Finance.

'The Company has been alive to every opportunity to expand the scope of its business and believes that growth will come, not so much at the expense of its competitors in the asbestos cement industry, but by increasing the per capita consumption of existing products and developing markets for new products. Plant and machinery are both modern and efficient and the Company is justifiably proud of the achievement of its research division.

'The Company is aggressive in the promotion of its products and it has taken an active part in the promotion of water conservation schemes. An instance of this is the financial support given the Water Research Foundation of Australia.'

PIPES LEAD
POSTWAR EXPANSION

Pipes had a special place in Thyne Reid's spectrum of Hardie products because of the engineering challenges inherent in them. They played such a major part in Hardies' expansion in the years Thyne Reid guided its destiny that Melbourne stockbrokers Davies and Dalziel, in their 1962 Investment Review of the company, estimated that they contributed 50 per cent of the company's profits, compared with 35 per cent from building products and 15 per cent from brake linings and other friction materials. The demand for asbestos cement pipes was growing at the rate of 15 per cent a year, the Review said.

For many years after the Second World War, pipes of all kinds were in such short supply that the only problems were production problems. A public authority that wanted pipes for a drainage scheme or water supply could only be told to put its name on the waiting list in the hope that in five or six or seven years its turn would come. To encourage public authorities to choose Fibrolite pipes, the

In the autoclave, silica, in the mix from which pipes (and sheets) were made, combined chemically with the excess lime in the cement, producing much stronger and more chemically inert pipes (and sheets) than those that were water-cured and air-dried.

Pressure-testing Fibrolite pipes at Camellia in the 1940s.

company often took up parts of their bond and debenture issues. Other forms of pipe, notably cast iron and steel, were in even shorter supply, and plastic pipes were still very much in their infancy.

Over and above their availability, deferred though it may have been, asbestos cement pipes had advantages for many projects. Price was one of the biggest, with asbestos cement pipes selling at 25 per cent less than steel pipes, and 50 per cent less than concrete.

They were much lighter than concrete pipes, their main competitor, and cheaper to transport from distant plants. For big projects, concrete pipe makers could set up local plants, but few projects justified that. Concrete and other pipes could withstand higher pressures than asbestos cement, but since most rural projects did not call for high-pressure capacity, this was not a problem.

As well as widespread use in water reticulation and sewerage schemes, asbestos cement pipes found an increasing role in irrigation, where they had many advantages. Open channels, which they often replaced, could lose up to 40 per cent of the water they carried, in evaporation and leakage. Pipes overcame that, as well as the problems of collapse, breakage and blockage with weeds and debris to which open channels were also prone. They took up less space, too, for the area around them did not have to be left uncultivated, and they were less subject to corrosion from fertilisers and soil chemicals than open channels were.

Conduit for electrical and telephone wires was another growing market for

asbestos cement pipes. As well as the higher demand for both these services, it was becoming a more common practice to put wires underground, which added to the need for conduit.

At the end of the Second World War, the only modern pipe-making machines Hardies had were two Mazzas at Camellia (Sydney), installed in 1937 and 1938, and one at Brooklyn (Melbourne), installed in 1938. Auckland had a 1940 Magnani machine, Rivervale (Perth) still had a 1929 Sutton machine, and Newstead (Brisbane) a 1935 Sutton.

A modernisation program began in January 1951, when two Magnani pipe-making machines were installed at a new plant at Welshpool, in Perth. Sutton pipes made in Western Australia had been far from satisfactory, and the bad impression they had created took some time to fade. Part of the problem had been sulphate attack on pipes in the Perth area, a problem that was overcome by autoclaving.

Until then, all pipes had been water cured for fourteen days, then air dried for fourteen days. This called for large water tanks and a lot of stacking space. Autoclaving overcame that, as well as the problem of sulphate attack, because it did not leave behind any free lime in the pipes to react with sulphates.

In the autoclaving process, the pipes, after leaving the quick-drying oven attached to the machine, were run without delay on trucks into the autoclaves, which were large steel cylinders. Here, under controlled heat and steam pressure, they were cured for about eight hours, after which, except for testing and finishing, they were ready for use.

The process called for a change to the original mix, silica replacing some of the cement. In the autoclave, the silica combined chemically with the excess lime in the cement to produce much stronger and more chemically inert pipes than those that were water-cured and air-dried. Traditional cement mixtures allowed to air dry reach 80 to 90 per cent of their setting capacity in about twenty-eight days, but never set completely. A silica-cement mix in an autoclave reaches about 99 per cent of its setting capacity in eight hours. An added advantage was that silica was cheaper than cement.

Getting the autoclaves made and into operation was a major problem. Each vessel was almost 2 metres in diameter and about 30 metres long, with self-locking doors, and had to be capable of withstanding severe pressure. Autoclaving gradually spread to all pipe and sheet plants, but this was to take some years.

A second Magnani machine was installed at Penrose (Auckland) in 1952. Brooklyn got a second Mazza machine in 1958 – the Premier of Victoria, Henry (later Sir Henry) Bolte, performed the official launching on 10 July – and a third in 1961. Queensland got a new pipe machine, a Mazza, in 1959, at a new plant at Meeandah, which the Premier of Queensland, Frank Nicklin, opened on 22 July. Queensland got a second Mazza, also at Meeandah, in 1968.

South Australia got its first pipe machine, also a Mazza, in November 1961, at Elizabeth. The Premier of South Australia, Sir Thomas Playford, opened the new plant on 1 March 1961. Before that plant was built, the Engineering and Water Supply Department of South Australia had ordered 500 miles of different-sized pipes, and these had been supplied from Victoria and New South Wales, all by road, over a contract period of two or three years. Construction of this plant in South Australia was a major step forward in the company's relationship with the

ERIC COHEN: WORLD CLASS EXPERT IN FIBRO-CEMENT

One development that gave Hardies a competitive advantage in the manufacture and sale of fibro-cement pipes in the late 1950s and the 1960s was the Cohen roller, which provided the extra compaction needed to maximise the advantages of autoclaved pipe.

Eric Cohen's idea was to cut a simple pattern into the surface of the top rubber roller on the Mazza pipe-forming machine, so that the roller face was made up of a series of raised areas about 6 millimetres square. This allowed very high local pressures, and gave the same effect as a 'sheepsfoot' road roller, from which Cohen is said to have taken the idea.

Eric Cohen joined the Group in 1944. His career took him through fibro-cement production in both building products and pipes.

He was a Director of various subsidiary companies and was appointed to the Parent Board in 1971. He retired as General Manager, Research and Engineering in mid-1980, and as a Director of James Hardie Industries Limited in December 1980.

Opposite: Hardies' 'Great Thirst' advertising campaign extolled the virtues of water conservation and development. It was introduced in 1961 and continued for some years.

South Australian Government. Although Playford had long wanted such a plant, as part of his ambition for the industrial development of South Australia, the company had been reluctant because South Australia was the only state with price controls. It had come to see, however, that these were always realistically applied.

The two Magnanis installed at Welshpool in 1951 had outlived their economic life and ceased production in 1961. For the next five years, Western Australia was supplied with unfinished pipes from the eastern states, lathes and testing equipment being installed at Welshpool to complete them. This arrangement lasted until 1966, when a Mazza was installed. It was launched on 22 March by Charles (later Sir Charles) Court, the future Premier of Western Australia who was then Minister for Industrial Development. In New Zealand, Penrose got a second Mazza in 1966.

A major technical innovation Hardies originated in the early 1950s was electrolytic stretching of pipes, so that the steel mandrel on which they were

Fibrolite pipes being laid in Sydney, in the late 1940s or early 1950s.

formed could be removed more easily. The idea arose at an informal brainstorming session held at Camellia one day in 1950 to try to think of better ways of removing the mandrels, which in those days was done more or less by brute force. Among those present were Jonah Adamson, who was Managing Director, Frank Page (Chief Engineer), Jack Henderson (Works Manager), Ian Archibald (Chief Chemist), and Ted Heath, an industrial chemist and future managing director.

Among the many ideas put forward, most of them not very useful, was one from Ted Heath. Passing a very heavy direct current between the green asbestos cement and the mandrel, he suggested, would set up electrolysis in the water content. Oxygen bubbles would form on the outside and simply escape, but hydrogen bubbles would form between the pipe and the mandrel and break the bond between them.

The idea seemed to be good enough to be worth trying there and then. They

Fibrolite pipes at the Lake View and Star gold mine, Kalgoorlie, Western Australia.

found an old electric welding machine, which would supply the current needed, and rigged it up to test the idea. They were soon convinced it would work. They saw that many steps were needed between their experiment with the welder and getting the idea to mass production stage. This proved to be so, and much development work took place, including power extraction of the mandrel, before all the engineering problems were sorted out.

In 1956, Hardies decided that all pipes made at Camellia would be subject to inspection by the Public Works Department. Until then the resident PWD inspector had examined only pipes intended for PWD contracts. The new practice gave users even greater confidence that all Hardies' pipes were made to the highest standards.

In July 1961 the New South Wales Department of Public Works approved Fibrolite sewer pipes for towns and cities in the state, and full-scale marketing of them began in September. By the end of the year the company had contracts for several New South Wales towns. By September 1964 about twenty large New South Wales country towns and cities had installed Fibrolite pipes for sewerage, and many others followed later.

Until 1961, Hardies had the Australian and New Zealand market for asbestos cement pipes entirely to themselves. Then Wunderlich Ltd and Humes Ltd formed a £1 million company, Wunderlich-Hume Asbestos Pipes Pty Ltd, and set up pipe factories in Sydney and Melbourne. After losing money for three years, they closed down the plant and Hardies agreed to buy them out. On 15 July 1964, Hardies bought all the issued capital for £450 000, equal to nine shillings for each of the million shares.

The price might have been higher, had it not been for the penny-tossing talents of Alan Woodford, one of the Hardie negotiating team. The two parties were still about £25 000 apart in the price at which they were willing to settle the deal, and time was running out for the Hardie team. The company was about to announce its plans to open an asbestos pipe plant in Malaysia, in association with Turner &

An autoclave on its way to a Hardie plant in Perth.

Opposite: Large diameter pipes being loaded for export.

127

Newall and Eternit. Humes already had a pipe factory there, and had they known of Hardies' intentions they would probably have bought the Wunderlich share in Wunderlich-Hume rather than sell their share to Hardies.

To close the deal, Woodford suggested the traditional Australian way of settling such a difference. This was agreed, but not without some reluctance on the part of the Hume people. Woodford tossed the penny and won. Frank Page, who knew Woodford well, averred that he had trained himself to know the number of times a given flick would turn a penny over. Page had seen him lose only one toss in twenty years.

To increase its pipe sales, and to develop in official circles and the community at large an awareness of the importance to Australia of conserving and making better use of water, Hardies began its Great Thirst advertising campaign in 1961. This was so well received that it had the unique distinction for an advertising campaign of receiving an honourable mention in Federal Parliament, when it was noted in a speech on water development as 'a splendid example of truth in advertising'.

Under the careful management of Ron Bolton and consultant George Dowman, the Great Thirst campaign was developed step by step over the next few years to cover such aspects as what proper water management can achieve, what progress had been made to date with water resources and development, the amazing increase in productivity that results from irrigation, and the immediate future for water development in Australia.

During 1962, the Brooklyn factory began to make low head-pressure Class 25 pipe for use mainly in flood irrigation projects. During the latter part of 1962, Hardies began to market asbestos cement irrigation pipe fittings made by an Adelaide firm, Irrigana Products Pty Ltd.

By June 1963, the new Supertite pipe joint, approved a year earlier by the New South Wales Public Works Department, was being marketed in all states. By early 1964, it was generally accepted throughout Australia for telephone conduit. Also in 1963, Brooklyn began making pipes for road drainage in Victoria.

Fibrolite pipes being transported to an outback mining township
in the early 1960s.

CHAPTER TWENTY-TWO

FROM FIBROLITE TO HARDIFLEX

One trauma the James Hardie group was spared at the end of the Second World War was a switch from wartime to peacetime production. Most of its products were just as useful in peace as in war, and there was a backlog of demand for them.

What the group knew best at the time was making Fibrolite sheets, both flat and corrugated, and after the war this continued to be one of the main bases of its business. It was in fact the base from which it switched its emphasis to asbestos cement pipes.

Labour shortages in the early postwar period led to greater interest in mechanisation. Hardie technical staff and tradesmen designed and built new machines to reduce the labour content of various operations. During this time the automatic Super Six corrugating machine was built and installed, eliminating much of the heavy work and increasing production.

For many years after the war, housing had a high priority in Australia. As the Commonwealth government had said in its 1945 White Paper on Full Employment in Australia, 'more houses' was an objective on which all Australians could agree. The war had created a chronic shortage of housing and building materials, and the new immigration policy accentuated it, as did the rapid return of so many servicemen.

To cope with the postwar housing shortage, whole suburbs of Fibrolite houses were built. Houses like this were eagerly sought after.

For a time, more than half the new houses were built by governments, both state and federal. They were concerned to minimise costs, and Fibrolite, in the form of both flat and corrugated sheets, certainly helped to do that. In the second half of the 1940s and much of the 1950s, the major problem seemed to be getting enough production from existing plants to meet demand. Although new sheet machines were installed from time to time, most of the new plants and equipment started up during this period were for pipes.

Even with the heavy demand, the promotion of Fibrolite continued steadily. An Asbestos Cement Homes Exhibition toured Australia during 1949, with models and photographs of architect-designed homes. An exhibition of asbestos cement homes at the Melbourne Gas Company's showrooms in Flinders Street, also in 1949, featured designs by architects from all over Australia, with models of the winning entries. John B. Reid, a future Chairman who was then an undergraduate, sometimes manned this exhibition; he learnt a lot about what people wanted in their houses at the time.

In 1957, Jock Reid added to his role as Victorian Manager that of head of the new national Market Development Division, which operated from Head Office in Sydney, and Harry Howarth, a master builder, was appointed Product Development Officer. Howarth at first handled all products, but he later concentrated on building products, while others handled pipes and other lines.

Another marketing step was the launch in 1958 of the building products showroom on the ground floor of Hardies' head office in Sydney. It opened to the public on 11 July, after a private preview the day before for metropolitan newspapers and trade journals. It was designed by Gordon Andrews, who later designed Australia's new decimal currency notes. An exhibition held in the showroom in 1959, called 'Sydney of Tomorrow', featured a model of the proposed Sydney Opera House.

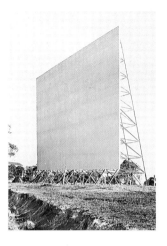

Drive-in screens, which began to appear all over Australia in the 1950s, were often made of Fibrolite.

Architect-designed houses incorporating Log Cabin siding and corrugated Fibrolite roofing helped improve the image of 'fibro' for suburban homes in the early 1960s.

Opposite: Autoclaved Fibrolite was introduced in all states in the late 1950s and early 1960s.

To overcome discrimination against fibro-cement houses by lending institutions, Thyne Reid in April 1949 persuaded the Commonwealth Bank to increase its maximum loan for them from £2000 to £2250, the same as for timber-sheathed houses. The Commercial Banking Company of Sydney soon did likewise.

Opposite: Continuing publication of booklets showing attractive modern homes made from Fibrolite steadily improved its image. Although this booklet had an artist's impression of Fibrolite homes, it contained many photographs, as definite evidence that such homes did exist.

As the only manufacturer in Australia that made building materials from fibro-cement only, Hardies could afford to promote them with vigour. Wunderlich, their only major competitor in fibro-cement products, also made and marketed terracotta, aluminium and plastic building materials, sales of which would be eroded by increased sales of its fibro-cement products. Hardies' top management never sought to increase sales by winning fibro-cement business away from Wunderlich but by increasing the overall market for fibro-cement building materials. This approach did not extend to all sales levels, however, and an excess of sales energy sometimes went into winning business away from Wunderlichs rather than to increasing the total market for fibro-cement.

One move that strengthened Hardies' share of the market was the purchase, in 1956, of Wunderlich's half-share in the Adelaide operation the two companies had set up jointly during the Second World War.

The first new Fibrolite product since the introduction of Tilux in 1929 came in April 1957, when Striated Sheet and Asbestolux Insulation Board were introduced. Another new board, Shadowline, first sold in October 1958, found ready acceptance for external walls, gable ends and fences.

One major process improvement, autoclaving, first applied to pipes, was equally applicable to sheets, and the first James Hardie autoclaved Fibrolite was

The introduction of vegetable cellulose into fibro-cement in the early 1960s led to the development of Hardiflex, a new type of sheet that was lighter, more flexible and easier to work with. It was launched in Victoria in 1964 with stage promotions, and was soon being sold throughout Australia and New Zealand.

made at Camellia in 1957. It was first sold in the drier western areas of New South Wales, where the old air-dried sheets tended to crack. In time, Camellia produced only autoclaved sheets, which were at first known as Western Quality.

By January 1959, all Fibrolite sold in New South Wales was autoclaved. Autoclaving of sheets was introduced to Victoria in 1959, and to Queensland, South Australia and Western Australia in 1961. The product was meeting with immediate acceptance and favourable comment through the building trade, the Chairman noted in his review of the year to 31 March 1961. Increasing demands led to a need for a sixth sheet machine at Camellia, which went into production in September 1959.

In January 1960, New Tilux replaced the original Tilux sheets, which had first been made by a French process in 1929. New Tilux, with a marbletone pattern and available in six colours, had taken four years to develop. It had involved buying a 5000 tonne press overseas, installing it and a sanding machine, evolving a highly technical colouring process, building a new factory at Camellia and comprehensive promotion and marketing efforts. New Tilux sold at the same price as the old Tilux it replaced, and demand for it was soon five times that of the old. The range was extended in 1963 to include Tilux weave pattern.

Although the technical aspects of New Tilux were developed in some depth, marketing was given scant regard. The choice of colours, for instance, was usually decided by a quick poll of female employees in the sales office.

The 5000 tonne press was also used to make thick compressed sheets, by pressing several standard sheets together before they had set firm to form half-, three-quarter- or inch-thick sheet. They were ideal for such uses as partitions in toilets, steps in stairways, and balustrades on home unit blocks. The brightly coloured balustrades on the Housing Commission's sixteen-storey home unit blocks at Waterloo, Sydney, completed early in 1966, were all made with James Hardie thick compressed sheets.

The success of New Tilux led to the introduction of sheets made of the same material and coloured by the same process, but produced in a variety of single, plain colours. This product was called Colorbord and was first sold in September 1960, for use in both external and internal infill panels in low-cost curtain wall construction for modern commercial, industrial and domestic buildings. Other new sheet styles introduced were Weatherboard, Log Cabin and Ranchline.

A major technical breakthrough came in October 1963, when a six months' trial of a new, all-purpose building sheet containing vegetable cellulose was started in the Yallourn area of Victoria. It was the first major step in producing an asbestos-free fibro-cement.

The trial showed that the new product, called Hardiflex, was lighter, more flexible and easier to work than Fibrolite. It met one basic requirement that had been set for it, that its performance properties had to be at least equal to the sheet it replaced. It was launched throughout Victoria in June 1964 with stage promotions by selected salesmen in all large Victorian towns and cities, and finally in Melbourne. It was soon being marketed throughout Australia and New Zealand.

The promotion of Fibrolite panels both inside and outside the home expanded demand. As well as flat and corrugated sheets, profiles included Striated and Shadowline.

CHAPTER TWENTY-THREE

A NEW DEAL FOR
THE CINDERELLAS

Part of the reorganisation of Hardie interests in the 1950s was a new deal for the Cinderellas of the company, the brake linings and insulation operations. Being small in relation to pipes and building materials, the company's main interests, they had not been given close attention. In 1957, for example, when the New South Wales Railways asked Hardies to consider making non-metallic railway brake blocks, the company decided it already had too much on its plate technically, and declined the opportunity.

The solution to the Cinderella problem seemed to be to give the smaller divisions their own executives and separate them physically from the larger operations.

In 1958, a second brake lining factory was completed at Camellia. To increase Hardies' share of the retail brake linings market, the company took over Better Brakes Holdings Limited early in 1959, issuing one £1 James Hardie share plus 3 shillings in cash for every six Better Brakes 5 shilling shares. This led to the issue of 183 155 Hardie shares as part consideration for the 1 100 000 Better Brakes shares. Soon after this, the company created a new brake lining brand, Safety Circle, to be sold alongside Hardibestos.

In 1959, Hardies looked again at the subject of railway brakes and made a submission to the New South Wales Railways on non-metallic brake blocks. In 1961, they won a long-term order away from Turner & Newall.

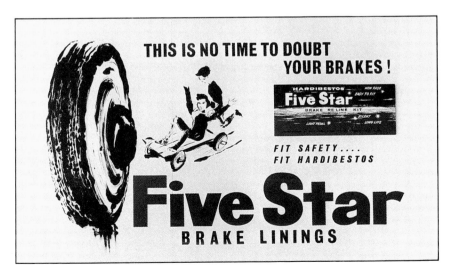

A poster advertising Hardibestos Five Star brake linings.

Above: Checking a clutch plate for wear.

Above right: A dynamometer used to test brake linings at the Hardie–Ferodo plant at Smithfield, New South Wales.

By June 1961, Hardies had agreed with Turner & Newall to form a friction materials company. Turner & Newall had decided to start producing their Ferodo brake linings and other friction products in Australia. They had hopes that Hardies would join them, but if that could not be arranged, they would go ahead on their own. They already had a site in Victoria, so their intentions were serious.

Negotiations began in Sydney with Turner & Newall's Deputy Chairman, Geoffrey Sutcliffe. Hardies' representatives were Frank Page, Alan Woodford, Jack Knutson and Don Walker. The talks went on for four or five days before Sutcliffe was joined by one of Turner & Newall's financial experts.

Hardies would agree to join Turner & Newall only if they could manage the Australian company. Turner & Newall accepted that Hardies knew the Australian market better than they did, and that the expanding Better Brakes chain gave them a major share of it. They were therefore quite happy to take a minority position. The deal was quickly arranged for a new company, Hardie–Ferodo Pty Ltd, to be formed, with a capital of £3 000 000, contributed 60 per cent by Hardies and 40 per cent by Turner & Newall. Hardies' contribution was in the form of assets, including goodwill.

The new company was launched on 2 April 1962, with Frank Page as Chairman, Geoffrey Sutcliffe as Deputy Chairman and Alan Woodford as

Managing Director. The other Directors were Ian Archibald of Hardies and Cliff Rush, an Australian representing Turner & Newall.

Hardie-Ferodo got off to a good start, its products enjoying wide support in the automotive, railway, transport and heavy industry fields. Hardies had made linings mainly for American-style cars, Turner & Newall mainly for British-style cars, so the products they brought with them into the new enterprise were complementary rather than competitive. At the same time, there were major economies of scale in making them all in the one place.

Hardie-Ferodo soon needed more factory space. Provision could have been made at Camellia by extending the existing factory, but this would have been only a short-term solution, and the cost would have been out of proportion to the benefits.

Frank Page and Alan Woodford set out to find a site for the new plant, away from Camellia but not too far away. They found one of about 9 hectares at Smithfield, about 10 kilometres to the south-west, which would suit their needs, provided they could buy five adjoining blocks, then occupied mostly by poultry farms. Four of the owners sold willingly enough, but the fifth, who owned the vital corner block, would not budge.

Alan Woodford went to see him, and, sitting around his kitchen table, they

Above: The Hardie – Ferodo proving ground at Pitt Town, New South Wales, was opened in October 1964.

Above left: Dave Deane (right) and Charles Stapley discuss brake performance with racing driver Leo Geoghegan.

worked out a deal. It turned out that the man was almost blind and did not want to move to a new, unfamiliar house. Woodford won him over by offering not only to find him a new site, but also to move his existing house to it.

In March 1964 the Board approved the transfer of Hardie–Ferodo Pty Ltd to a new single-storey factory to be built on the new site. The estimated cost of this was £1 200 000, but £400 000 was expected to be recouped by selling the existing factory and land at Camellia to James Hardie. This arrangement had Turner & Newall's agreement.

A new Hardie–Ferodo brake-proving ground was officially opened at Pitt Town, near Windsor, on 27 October 1964. The oval-shaped, built-up track, 2 kilometres long, was on the site of a disused wartime airstrip. It was soon in daily use by a fleet of specially equipped company vehicles and those of other bodies, such as the New South Wales Police, for research into brake and clutch design, and vehicle performance.

In 1959 Hardies set up a research and pilot plant at Camellia to look for better ways to make insulation materials, mainly 85 per cent magnesia, production of which had started at Camellia in 1930 and been increased in 1942.

The research led to development of the Mark II Process, which came into use in 1961. It involved pressing as well as chemical setting of the product. Because control during manufacture was greatly increased, the new process enabled insulation blocks to be precision moulded, a considerable advance.

One of the Hardie – Ferodo test fleet about to start a test program to evaluate a new friction material at the Hardie – Ferodo proving ground at Pitt Town, New South Wales. All brake-lining components had to pass rigorous tests before factory production began.

The Hardie – Ferodo plant at Smithfield was opened in March 1964.

CHAPTER TWENTY-FOUR

THE CHAIRMAN'S RIGHT-HAND MAN

For much of the time Thyne Reid was Chairman of the Hardie Group, 'Jonah' Adamson was his right-hand man. He recruited him in 1947 as his Personal Assistant, and appointed him Chief Executive Officer in 1948 and Managing Director in 1952. Adamson was still in that role in 1964, when Thyne Reid died.

Adamson, whose full and correct name was John Thyne Adamson, was the son of the John Adamson who had come from England in 1927 to be Sales Manager of Hardie Rubber. His mother was Constance Thyne, and there was a family connection with the Reids. Young Jonah came with his parents from England. He came to be known as Jonah because of his initials J.A. (for John Adamson).

Frank Page, who was for many years Hardies' Technical Manager, and for a period Deputy Chairman, was a contemporary of Adamson at the University of Sydney. He recalled him as a 'professional 51-percenter', who did only as much as he had to do to get through the exams, a not uncommon trait among university students. When his judgment failed, he got 49 per cent and had to do supplementary exams. He graduated in science, only to wish later that he had done law.

When he graduated, about 1936, he joined the British Colonial Service, which sent him to Oxford for training and then posted him to Nigeria. When the Second World War began, he joined the Royal Air Force, did his early training in Rhodesia, and became a flying instructor. He is said to have wanted to be a fighter pilot, an ambition thwarted by his large build. He became a bomber pilot instead, and at the end of the war was ferrying bombers around Europe. After the war, the Colonial Service sent him to Malaya. Thyne Reid met up with him in Singapore and persuaded him to join Hardies.

Adamson soon applied himself to the task of developing a plan to reorganise the group. He knew that Hardies' future would depend on people, and he began a fairly systematic assessment of people the company already had, going round all its operations in every state, seeing what made things tick, and meeting people in the process. He almost surely had a part in the notion that the company needed a Personnel Manager, and the first one was appointed in 1951.

To help form his own views, and no doubt to give a sense of participation and commitment, Adamson at one stage wrote to all branch managers asking for their views on his planned organisation manual. Only two bothered to reply. One of them was Jock Reid, who was familiar with the project, the other Alan Woodford, who had no idea what an organisational manual was when he was asked but made the effort to find out.

John (Jonah) Adamson
(right) with Queensland
Manager Bill Sauer (left)
and guest.

By the early 1950s, Adamson could see clearly that Hardies would need to develop a better sales organisation. 'There is no doubt that over the past ten years or more, selling conditions have been abnormal,' he wrote. 'We have been able to place everything we have made and have large backlogs of orders. Throughout this period, the company has enjoyed a highest rate of prosperity. Profits have been good. Personally, I am concerned at the prospect that when we have to meet keen competition, our selling force will be untrained and softened by the lack of a need for an aggressive selling campaign over such a long period.'

He arranged for Alan Woodford to move from Perth to Sydney to be New South Wales Sales Manager. Woodford had done well in selling the idea of fibro-cement in South Australia, and had made a point of developing a sales force and improving relations with such people as architects in the four years or so he had been Manager in Western Australia. He had also devised a method of assessing how much of the company's products went into 'sundry uses', rather than directly into houses.

Closely related to the more formal organisation of the company and its many activities was the question of budgetary control. Until Adamson took an interest in the matter, the company had various budgets for individual operations but no system of overall, company-wide budgetary control.

Adamson struck a lot of resistance to the ideas of a structured organisation and budgetary control. Many people, at various levels of management, saw structured organisation as so much nonsense, an attempt to make the company into something like the public service – an assertion that came readily to mind in view of Adamson's period in the British Colonial Service.

The first steps in budgetary control brought much the same reaction. Many people feared and resented the idea. They saw only that, for the first time, there would be some way of gauging and supervising their efforts. Slowly, however, they also came to see that budgetary control could help them.

Woodford 'saw changes in the attitude of so many people after the first twelve or eighteen months'. They came to realise the advantages of budgeting, and it became part of their daily routine. Within two years, about 95 per cent of those concerned were converted.

'The days were gone,' Woodford said, 'when somebody could run a little operation all tucked away in some corner of Australia as their own little world nobody could really interfere with, when what they told head office, or what they told anybody, was their own business.'

For a while the pendulum swung too far the other way, Woodford felt. Some people 'adopted an attitude for a while that everything in the budget was sacrosanct'. It took them time to accept that there was such a thing as a bad budget, and that failure to comply with a bad budget was not so serious as they might think.

One problem that had to be sorted out was the separation of Head Office people from New South Wales Branch people. Until that had been done, there was little hope of allocating responsibility for the control of personnel costs.

Although Adamson developed a reputation for being domineering, those who knew him well say this was more apparent than real. Although he was inclined to 'fly off the handle', he was always willing to consider other points of view if they were carefully presented. Those who took the trouble to study his modus operandi soon came to see that the best way to get an idea through to him was to put it on paper, as succinctly as possible, for he had little patience with long and ponderous reports. He believed in putting people in place to take care of the detail and leaving it to them.

Two of his favourite utterances were 'Softly, softly, catchee monkey' and 'He who carries a big stick must walk gently', suggesting he did not favour confrontation. When he was Production Manager at Camellia for a period early in his career with Hardies, he told Jim Rhys-Jones, his Plant Manager, that he would allow him a quota of two arguments a year with the sales people. Beyond that, his back-up could not be taken for granted.

One of his habits, if he had to convey some news he knew would produce an unfavourable reaction, was to have it delivered late on a Friday afternoon. He'd be out of the office by the time the expected explosion came. By Monday morning, most people would have cooled off.

For some decades, Fibrolite was promoted by means of permanent show homes on city showgrounds. This brochure was issued at the Perth show home.

CHAPTER TWENTY-FIVE

FAREWELL TO HARDIE RUBBER

In 1960 the shareholders in Hardie Rubber Co. Ltd accepted a takeover offer from H.C. Sleigh Limited, and Hardie Rubber ceased to be part of the Hardie Group. The name survived for a few more years, then gave way to Firestone.

The rubber enterprise had begun in 1899, when a man named Duval began making rubber heels for shoes in a convict-built factory in Paddington, Sydney, which had at times been a gin distillery and a tannery. In 1900 the firm became known as the Colonial Rubber Company.

By the start of the First World War it had expanded its range to include milking machine parts, waterproofed materials and a wide range of hoses. In 1914 it began to make solid rubber tyres for motor vehicles and in 1917 pneumatic tyres.

After the war its prosperity waned, and by 1924, as the Colonial Rubber Co. Ltd, it was in liquidation. Andrew Reid became interested in buying some of its machinery, but was persuaded by the firm's employees in April 1924 to take over the company and keep it in business.

For a time it traded as Hardies' Colonial Rubber Works, but in December 1924 it was sold to a new company, Hardie Rubber Co. Ltd, in which the Hardie group held a controlling interest, with Andrew Reid as Chairman. The other Directors were George Sutton, Stewart D'Arrietta and Rowland Anderson, a Sydney master tanner. Chisholm Cameron was Secretary.

In 1929 Reid entered into an agreement with North British Rubber Coy Limited, of Edinburgh, the largest general rubber works in the British Empire, for technical assistance. John Adamson, who had worked with North British, came from England to Hardie Rubber in 1927, originally as Sales Manager. He became a Director in 1929 and spent the rest of his working life with Hardie Rubber, taking over from George Sutton as Managing Director in 1940.

A serious fire on 5 November 1931 destroyed the mill room, mixing room, raw materials store and the offices. The loss, £48 266, was covered by insurance. The section was rebuilt at once, but the company was hard pressed to fulfil its orders while this was being done. In 1932 it acquired the Anchor Rubber Company.

By 1939, Hardie Rubber had more than 500 employees. Among the new products they produced during the war were special fuel lines for the armed forces. In 1944 the Sydney Stock Exchange accepted Hardie Rubber for listing.

On 1 July 1945 Hardie Rubber acquired the assets of Progress Rubber Coy Ltd, which made tyres and other rubber products at a factory in the Sydney suburb of Auburn. The consideration was 40 010 ordinary shares in Hardie Rubber, with the right to subscribe to and pay for a further 10 000 shares. As well as the 50 010 shares for the Progress Rubber acquisition, Hardie Rubber issued a further

49 990, making the total new issue up to 100 000, all at par, which was £1.

Frederick Holbrook, who was Managing Director of Progress Rubber, became a Director of Hardie Rubber, and continued to manage the Auburn plant until he died, in 1955. At the same time as it acquired Progress, Hardie Rubber set up a Board of Associate Directors, to give employees an active interest in the company's affairs. One of the original members of this board, William Parry Scholes, later became Managing·Director.

As part of the company's early postwar expansion, two completely new factories were set up in the Illawarra District, in keeping with the New South Wales government's decentralisation policy. The first of these, at Thirroul, started production in October 1946, making rubber shoes and clothing, and the second, at Bellambi, in December 1948, making wet-weather footwear, knee boots and similar products.

In 1956, to expand its operations in Queensland, Hardie Rubber acquired General Rubber and Acme Rubber, and a year later began making Hardie tyres

The Hardie Rubber factory at Paddington, 1953.

and other products there. In 1957, to expand its retail outlets in New South Wales, it acquired the Tyre Recapping Company. Further retail outlets were acquired in 1959.

Thyne Reid took an active interest in Hardie Rubber, and the company pursued technical excellence with the same enthusiasm as the other Hardie enterprises. 'The factories in which Hardie products are made include Hardie designed and Hardie built machines which equal and often surpass the best standards of the world,' the 1959 Annual Report observed. This may have been a little puffery for the benefit of would-be takeover bidders, but the report gave examples to back the claim.

One was a three-storey-high calendar train, designed and built by Hardie engineers in 1951. This machine was the first in Australia to pre-treat tyre cord and impregnate it with rubber in one continuous operation. Another was the first automatic truck-tyre moulding machine made in Australia. It too had been designed and built by Hardie engineers, and its Hard-i-matic design was covered by patents. Hardie Rubber also made the only seamless-back tennis shoes available in Australia at the time, under a licence from tennis star Jack Kramer.

Although it had grown steadily and had nearly 2000 employees by the end of the 1950s, Hardie Rubber still had only about 10 per cent of the Australian tyre market, the rest being divided between Dunlop, Olympic and Goodyear. The industry had become extremely competitive, with considerable over-capacity and an increasing tendency to sell through tied outlets, including the one-brand service stations which first appeared in Australia in the early 1950s. Stations that sold only one brand of petrol were tending also to sell only one brand of tyre.

The position was about to be aggravated by the opening of a new Goodrich tyre factory near Melbourne. Hardie Rubber dividends had gradually fallen from 10 per cent – first to 8 per cent, then to 6 per cent. Its shares had sold well below par, giving rise to rumours from time to time about likely takeover bidders. A name often mentioned was Firestone, who were expected to enter the Australian market at some stage.

The bid, when it did come, was from H.C. Sleigh Limited, which had the nation-wide chain of Golden Fleece service stations. It seemed like an ideal arrangement. Golden Fleece needed a tyre brand to sell, and Hardie tyres needed more retail outlets. The Directors of Hardie Rubber advised shareholders on 19 December 1959 not to sell until they had heard details of the bid. The share price rose that day by 2s 3d to 26s 0d, which gave a total rise of 7s 3d on the previous month's low of 18s 9d.

Sleigh announced on 22 December 1959 that it would offer two of its 5s 0d shares for each Hardie Rubber £1 share. There never seemed to be any doubt that the offer would be accepted, and it was. Sleigh issued shares with a face value of £1 050 279 and a market value of £3 421 000.

At the time of the bid, Thyne Reid was Chairman of Hardie Rubber and William Scholes was Managing Director. Also on the Board were John Adamson, Stewart D'Arrietta, Chisholm Cameron (who was no longer Secretary), Howard Wilkie and Donald Rosie, who had been Managing Director of General Rubber.

Sleigh continued Hardie Rubber in its own name for some years, and did well with it. It sold 70 per cent of the shares in October 1966 to Firestone, and the Hardie name soon disappeared from tyres and other rubber goods.

CHAPTER TWENTY-SIX

PROGRESS AT
HARDIE TRADING

Hardie Trading's main contribution to the war effort was through Spartan, and through its continued importation and distribution of vital materials. To help cope with the wartime workload, the Spartan offices in Sydney were moved from Elizabeth Street to much larger premises in Commonwealth Street. In March 1943 a fire destroyed much of Spartan's Melbourne factory in West Footscray, and it was replaced with a much larger and more modern one. Some Spartan lines, including paints, were made in Perth during 1943. Land was bought in Brisbane in 1944 for a factory, but owing to the wartime shortage of building materials it could not be built until 1946.

Steady expansion had created a need for more capital, so in 1945 Hardie Trading Limited was formed as a public company, with a nominal capital of £500 000, of which £150 000 had already been issued. It soon issued 75 000 5 per cent cumulative preference shares of £1 at par, and 75 000 ordinary shares of £1 at a premium of 7s 6d. The whole issue was oversubscribed threefold within a few minutes of opening. Soon after the public company was formed, Thyne Reid stepped down as Chairman in favour of his younger brother, Jock, but he kept his seat on the Board.

Spartan Paints became a major Hardie Trading subsidiary.

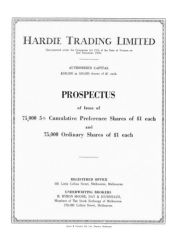

The original prospectus for
Hardie Trading Limited.
The company went public
in 1945.

Export of Spartan products to India and Malaya, which had been interrupted
by the war, resumed in 1946. At this stage shortages of raw materials meant that
such lines as lacquers and enamels could not be made in sufficient quantities to
provide for export as well as local markets, but large quantities of rot-proofing
compounds, polishes and automobile accessory lines were. Soon after the public
float, Hardie Trading sent Kevin Gray, Manager of its Chemical Department, to
the United States and Canada to study developments and seek new agencies.

Adjusting the manufacturing side of the company to peacetime production
brought few problems. Such as did exist came from shortages of raw materials and
of such packaging materials as tinplate, bottles and drums. The company had
hoped to have big new factories available to boost production, but building
permits for these had so far been refused, the Chairman said in his address at the
first annual meeting, in October 1946. By then Bob Goss, the Production
Manager, was in the United States, looking into the latest developments in paint,
lacquer and enamel manufacture.

As trading conditions after the war became clearer, Hardie Trading took steps
to switch its sources of supply from the United States, which involved hard-to-get
dollar currency, to British and European sources, which did not.

In 1948 Hardie Trading acquired L. Horscroft Pty Ltd, which made
commercial and industrial laundry and dry-cleaning equipment. Les Horscroft
had sold Hoffman pressing machines, which were imported from the United
States, through most of the 1930s. When the war cut off his supplies, he arranged
with Bob Amott of Rapid Machinery Company, of East Brighton, to make
presses. Amott was already making some laundry equipment.

Horscroft, Amott and a third man, Basil Raphael, developed some kind of
partnership. Their firm worked on war production, making trailer-mounted dry-

Hardie Trading acquired
L. Horscroft Pty Ltd,
commercial and industrial
laundry and dry-cleaning
machinery manufacturers,
in 1948.

cleaning units for the army, parts for Beaufort guns, and bomb racks. After the war, the partnership broke up, and Horscroft carried on the business until he died, in 1947. Hardie Trading acquired it from his estate for £74 000. By then, Horscroft had a large and efficient plant at Moorabbin.

In 1950 Hardie Trading Limited bought all the issued capital of the Sydney trading company, James Hardie Trading Coy Pty Ltd, which until then had been a subsidiary of Hardie Investments Pty Ltd. The Sydney company had its offices and warehouse in Gosbell Street, Paddington, where it traded in much the same way as its new parent. It too had manufacturing interests, with a factory at Botany which made such successful lines as Repo and Auto Cream car polishes and rubbing compound. It made a complete range of industrial adhesives and sulphonated oils, cotton padding for laundry and dry-cleaning pressing machines, and vinyl recording biscuits for the manufacture of gramophone records.

The purchase of James Hardie Trading Coy Pty Ltd brought with it that company's subsidiary, James Hardie Trading Pty Ltd, of Brisbane, and the other half of the New Zealand company, Hardie Trading Co. (N.Z.) Ltd, which was based in Auckland, with branches in Wellington and Christchurch. The New Zealand company was sales agent for the manufacturing interests of the Hardie Trading group, and was a distributor of industrial raw materials and machinery.

Then came a series of expansionary moves. In 1954 Hardie Trading acquired Proud Brothers Pty Ltd, established in 1870, which made foundry facings for the foundry industry. It had a factory in Dudley Street, West Melbourne and one in Alexandria, New South Wales. In 1957 Hardie Trading formed Peco-Hardie Pty Ltd in conjunction with the Projectile & Engineering Co. Ltd, of London, to make injection moulding machines in Australia. Hardie Trading had previously imported them.

Victorian Premier Henry (later Sir Henry) Bolte and his wife examine the mural at Hardie Trading's new headquarters at 594 St Kilda Road, Melbourne, at the official opening in 1962. Looking on are the Chairman, Jock Reid, and his wife.

The next acquisition was Colours & Chemicals Pty Ltd, in 1954, which made a wide range of products, including naphthenate driers for the paint and printing ink industries, and copper compounds for rot-proofing. Then, in 1962, came Wilco Products Pty Ltd, which made Wilco electrical switchgear and allied products. In 1963 Horscroft began to make a range of machines for the textile industry, and acquired a plant to make its laundry and dry-cleaning products in New Zealand.

By the end of the 1950s, Hardie Trading and Spartan Paints had grown to such an extent that they needed new offices for their sales and administration staff. The Board bought land and built modern offices at 594 St Kilda Road, Melbourne, and in Commonwealth Street, Sydney. The Melbourne offices were ready for use in 1962, Sydney in 1964. As Hardie Trading Limited board meetings were held in Melbourne, and Thyne Reid lived in Sydney, John B. Reid (Jock's son and Thyne's nephew) began to attend as Thyne's Alternate Director.

In 1962 new Hardie Trading headquarters at
594 St Kilda Road, Melbourne, replaced the Little
Collins Street premises.

PART FOUR
MARKETERS

JOCK REID

CHAPTER TWENTY-SEVEN

JOCK REID
TAKES THE CHAIR

On Thyne Reid's death, his younger brother, Jock, took over as Chairman of the fibro-cement side of the Group. He had been Chairman of Hardie Trading Limited and Mercantile Credits Limited since 1945, when Thyne had given them up so he could concentrate on fibro-cement manufacture, with its higher engineering content.

Jock Reid was well acquainted with all aspects of the Group. As Andrew Reid's son, and later as an employee and executive, he had been hearing about it almost every day of his life from the time he was old enough to understand. He joined it in 1923 at the age of twenty and had been with it for more than forty years by the time he became its Chairman.

Jock, christened John Thyne, was Andrew and Peggy Reid's second son, born at Randwick on 15 October 1903. His mother began to call him 'Jock' when he was quite young, and the name stuck. The family moved to Wahroonga in 1910, and Jock lived in the family home there until he married, in 1929. He met James Hardie once, about 1911, when Andrew took him along on one of his frequent trips to Melbourne. He remembered Hardie as a very old man, as he would have seemed to the eyes of an eight-year-old.

For a time, Jock went to school at Turramurra College, a day school. In February 1917 he enrolled as a boarder in Macarthur House, part of The King's School in Parramatta, but he became ill there and in June 1918 he left. He had a private tutor for a short time, until his father took him to Scotland, where he attended the Edinburgh Academy. He played Rugby football there 'rather indifferently', to use his own words, and cricket 'only slightly better'. He also recalled, many years later, that rationing and First World War shortages were still very much in evidence in the meals he was given.

Andrew suggested that Jock might like to go to Oxford and do an Arts degree, which would make him a 'more cultured gentleman'. But Jock chose instead to start work as an office boy in the stores office of Watson Laidlaw & Co. Ltd in Glasgow. The firm made machinery such as laundry hydro-extractors and sugar mill centrifuges, for which Hardies were the Australian agents. Jock's time in Glasgow, he later recalled, brought him into close touch with the Scottish working man, and gave him some idea of the problems of parents who, although on low wages themselves, often had high ambitions for their children.

Unbeknown to Jock, Andrew had arranged to refund the weekly wage of 17s 6d ($1.75) that Watson Laidlaw paid him. After his father's death, he discovered among his papers Laidlaw's letter dated about a year after he started with them,

Opposite: Jock Reid was Chairman during a period in which marketing took an increasing role in the Group's success.

Jock Reid shows South Australian Premier Don Dunstan over Hardies' new South Australian plant at Birkenhead. 'Rowley' Hudson, South Australian Works Manager, is in the centre.

saying they no longer needed the subsidy. Jock's actual living expenses were in fact £2 5s 0d ($4.50) a week, well above his income of 17s 6d. He used to send a detailed monthly account of his expenditure, down to the last penny, to an Edinburgh solicitor, who refunded it to him. No doubt Andrew's Scottish respect for good accounting was behind this.

During his two years in Glasgow, Jock Reid studied accounting at night. He also often found the time, and the necessary shilling, to go to hear the Scottish Orchestra at St Andrew's Hall. Each Sunday he went to Lansdowne Church, where he became friendly with the minister's sons. He also met the minister's fourteen-year-old daughter, Gladys, whom he married eight years later, in 1929, on another visit to Scotland.

Back in Australia, Jock Reid began work in the Sydney office of James Hardie & Coy Ltd, in 1923. For a time he worked as assistant to Stan Strachan, in the mail room, where one of their daily chores was to put the incoming mail neatly on the desks of the important people before they arrived. Later he moved to the Audit Department, another training ground for young men with no special skills.

After some time there, he was moved to the Chemical Department under William White, whom he described as 'a hard task master and rather intolerant of anyone thinking for himself'. 'Willy' White's usual test for would-be office boys was to give them a sum to work out, involving the multiplication of tons, hundred-weights and quarters. Perhaps in the case of the Chairman's son he deemed it politic to skip that test. That may have been just as well, for those who knew Jock Reid say they doubt that he could have passed it.

White obviously had no need of assertiveness training; as Jock recalled, he was not averse to sending an office boy into the next-door building to tell a painter there to stop his annoying whistling. One of White's major achievements was to arrange the Re-po car-polish agency for Hardies.

Young Jock kept the stock books and consignment stock records for a time, just as his son John Boyd Reid did thirty years later in the trading company. He escaped from them when somebody saw the need for a new salesman. He was given a list of former customers who had not bought anything for a year, and told to go and see them. He did not have a car, and his territory stretched from Botany to Liverpool, and from Chatswood to Manly, with Newcastle added later. If there had been a prize for the most unsuccessful salesman, he said, he would certainly have won it.

Jock Reid in younger days.

But he did have his moments. One hot day, working his way through Botany, then consisting mostly of sandhills, he remembered that Wrigleys, the chewing gum manufacturers, had a beautifully cool building. He dropped in there for a breather and justified his presence by asking to see the purchasing officer. He sold (or perhaps it would be truer to say the purchasing officer bought) 10 hundredweight (half a ton) of gum arabic, 4 hundredweight from stock and 6 hundredweight from a shipment due in a month. Hardies normally expected to sell gum arabic only a few pounds at a time, but this sale was for 1120 pounds.

Jock's major success in his early days was the result of a mistake. He cabled an order to an overseas principal for 500 tons of chloride of calcium, instead of the 50 tons intended. All 500 tons came in one ship. As luck would have it, that ship was the last to arrive before a strike closed down all British ports for seventeen weeks. Chloride of lime, then used in refrigeration, was in great demand as summer surged on, and the company sold every ton at a very good price. Luck was against Jock, though, when he managed to get the company's first indent order for six months from Globe Worsted Mills, only to have Hardies lose the agency before the goods could be delivered.

In the late 1920s, when the Sydney office agreed to sell products from the new Spartan factory in Melbourne, Jock was seconded to Harry McClure, a tanning supplies salesman, and they were given the job. They knew little of the products or the market, and were given scant help from the company. Jock found a friend in a Mr Hodgson, Works Manager of Smith and Waddington, well-known Sydney motor body builders of the time, who taught him a lot about the market for automotive finishes and even gave him some orders. Only later did Jock find out that Hodgson had a reputation for terrorising salesmen.

In his Spartan role, Jock called at the Randwick Experimental Workshop of the Royal Australian Air Force, where Wing Commander Lawrence (later Sir Lawrence) Wackett was building the Widgeon I, a single-engined amphibian aircraft. Jock suggested the craft should be finished in Australian-made Spartan products rather than the American Berryloid that Wackett had intended. Wackett agreed that an Australian finish for an Australian plane was a good idea, and Jock learned from him how to use a spray-gun and sandpaper and rubbing compound. They used a lot of product and a lot of energy, but they did produce a beautiful finish.

In 1932, when George Gregson wanted to go overseas — to South Africa for some big-game shooting and to Europe on business — Andrew Reid arranged for Jock, now twenty-nine, to go to Melbourne to take charge while he was away. In those days, trips like the one Gregson intended took six to eight months, so it was important to have a good deputy on the job. Jock became a Director of Hardie Trading Pty Limited and was to live in Melbourne for the rest of his life.

He became Victorian Branch Manager of the fibro-cement business in 1936, while continuing his active interest in the trading company. Soon after Hardie Trading became a public company, in 1945, he took over from Thyne as its Chairman. On Thyne's death, he was the natural choice as Chairman of the fibro-cement company and the holding company; he had been Deputy Chairman of both since 1957. He continued as Group Chairman until he retired, on 25 October 1974.

As a young man, Jock Reid was a keen pilot.
He gave up flying once he became a family man.

CHAPTER TWENTY-EIGHT

BUILDING ON BUILDING PRODUCTS

All through Jock Reid's period as Chairman, Hardies continued to make steady progress in their fibro-cement activities, both in building products and pipes. To concentrate effort on the special needs of the two markets, each was given its own separate marketing management.

In building products, the company continued to look for new uses for fibro-cement but never forgot its base market, in housing. 'All-fibro' houses had ceased to be built, but more and more fibro-cement went into most new houses in Australia and New Zealand, in an increasing range of uses.

Jock Reid continued to encourage the new approach to advertising already started in Thyne Reid's time. It set out to show and encourage the wider use of Hardie products in every type of building and expanded into a national program. Hardiflex in particular was finding a greater range of uses. Its cellulose fibre content made it more flexible than former fibro-cement sheets. Autoclaving made it whiter and also able to be painted immediately, because it did not react chemically with paint. It was being supplied to all parts of Victoria by early 1965, to counter the competition from Goliath fibro-cement sheets made in Tasmania.

In New South Wales, a new, more highly automated machine was brought into production in that year to help supply the growing demand for flat sheets faster and more efficiently. South Australia also got a new sheet machine at about the same time.

Continuing capital investment of this sort was needed, the Chairman said in one of his Annual Reviews, to meet the needs of expanding markets, develop new products, replace obsolescent plant, increase efficiency and lower costs. The new machines had greater capacity than was currently required, but he expected this to be fully utilised within two years. The return on capital might be low in a new machine's early years, but the Board felt justified in having capacity in reserve to meet future demand. The investment was largely financed from internal sources, with worthwhile help from taxation investment allowances.

The long-term outlook for the housing industry was bright, but the industry needed to become better co-ordinated and more efficient, the Chairman said in his 1966–67 Annual Review. The stop–go economic conditions in which it operated made progress difficult, and varying building regulations and divergent interpretations of them hindered the adoption of many technological advances. He also said that major goals for the industry should be a more realistic and stable system of finance for homes, and a determination to unify building codes and keep them up to date, so as to permit the use of improved products and methods.

For the headquarters of the ANZ Banking Group at Martin Place in Sydney, more than 11 000 square metres of Hardie compressed sheet were used as a base for tiles on the infill panels.

Hardiflex, which had had such a good start in Victoria, was on sale in all states by early 1967. With all the virtues of Fibrolite, plus the added advantages of extra flexibility and a greater range of uses, it proved popular with the building trade. Another building board, Versilux, an improvement on Asbestolux, was added to the range. It was developed mainly for internal linings, for which neither Fibrolite nor Hardiflex had won wide acceptance. Versilux offered better appearance and sound absorption and superior jointing. It also came in a size range more useful for the type of house then being built. The range of Tilux colours and patterns was expanded, and demand for it held up well. Colorbord was released in a new colour range, and it sold well in all states, taking fibro-cement into new markets.

Competition from alternative materials in both building products and pipes kept people on their mettle, Jock Reid said in his 1967–68 Chairman's Review. They were confident, however, of fibro-cement's future, and the Group had acquired suitable sites to expand its manufacturing in each state: at Strathpine in Queensland, St Marys in New South Wales, Elizabeth in South Australia, Spearwood in Western Australia, and Brooklyn in Victoria. The former Hardie–Ferodo site at Camellia was also available for fibro-cement production, a new brake-lining plant having been built at Smithfield.

Towards the end of the 1960s, in their ceaseless search for new applications for fibro-cement, Hardies looked for ways to renew interest in its moulding potential. One example was the large facing panels on a drive-in shopping centre in the Brisbane suburb of Indooroopilly. Each panel had a decorative symbol moulded into it. Many similar uses followed.

Left: Special orders added to the demand for fibro-cement products. Hand-moulding window surrounds for the Flotto Lauro Building in Perth (above). Each of the 416 panels was painted bright blue with polyurethane paint. Each square panel weighed only two tons, much less than comparable materials. This meant substantial savings in costs, as only five men and a small, low-cost crane were needed to place the panels. The Flotto Lauro Building in North Sydney has similar panels, painted red.

Opposite: During the years Jock Reid was Chairman, the Group continued to encourage the use of Fibrolite in such applications as fencing.

The upper storey of this Sydney home of the early 1970s was clad with light-weight Hardiplank.

Familiar products were selling well for some unfamiliar uses. Canal retaining walls for land reclamation and quay developments were being made from fibro-cement, which proved both durable and effective. In one case, a new 20 kilometre flume to carry brine for making industrial salt was built with more than 60 000 sheets of corrugated Fibrolite.

Thick compressed fibro-cement sheets were in steady demand for curtain walls, verandah and bathroom flooring, toilet and shower partitions in public buildings, balustrades for bridges and balconies, permanent formwork for bridge decking, and impervious sub-flooring in such household wet areas as bathrooms and laundries, where they were used to form a base for ceramic tiles and other surface coverings. Savings in weight, labour and structural costs, plus great strength, were expected to ensure steady sales growth for these thick sheets.

New products such as Hardiplank and Highline were well accepted. Free-standing fibro-cement sheets were widely used for fencing, where they had the advantage of being rot-proof and almost maintenance-free. Fibro-cement fencing became very popular in Western Australia.

Hardie products in housing won the approval of the well-known Australian architect Robin Boyd, who chose Queensland architect John Dalton's award-winning Home of the Year to be featured as an example of good Australian architecture at Expo 70 in Japan in 1970. The home included various Hardie products, both inside and out.

A new building products plant in Western Australia went into production in June 1970. The plant, which cost $2.4 million and was one of the most modern in the world, was built mainly to make Hardiflex for the Western Australian market. Its commissioning coincided with Hardies' fiftieth anniversary of moving into the state.

Although much of the increase in demand for fibro-cement in the early 1970s was for non-housing uses, more fibro-cement than ever was going into houses in one way or another. This was helped by the development of such products as New Versilux, an improved internal lining board, and Hardibord seamless underlay for ceramic and vinyl floor tiles.

Throughout the period Jock Reid was Chairman, the Group put steady effort into new products and new raw materials, either by research and development at Camellia and elsewhere, or by buying small businesses and developing them. Some products, such as Hardiflex and Versilux, became success stories. Others, such as woodchip boards and cement-bonded woodchip hollow floor blocks for high rise buildings, did not.

In the early 1970s, quiet conditions in the Australian housing industry led the company to look for markets overseas, as well as at local non-housing uses, such as those already described, in which it had already met with some success. Worthwhile export markets for building products were found in Japan, Singapore, Malaysia and the United States.

Fibro-cement building materials were promoted for use in such re-cladding jobs as this facelift to an old weatherboard church.

A Vice-Regal inspection of the South Australian plant in the 1960s. From right: 'Rowley' Hudson, South Australian Works Manager; Sir Edric Bastyan, Governor of South Australia; Jock Reid; Frank Curtis, President of the South Australian Chamber of Manufactures; John B. Reid, State Manager for South Australia.

CHAPTER TWENTY-NINE

SURGING AHEAD IN PIPES

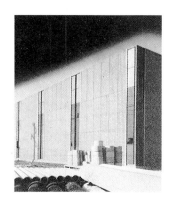

Fibrolite pipes continued to provide much of the Group's growth in the second half of the 1960s and the first half of the 1970s. The period saw steady growth in the volume and range of pipes offered, and in the variety of tasks for which they were used.

A new Perth pipe plant at Welshpool was officially opened on 22 March 1966. Speakers for the occasion included Charles (later Sir Charles) Court, Western Australia's Minister for Industrial Development, who lauded the part Hardies had played in Western Australia since they had built their first branch plant, at Rivervale, in 1920.

The company was a big user of Western Australian products, Court said. The fine new factory, turning out pipes that were 90 per cent made in Western Australia, was itself also 90 per cent made in Western Australia. The new pipe plant would help fill orders for the large-scale development of Western Australia then taking place, including the new iron ore mines and towns. Court officially turned on the power at about 10 am, then toured the plant.

A section of the new pipe plant at Welshpool, Western Australia. The building was awarded a citation for outstanding design in 1970 by the Western Australia Chapter of the Royal Australian Institute of Architects.

Eric Cohen, later a Director of James Hardie, tries a new joint on a Fibrolite pipe.

To provide for future expansion in Western Australia, the company bought 18 hectares of land at Spearwood. It was in a developing industrial area, with rail and other services readily available. The purchase seemed desirable, since the Rivervale and Welshpool sites were operating almost at capacity.

The Board had approved construction of a second pipe-making machine at its Meeandah works in Brisbane, the Chairman reported in his 1965–66 Annual Review. This would meet the growing demand for pipes of all types, notably those of larger diameter than could be produced by the existing machine. In his next Review, he was able to report that the new machine was in production.

The drought in the eastern states, and its effect on rural incomes, depressed pipe sales during 1966–67, but they recovered soon after. Developments in pipes in 1967–68 included perforated pipes for soil drainage and stormwater drainpipes and fittings. Low-head Fibrolite irrigation pipes were replacing open irrigation channels, effectively saving water, reducing both the irrigator's labour and the cost of maintaining channels, and taking up far less irrigable land than open channels.

During that year, the size range of pressure pipes was extended, and all states could now supply all sizes. This gave Hardies a larger share of the pipe market for the bigger projects then under way in Australia. The company had also won the contract to supply Fibrolite water pipes to the Commonwealth Department of

Large-diameter pipes were used in power stations to transport coal ash, in the form of a slurry, from the boilers to the settling ponds. This work had previously been done by fleets of trucks.

Above: Many Fibrolite pipelines stretched for considerable distances across inhospitable country.

Right: Pipes were important enough to feature on the front cover of the 1971 Annual Report, the first on which the company used a colour photograph.

Works, then the leading construction authority in Australia's external territory of Papua and New Guinea.

A major new power station on the east coast of Australia had reported that a dust disposal system using Fibrolite pipes was extremely efficient. Another power station was about to be equipped with the same system, which did not need the usual rather expensive fleet of hopper-equipped trucks to dispose of the dust.

Large-diameter trunk mains for water supply provided a steady demand for Fibrolite pipes, which were widely used in the new mining towns and mining operations being developed in many parts of Australia. Some mining operations,

Above: Harditube plastic pipes ready to be installed at a macadamia nut plantation at Dunoon, near Lismore, New South Wales.

Left: Large-diameter Fibrolite pipes were used for bore-casing in bores sunk to help ease groundwater pressure in open-cut mines.

including coal and ore washing, needed large volumes of water, which in one case was drawn more than 65 kilometres through Fibrolite pipes. Fibrolite pipes had been approved in all states for sewerage lines. Many towns were at the time planning sewerage schemes, and pipe stocks were held at Hardie plants in each mainland state and at other strategic places.

To strengthen its grip on the growing pipe market, Hardies acquired Montpelier Foundry Pty Limited, in Hobart, Tasmania, in December 1969. Montpelier had long been a manufacturer of cast-iron fittings for water and gas pipes. The foundry shareholders wanted to dispose of their interests, and Hardies took the opportunity to acquire a company from which they could draw the major part of their needs in pipe fittings.

New types of fittings, for use with pipes of all kinds, were added to Montpelier's product range. As well as supplying Hardies' needs, the foundry made castings in iron, aluminium and bronze, for industry, mining companies and government and semi-government authorities, working to close metallurgical and physical tolerances when required.

To meet growing competition from plastic pipes, mainly in the smaller diameters, the company formed Hardie Extrusions Pty Ltd in 1970–71, and built a factory at Altona in Victoria to make them. Its first poly-vinyl chloride pipes (Harditube) were sold early in 1971. The selling approach adopted, 'AC + PVC' (asbestos cement plus poly-vinyl chloride), stressed the advantages of each type of pipe. Hardies could now offer complete pipe systems for pressure and non-pressure uses, in diameters from 12 millimetres up to 600 millimetres.

Pipe sales increased, too, as funds became available to government and local authorities to expand water supply and sewerage services. One major export order during 1972–73 was for pipes and cast-iron fittings to provide water supplies for forty-two cities in Indonesia.

Fibrolite pipes being loaded for export. Hardies
won many large export orders in South-East Asia in
the 1960s and early 1970s.

CHAPTER THIRTY

UPS AND DOWNS
IN NEW ZEALAND

Hardies in New Zealand had to ride the ups and downs of the country's economy as it went through the hard times of the 1960s and 1970s. But the company never faltered in its steady growth and its faith in the future. In 1964–65, for instance, the parent company did not draw a dividend from New Zealand, choosing instead to leave profits there to expand local production capacity.

A new pipe-finishing plant that began operation in New Zealand in 1964 helped to reduce costs and so to stabilise Fibrolite pipe prices there. Demand for pipe in New Zealand was such that within a year the existing pipe machine had to be replaced by a more efficient unit, which came into production in mid-1966.

Devaluation of the New Zealand dollar in 1967–68 led to a drop of $A697 318 in the value of the parent company's overseas subsidiaries. It also meant, of course, that future profits from New Zealand would have a lower value in Australia.

As in Australia, fibro-cement building materials were in steady demand in New Zealand, both for housing and other uses. Hardiflex was soon popular there, having been introduced in 1969–70. Moulded panels were being used on many high rise buildings, and Fibroplank weatherboards became a popular material for houses.

Hardie Trading's New Zealand headquarters in Auckland, in 1966.

Shadowline Wall Panels and custom-moulded infill panels were used for the Warkworth Satellite Earth Station built for the New Zealand Post Office in the early 1970s.

In a move similar to the acquisition of the Montpelier Foundry in Australia, in 1969–70 the New Zealand company bought Utility Castings Limited, a foundry business that made castings for pipe fittings.

In 1970–71 large quantities of Fibrolite pipes were ordered for the new aluminium smelter being built at Bluff, on the southern tip of the South Island, where alumina from Australia would be smelted to produce aluminium. This was one of several large-scale water supply projects in New Zealand for which Fibrolite pipes were specified.

Building products and pipes were both exported from New Zealand, mainly to the South Pacific Basin, where the growing tourist industry created a demand for buildings for which Hardie products were very suitable. The new airport buildings at Nandi, Fiji, in which fibro-cement products were used extensively, were a good local advertisement for Hardie products.

CHAPTER THIRTY-ONE

A CONTINUING ROLE
FOR RESEARCH AND
DEVELOPMENT

Research and development played a major role in Hardies' progress all through the period in which Jock Reid was Chairman. He made regular references to them in his Annual Reviews, becoming more expansive almost every year and acknowledging the help Hardies had received from the Industrial Research and Development Grants Board.

Continuous research and development ensured the sort of product improvement and innovation that kept fibro-cement building materials and pipes selling strongly. It also led to cheaper, better methods of manufacture, a factor that became more and more vital as the stable costs of the late 1950s and early 1960s gradually gave way to a new period of inflation in the late 1960s and early 1970s.

The Research and Development Division was reorganised and extended in 1966. To help ensure close co-ordination with the realities of the market place, in 1967–68 the company set up a Products Committee to work with the Research and Development Division to extend the range and uses of its various products. At that stage, Hardies had deliberately developed their manufacturing capacity ahead of demand and were keen to take up at least some of the slack.

In 1973 the Research and Development Division moved into a new $3 million Research and Engineering Centre near the New South Wales fibro-cement plant at Camellia. The move grouped in one building research and development facilities that until then had been scattered through the Camellia plant. It would now be possible to exercise more vigorous direction and control over the Division's work, and to venture into wider fields of investigation.

Research continued to promote a better understanding and more efficient use of raw materials. The company's work in these areas was reinforced by associations with the University of New South Wales and the University of Aberdeen in Scotland, as well as with the Commonwealth Scientific and Industrial Research Organization and specialist consultants in selected fields. All these approaches were co-ordinated by Hardie staff.

The company's research work aided the development of such new uses and products as wall cladding, floor slabs, fencing panels and surface coatings on fibro-cement sheeting. In pipes, it led to improvements in manufacturing techniques and the design of fibro-cement pipe joints. A new use of fibro-cement piping as bore casing was developed, with special applications in the brown-coal fields of Victoria.

Considerable work was done on the production and testing of a poly-vinyl chloride pipe joint, sold as Hardiseal, that was new to Australia. Improved quality

Continued research led to improved quality and durability for such products at Tilux.

SPEAKING OUT ON EXPORT

By the early 1970s, Hardies had developed good markets for both building products and pipes. The company had taken advantage of various government incentives and allowances, as the government had clearly wanted Australian manufacturers to do.

Then, early in 1973, the Whitlam government announced the probable end to export incentives and market development allowances. It was to be hoped, Jock Reid said in the last of his Chairman's Annual Reports, for 1972–73, that the government would consider how tenuous a hold many Australian exporters had on their overseas markets. In many cases, only the export incentives made it possible for exporters to develop markets, as the profits earned initially would not justify the cost and effort involved.

At a time when Australian overseas balances were high, the Chairman pointed out, there might not seem to be a need for continued effort in manufactured exports. But there had been times when these balances were seriously depleted, when the business community had been urged to go out and sell overseas. These times might come again, and potential overseas buyers of Australian goods might not look kindly on stop–go policies towards their supply. There was no shortage of competition for world markets, and competitors were well supported by their own governments.

control techniques won both Harditube and Hardiseal a greater share of the market.

One of the Division's objectives was continued improvements in the quality and appearance of Hardie products. This resulted in the development of New Versilux internal lining board, Hardibord seamless underlay, and improved quality and durability for Colorbord and Tilux.

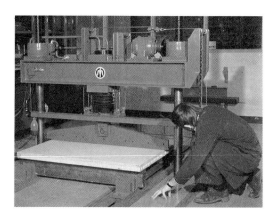

In the Research and Development
Centre at Camellia, New South Wales.

CHAPTER THIRTY-TWO

SPONSORING THE HARDIE-FERODO 500

One day in 1968, Dave Deane, one of the longest-serving employees of the Hardie brake linings activities, walked into Alan Woodford's office at the old Hardie–Ferodo plant at Camellia and asked him if he would like to sponsor the annual 500 mile motor race at Bathurst's Mount Panorama Circuit.

Deane, who was also a long-standing member of the Australian Racing Drivers' Club, knew that the club was in need of a sponsor, since the previous one, the Irish tobacco company Gallaher, had decided to withdraw. Until Gallaher had taken over the sponsorship, two years before, the race had been the Armstrong 500, which that firm used to promote its shock absorbers. The club needed any sponsor it could get, but it preferred one from the motor industry.

Woodford warmed to the idea at once. Coming in as sponsor at this stage fitted in neatly with Hardie–Ferodo's move to its new plant at Smithfield. The cost, $12 000 a year, was modest enough. That, plus the gate money, covered the club's costs in organising the event and left something for profit.

The deal was soon arranged over the phone, and the details tied up later in a meeting between Dave Deane, George Hibbert and John Hinxman, the club secretary. Dave Deane entered into the sponsorship with such delight that he had new business cards printed, describing himself as 'Manager of the Motor Racing Division'. A new rule was that all cars had to be fitted with Hardie–Ferodo brake linings. Apart from the boost to sales, this was expected to give Hardie–Ferodo new insight into how its products performed under severe stress.

The 1968 Hardie–Ferodo 500 proved to be very successful. Advertising was allowed on cars for the first time, and firms were falling over themselves to sponsor them. One great benefit of the race from Hardie–Ferodo's point of view, and from that of any sponsor who managed to get an advertisement on a car, was that it was nationally televised on the Channel 7 Network. The 1968 telecast (in black and white) was estimated to have been seen by a million and a quarter people.

Although the rules about classes had been changed several times since the first Armstrong 500 was run at Phillip Island, Victoria, in 1960, the race was still seen as one that put ordinary production touring cars to the test. Since people saw a connection between cars they might aspire to own and those that raced at Bathurst, car manufacturers vied keenly to do well there.

The first Hardie–Ferodo 500 at Bathurst in 1968 began the V8 era of touring car racing in Australia. Holden, with its new Monaro GTS 327 and newly formed Holden Dealer Team, was in direct competition with Ford, with its proven four-door Falcon GT and strong factory backing. But neither the Holden nor the Ford

The Hardie bridge at
Bathurst, built in 1978.

team was to win. The 1968 Hardie–Ferodo 500 went down as the last Bathurst long-distance race to be won by a true 'privateer'. Bruce McPhee, sponsored by his local Holden dealer, drove his Holden all but one of the 130 laps it took to cover 500 miles. He won by just over three minutes from the first of the Holden Dealer Team cars. McPhee achieved his 129 lap total by a neat application of the rules of the day. These specified that a co-driver was mandatory, but did not say how far he had to drive. McPhee's co-driver, Barry Mulholland, obligingly completed just one lap.

Other regulations also had odd effects. One of the most frustrating rules was that if a car broke down on the circuit, only the driver could get it going again. When Jim McKeown's Ford Team Falcon broke a wheel bearing, he walked back to his pit, shouldered a new axle and bearing assembly and lugged it back up the mountain, taking a mechanic with him, but only to give advice.

In 1973, with the switch to metrics in Australia, the distance was changed from 500 miles to 1000 kilometres, and the race became the Hardie–Ferodo 1000. This

A PRODUCT WITH POLISH

One steady but unspectacular line in the many Hardie Trading manufacturing activities was Re-po car polishes. Hardies first began to make them at their Botany factory in 1931. The company's long experience with the product was backed technically by a licensing arrangement with a prominent United States manufacturer.

Re-po Polish & Cleaner, with its unique handle on the neck of the bottle, was the key Re-po line from the early 1930s. In the 1960s, the range was extended, to include Re-po Auto Creams and Re-po De-luxe, formulated specially for the acrylic, enamel and lacquer finishes then being used on new cars. In the late 1960s Re-po Rapidglo joined the range, with the Re-po Wash & Wax sachet coming soon after. Re-po was exported to many parts of South-East Asia from the 1950s on.

Other lines made at the Botany factory included vinyl resin compounds (used to make gramophone records), sulphonated oils and adhesives, and a range of flexible PVC extrusion compounds for specialised industrial applications. The company found export markets in South-East Asia for its PVC compounds for the gramophone record industry. The Botany plant also made galvanised wire coathangers, and a complete range of soaps, waterproofing and retexturing agents, paint removers and knitted cotton padding, all designed for the dry-cleaning and clothing industries.

In the early 1970s the factory formulated and made a range of plating solutions for the electroplating industry. They were well received by the trade and distributed by all branches throughout Australia and New Zealand.

A 1958 advertisement for Re-po.

took 163 laps instead of the previous 130. Since cars were going faster and faster, the extra distance was of no great consequence. To increase their television exposure from the race, and to reduce the risk to people crossing the track, in 1978 Hardies built the new spectator bridge across the circuit. Thousands of starlings were duly grateful and took to roosting on it.

The publicity benefits from the race increased steadily as it grew in stature. In some years, estimates of the television audience ran as high as 8 million. The race also had a lot of exposure in the print media, on radio, on film and in books. Australia's best-selling motoring book was on the race. The name was changed to the James Hardie 1000 in 1981, after Ferodo sold its interest in Hardie–Ferodo to James Hardie Industries Limited.

CHAPTER THIRTY-THREE

GEORGE JACKSON: HARDIES' MR TRADING

George Jackson's predecessor as Managing Director of Hardie Trading Limited, George Gregson, held the job for almost forty years — from 1913 to 1953. Jackson had it for almost twenty years — from 1953 to 1972. For a company to have had only two Managing Directors in almost sixty years may not be a record, but it is certainly unusual.

When George Jackson decided to retire as Managing Director of Hardie Trading Limited in 1972, at the age of sixty, he had been with the Hardie Group for forty-five years — more than half the period of its existence.

He saw nothing odd in stepping down before he reached the standard retiring age of sixty-five. He and the Chairman had discussed that subject off and on over some years, and had agreed that about twenty years was long enough for anybody to carry the heavy load of being Managing Director. Jackson had been in that job for twenty-one years.

Jackson joined the company in 1927, but only on his second attempt. His first application for a position as office boy was turned down, and he spent six months with an insurance company. On his second attempt Hardies saw the light, and he started with his second and last employer.

In seeking any sort of a job at that stage, he acted against his father's wishes. He abandoned a scholarship for an engineering diploma course at what was then the Working Men's College and later became the Royal Melbourne Institute of Technology. He never had any regrets about that, for he was convinced he would have made a poor engineer.

He soon found that Hardies had their standards. A hat was compulsory, a conservative suit a must — except perhaps on Saturday morning, when you might get away with a sports coat and slacks, depending on whether George Gregson had turned up dressed to go shooting or golfing that afternoon. Those were only the superficial standards. He also soon found that Hardies had a good reputation for their ethical and personal standards.

Jackson began at the West Footscray plant, which at the time had an early warning system that signalled Gregson's departure from Little Collins Street in his Citroen, bound for the factory. One day, however, the system failed, and Gregson arrived to find the future Chairman, John Thyne Reid, and the future Managing Director, George Jackson, engaged in a spirited demonstration with the Chief Chemist, Hesketh, of the techniques of fly fishing.

Jackson's time at West Footscray was abruptly terminated by a confrontation with Ern Viret, the Factory Accountant, which led to his being switched to the job of Sales Clerk in the city office. He often said later that he did not recommend giving your boss a clout in a moment of utter frustration as a sure-fire way of getting a promotion. But in his case the move seemed to have had its advantages, for it brought Jackson under the closer notice of George Gregson.

He was soon a part-time outside salesman for Spartan, which entailed seeking orders, on foot and by tram, from those accounts no other salesman wanted. He also called on architects, trying to convince them to specify Spartan for their projects. It was all good experience.

One day in 1934 George Gregson called Jackson into his office, said the company needed a Manager for South Australia, asked if he would take the job and got an acceptance on the spot. Next morning, having thought a little more deeply on the subject, Gregson asked Jackson how old he was. He was a little surprised to hear his new Adelaide manager was only twenty-three, for he had thought him to be twenty-seven. But he stuck to his word, and George Jackson spent the next fourteen years in Adelaide, building a very good business there. Jackson started in Adelaide at a salary of £6 a week. This was later increased to £6 10s 0d, and it was on this salary that he was married and, as he put it at his farewell dinner, 'managed to have a reasonably comfortable existence'.

George Jackson, who was Managing Director of Hardie Trading Limited for twenty years.

Sales turnover in Adelaide in 1934 was about £1250 a month, of which Spartan sales were about £450. This was about a break-even situation, and hardly justified anything better than the galvanised iron buildings and dirt floors that then comprised the company's South Road premises. They had previously been a fibrous plaster factory.

Both the sales volume and the premises improved in time. Jackson acted as manager, salesman, accountant and even storeman at times. On one occasion, he was a painter's labourer, with Eric Sangwell as the painter. Jackson counted it as one of his achievements, he said, that he persuaded the company to start some

While George Jackson was Managing Director, Hardie Trading established Glas–Kraft to make laminated reinforced papers and foils for the building and packaging industries.

paint manufacturing in Adelaide. It was a start that led to setting up the Woodville North plant in 1948.

Jackson became a Director of Hardie Trading Limited in 1945 and in 1951 came back to Melbourne, in readiness to take over as Managing Director on Gregson's retirement in 1952. One habit he inherited from Gregson was to avoid the subject of fibro-cement manufacture, along with the people involved in it, particularly if they happened to live in Sydney. He was a staunch supporter of a separate existence for Hardie Trading.

While Jackson was Managing Director, Hardie Trading expanded its own manufacturing activities markedly, acquiring Wilco, manufacturers of products for electrical contractors, in 1962, and establishing Glas-Kraft, to make laminated reinforced papers and foils for the building and packaging industries, in 1965. He became Chairman of both, and was Chairman of several other manufacturing enterprises, including Spartan, which were already subsidiaries when he became Managing Director of Hardie Trading. He was largely instrumental in setting up a new superannuation fund in 1953, which by the time he retired had assets of well over $2 million. He was very involved in the decision to build at 594 St Kilda Road, Melbourne, and to move most of the Hardie Trading Limited offices there.

At George Jackson's farewell dinner, his successor, Bill Butterss, spoke of the quality of his thought and expression, as shown in his correspondence, which was a model of clarity, strength, style, interest and sheer readability. His grasp of financial matters and his bewildering memory for figures were among his other outstanding attributes, Butterss said. A balance sheet and a profit and loss account

Hardie Trading acquired Wilco, manufacturers of products for electrical contractors, during George Jackson's period as Managing Director.

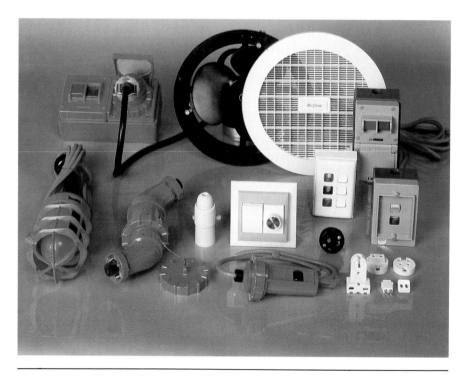

George Jackson was instrumental in the move of most of Hardie Trading Limited offices to the new premises at 594 St Kilda Road, Melbourne.

were to him like a musical score to a great pianist, full of interest and meaning, and capable of rapid and enlightened interpretation. Butterss had worked as Jackson's deputy for twelve months. Their frequent discussions had covered a wide range of subjects, not excluding the vagaries of the bowling green on the previous Saturday and the nature of the opposition next Saturday.

George Jackson said that in his retirement he would 'catch up on a lot of reading and play more bowls'. As well as resigning as Managing Director, he also resigned as a Director. He thought it unfair for a former chief executive to stay on, 'peering over the shoulder of the new man'.

CHAPTER THIRTY-FOUR

PROGRESS AT SPARTAN

In 1964 Spartan, the paint subsidiary of Hardie Trading Limited, added to its overseas technical links a licensing agreement with Jones–Dabney, a leading maker of surface coatings in the United States and a major supplier to the automotive industry there. This was expected to enable Spartan to expand its already substantial share of the automotive paint industry in Australia. To ensure that the company made the most of the opportunity, two senior technical officers from Spartan visited Jones–Dabney.

Exports of Spartan products continued to provide useful turnover in markets that could be classified as highly competitive, John T. Reid said in his 1964–65 Chairman's Report. This success showed the measure of service Spartan was able to provide, and that its costs were satisfactory. Australian consumers benefited from the high level of efficiency needed to succeed in world markets.

A year later he was able to say that Spartan's Automotive Division had made significant progress, including satisfactory sales of car finishes made under the Jones–Dabney licence. Spartan's laboratory facilities had been extended to enable it to increase its technical development program, vital to the growth of its four major divisions: Industrial, Architectural, Automotive and Floor Finishes. Each of the four released new lines in the next year.

Spartan marine paints were chosen for this hard-working Victoria Police vessel.

Inside the Spartan plant, Melbourne

In 1967–68, Spartan finishes were used exclusively on the new Victorian Arts Centre in Melbourne, which called for a wide variety of products of the highest quality. During 1969–70, the exteriors of Ansett aircraft were painted in Spartan Ultrathane. This product, developed over about two years, had to resist damage from fuel, fumes and oil and to withstand the wide extremes of temperature encountered by aircraft. Spartan always made much of its strong program of technical development. In 1969 it acknowledged the impetus this had been given by the Commonwealth Government's Research and Development Grants Scheme.

In the late 1960s and early 1970s demand for Spartan products was such that the company had to add plant at all its factories, at Footscray (Victoria), Botany (New South Wales), Belmont (Western Australia) and Athol Park (South Australia). In Western Australia, the former Hardie–Spartan sales office and warehouse were taken over to make way for the Mitchell Freeway, and a new office and warehouse were built at Belmont. In Queensland, a new office and warehouse were built to replace the very old buildings that had served for many years but were no longer adequate.

Marine paints were selling well. Spartan was the Australian member of the worldwide Transocean Marine Paint Association, which marketed a common brand of high-quality marine finishes that reflected the combined technical resources of a strong and highly competent group of paint manufacturers. Export sales were going up. Although the main market was in South-East Asia, Spartan products continued to be sold in such countries as Malta, against strong competition from European manufacturers.

Spartan's Floor Finishes and Chemicals Division was further strengthened in 1971 by means of a marketing and technical link with Spartan Chemical Co. Inc., of Toledo, Ohio, in the United States (the common name being coincidental). During 1971–72, Spartan Chemical Company was formed as a Division of Spartan Paints to specialise in polishes and cleaners, for which there was a growing market for modern buildings. Spartan Sanitation Chemicals, together with Spartan Floor Finishes, brought out a range designed to meet the needs of hospitals, institutions, and commercial and domestic buildings.

Spartan Sundry Trading Division bought in and marketed a range of items that complemented Spartan's own products. These included wallpaper, brushes, spray equipment, vacuum and polishing machines, abrasive papers, masking tape, buckets and a variety of equipment used in the automotive and automotive repair industry.

An Ansett-Elphin racing car on show at a Spartan trade display.
Spartan paints were also used on Ansett aircraft.

CHAPTER THIRTY-FIVE

HARDIE TRADING IN 1974

In 1974, the year Sir John Reid retired as Chairman, Hardie Trading Limited noted that obtaining supplies had been difficult during the year, especially raw materials and products that came from the oil and allied petro-chemical industries. The so-called energy crisis had meant a sellers' market, and many prime commodities had been on quotas for much of the time. This had led to customers overordering, which called for very careful judgment by the company's sales and administrative staff and a great deal of tact to sort out the inevitable cancellations and other problems.

The year had not been an easy one for other reasons. In spite of the tendency of some customers to order more than they needed of oil-related products in the hope of getting at least some, others had been careful with their ordering and had kept stocks down, because of high interest rates. Local manufacturers who bought their raw materials through Hardies were also worried about the volume of imported manufactured products. Added to this was the fear that consumers would have less buying power, as a result of the slow economic conditions. For all these reasons, Sir John said, he would be surprised if the level of consumption and hence industrial turnover were maintained.

Another problem was that the textile manufacturing industry, one of Hardie Trading Limited's major customers, had been seriously affected by changes in tariff policy and sharply increasing local costs of production. The Whitlam government had recently cut all tariffs by 25 per cent, in an attempt to hold down inflation by providing Australian industry with more competition and to spread the money available in the community across more goods.

After all this, the fact that the Brisbane floods, early in 1974, had caused some damage to the company's office and store there did not seem very serious at all. The staff had worked long hours under most difficult conditions, and there had been a quick return to work with a minimum of inconvenience to customers.

Hardie Trading's annual report for that year gave a more than usually detailed description of its many activities. They can be divided broadly into trading and manufacturing. Both were directed towards supplying the needs of other manufacturing industries rather than providing consumer products, although there were some exceptions.

The company had twelve sales offices in Australia and New Zealand: in Melbourne, Sydney, Brisbane, Newcastle, Adelaide, Perth, Hobart, Launceston, Burnie, Auckland, Wellington and Christchurch. All offices had accompanying warehouses, and, with minor exceptions in the smaller centres, they had separate departments for groups of products. When seeking overseas agencies, the company would highlight the fact that it had a sales network that covered all Australian states and the main cities in New Zealand.

As from 1 July 1974, all these offices would be identified as Hardie Trading Limited. Previously the Brisbane and Sydney and all three New Zealand offices had been known under other names, dating back to when they had been owned by the fibro-cement part of the Hardie Group.

Although they now occupied only a small niche in the overall trading activities, such lines as those with which James Hardie had started the company in 1888 — tanning supplies and machinery — still had a place in Hardie Trading Limited. As agents for Forestal Quebracho Ltd of England, the company offered Quebracho extract and a range of other supplies from many sources. It also represented Hodgson Tanning Products, an English firm that made a range of both vegetable and synthetic tans, as well as other tanning materials.

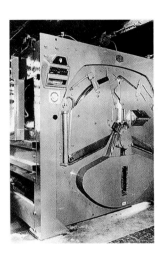

Capable of automatically washing and drying a tonne of laundry every two hours, this Horscroft-Milnor machine, supplied by Hardie Trading, was installed at Princes Laundry in the Melbourne suburb of Mentone.

Hardie Trading imported a range of raw materials in many forms from all over the world for the chemicals industry, and also bought raw materials locally for resale. It was sole agent for some lines, a non-exclusive importer for others, with customers ranging from the large steel and aluminium producers to small, highly specialised pharmaceutical manufacturers. It also sold resins, driers and other products made by its own subsidiary, Colours & Chemicals Pty Ltd.

The company carried a range of imported dyestuffs and other chemicals for textile yarn and piecegoods dye-houses, textile printers, garment dyers and paper manufacturers. As well as selling these specialised products, it offered a supporting laboratory technical advisory service manned by highly trained staff.

In engineering and transmission supplies, the company was developing sales of specialty machinery for particular sectors of industry. This was taking over from the traditional business of selling consumable supplies to the general engineering field. In the former category, the company now offered a range of liquid and aerosol filling equipment, compactors for reducing the bulk of waste materials, dishwashing machines for the institutional and catering markets, and vulcanisers for endless conveyor belts. In the transmission sector, the company continued to offer conveyor and other belting made in its own factory at Footscray. Such belting, in many a previous form, had been one of the steady lines in the earliest days of James Hardie's 'very good business'. The range included conveyor rollers, idlers and drums, and all types of industrial hose.

As agents for the British Moulding Machine Company, the company sold and serviced a range of foundry moulding machinery and associated equipment for all types of foundries. Its range of supplies for the foundry industry included coal dust, plumbago, bentonite and core-gum. As agent for the Great Lakes Carbon Corporation, it supplied graphite electrodes for electric steel furnaces and anodes for electrolytic processes in the chemical and metals manufacturing fields.

As sole distributors for its wholly owned subsidiary, L. Horscroft Pty Ltd, Hardie Trading handled a full range of laundry and dry-cleaning machinery for hospital and other institutional laundry plants and commercial laundries and dry-cleaners. Many other specialised items were imported from Europe and the United States. It also offered a full range of consumable supplies for both industries, including special soaps, detergents, additives, press padding and wire coathangers made by its own subsidiaries.

BLOOMER
BOILER
BY
HARDIE

A product manager specialising in technical presentation of mill furnishing such as felts and wires called regularly at all paper and board mills throughout Australia and New Zealand. He was supported by follow-up calls from the company's office in the area concerned. Hardies were the sole agent for Kenyon felts, of England.

Hardie Trading Limited sold prime metals such as chrome, nickel and copper to electroplaters and metal finishers. It had a range of plating solutions, rack coating, and polishing mops and compounds made by its own subsidiaries. It maintained a laboratory and full technical service from its main offices, and offered special filters and other mechanical and electrical plant components from both local and overseas sources.

As sole agent for Amcel (American Cellulose), of the United States, Hardies promoted and sold plastic moulding and extrusion compounds, such as Celcon and Celanex. These were formulated for specialised use in making parts for the automotive, electrical, air-conditioning and general engineering fields. For British

One of the largest of its kind ever made in Australia, this fully automatic oil-fired steam package, complete with stand, was made in Brisbane by the Bloomer Boiler Division of James Hardie Trading Pty Ltd in 1972.

Celanese, the company distributed acetate sheeting and film to the packaging industry, including see-through shirt-box lids, floral packs and vacuum formed packs, as well as Rocel, a plastic material used by spectacle frame makers. As suppliers of chopped strand mat and rovings, the company was closely allied to industries that used fibreglass, including boat, surfboard and swimming pool manufacturers.

As a supplier to textile manufacturers, Hardies offered a range of machinery and accessories for almost every operation. It was sole distributor in Australia and New Zealand for many European and American manufacturers whose products included all kinds of yarn production and preparation plant, weaving looms, knitting machines, finishing plant for both woven and knitted fabrics, and all components for dyeing yarns, fabrics and finished garments. It also supplied many auxiliary items such as yarn- and fabric-testing instruments and laboratory dyeing equipment, plus many consumable items, such as bobbins, cloth-finishing wrappers and all kinds of loom accessories, spare parts and attachments.

In its role as sole agent for Amcel, the company promoted the use of Arnel fibre and yarn in the fashion industry, and supplied the yarn itself to the weaving and knitting industry. It also acted as import and indent agents for other yarns and fibres from many parts of the world.

Although in general terms each Hardie Trading branch sold right across the range of products, the volume of particular lines through particular branches reflected local industry specialisation. Tanning supplies sold best in Melbourne, raw materials for gramophone records in Sydney, for instance. Brisbane had a wide range of trade, because as a smaller market it attracted fewer competitors for Hardies. One activity it alone among the Hardie branches engaged in was selling abattoir equipment and supplies.

CHAPTER THIRTY-SIX

FIRST MOVES IN SOUTH-EAST ASIA

In 1964 the James Hardie Group found itself suddenly presented with an opportunity to take part in a fibro-cement venture in Malaysia. Three overseas manufacturers — Turner & Newall of Britain, Eternit of Europe and Johns Manville of the United States — had agreed to set up a pipe plant there. Then Johns Manville pulled out. Jonah Adamson, who happened to be in London, heard of this from Turner & Newall and asked if Hardies could step into Johns Manville's place.

The answer was encouraging enough for him to phone Frank Page in Sydney and arrange for John Reid and Ted Heath to go to Malaysia and survey the pipe market there. John Reid, the Chairman's son, was then managing James Hardie & Coy Pty Limited interests in South Australia. Ted Heath was Federal Pipe Sales Manager, based at Camellia. Within two days, the two men were in Malaysia.

Compared to the feasibility studies of today, theirs was a 'once over lightly', as they later came to see. But they did conclude that the market was promising, and that there was a case for a sheet plant as well as a pipe plant. They phoned

The office of Hardies' Indonesian-Australian joint venture company, P. T. Harflex Asbes Semen, in the early 1970s.

The United Asbestos Cement Berhad plant at Ipoh in Malaysia, as pictured on the back of the James Hardie Annual Report for 1972. The plant went into production in 1966, making building products for sale in Malaysia and for export throughout Asia. Although a minority shareholder, James Hardie was responsible for managing the Malaysian company.

Adamson, who was still in London, to tell him. They asked if they should come to London to give their report in person. The line was so bad they could not be sure whether he had said 'Yes' or 'No', so they decided to go anyway. In London they created a good enough impression for the project to be handed over to them to implement.

John Reid became Chairman of the company formed to handle the venture, United Asbestos Cement Berhad. Ted Heath became a Director. David Macfarlane, later to be Managing Director of James Hardie Industries Limited but at that stage a young Pipe Sales Manager in South Australia, was sent to Malaysia as General Manager.

Back in Australia, the Group's top management looked on the project more with tolerance than with enthusiasm. However, this project and another that followed in Indonesia gave Hardies a window on the world, a window they had never had before. Until then, their only overseas ventures had been in New Zealand, where ways of doing business were much the same as those in Australia.

Machinery for the plant was designed by Hardies' own technical staff. It incorporated the results of the company's years of experience and research, and gave the Malaysian operation a start that was world class. Some of the more specialised equipment was sent from Australia, but most of it was either bought or built in Malaysia. The sheet-making plant began operating in 1966, on schedule, and its products soon found a ready market. The pipe-making plant began production in May 1967. Several Malaysian staff trained with Hardies in Australia and then passed their knowledge on to other workers at the plant.

The Malaysian company paid its first dividend, 5 per cent, for the year to 30 June 1969. It had developed useful export markets and was earning foreign exchange for Malaysia. Because the arrangement was that Hardies would manage it, it was also earning foreign exchange for Australia. It continued to do well, and paid 10 per cent in dividends in 1969–70, 12.5 per cent in 1970–71, 15 per cent in 1971–72, all tax free. In January 1973, the Directors made a one for four bonus share issue, and said they expected to be able to keep up the 15 per cent dividend on the increased capital. United Asbestos Cement Berhad employees continued to train in Australia, and James Hardie employees continued to visit Malaysia for training and consultation.

In 1969 James Hardie Asbestos Limited joined with local interests to set up P. T. Harflex Asbes Semen, a new company to make asbestos cement products in Indonesia. It was based on a small existing plant in need of major rehabilitation, at Kebajoran Lama, Jakarta. Hardies held a majority of shares in the early stages, because of the need for new capital, but an agreement was made with the Indonesian authorities that 51 per cent of the shares would be owned by Indonesian interests within ten years.

The Indonesian plant made a small profit in its first and second years, but not enough to warrant a dividend. It soon became well established in the roofing market, and its range of roofing accessories was extended. It began to move into flat sheets, which had not as yet been much used in Indonesia.

The James Hardie Asbestos Limited Annual Report for 1972 noted that the plant had been rehabilitated and new equipment added, but much more remained to be done to increase efficiency. A year later, training and upgrading of Indonesian staff were continuing, and the two companies were liaising closely on operating, technical and marketing matters. There had been some further expenditure to improve quality, and market prospects continued to be encouraging. There was some competition from imports, for the range of Harflex products did not yet supply all the market's needs.

Late in 1972 James Hardie Asbestos Limited announced plans to form a new company to build a new factory in Indonesia, at Tangerang in West Java, just outside Jakarta. It would make roofing sheets and other building products, and asbestos cement pipes for water supply, drainage and sewerage, as well as telephone and electrical conduit.

The government of Indonesia and the West Java provincial government were very helpful in planning the project, which the President of Indonesia approved on 4 June 1973. At that stage, the plan was to begin construction later in 1973 or early in 1974, with production of building products to start in 1975, and pipes in 1976. The project would be Australia's largest commercial commitment in Indonesia.

CHAPTER THIRTY-SEVEN

EDUCATING YOUNG JOHN

John B. Reid, about 1960, when he was State Manager for South Australia.

From John Boyd Reid's youngest days it must have been evident to his elders, even if not to him, that one of his career options would be to join the family firm and, in the normal course of things, rise to lead it. He was the grandson of Andrew Reid, who had led it for so long and done so much to make it what it had become. His father, John Thyne Reid, known as Jock, was Andrew's second son. The eldest, Andrew Thyne, known as Thyne, had no children.

None of this meant much to young John. He had no interest in business as a career. But then he had little interest in anything else as a career, either. At one stage it did occur to him that he would like to be a Presbyterian minister, following in the footsteps of his maternal grandfather and two uncles, all of whom were ministers of the Church of Scotland. But the idea does not seem to have driven him along too far. In his last year at Scotch College, in Melbourne, Reid worried a lot about what he would do next. He had decided he wanted to go to university, but not to do commerce. The University of Melbourne helped him make up his mind when it dropped Latin as a prerequisite for Law, and he opted for that.

During his university days, he developed a keen interest in debating, as befits a lawyer. This took him overseas, to the United States, under the sponsorship of New York's Institute of International Education. The Institute had been taking debaters to the United States from Oxford and Cambridge, but had not had any from Australia since 1935. Reid went with Robin Millhouse, from Adelaide, who later became Mr Justice Millhouse of the Supreme Court of South Australia.

When Reid finished his Law degree, Professor David Derham told him he must do his year of articles and be admitted to practice. Derham himself had skipped this on his own graduation, and had come to regret it to such an extent that he had gone back and done it later in life. Reid became articled to Jock Macindoe of Hedderwick, Fookes & Alston, the company's Melbourne solicitors. He completed his term with them and became entitled to practise as a barrister and solicitor in Victoria.

With that experience behind him, he opted for commerce after all. In 1954 he began work with Hardie Trading in Melbourne, at the premises in Collins Street where the ghost of James Hardie walked. It was here that the founder had moved the infant business in 1902, and spent so much on whitewashing walls and painting names on doors. It had been the home of the trading company for over sixty years. Young Reid's first task was on the debtors ledger, phoning people and asking them to pay their account. It was a fairly fiery induction into the world of commerce, as anyone who has ever had the job well knows.

After a short period at that, Reid shifted to the Chemical Department, where he worked on the stock-books — 'great thick things with heavy boards on them'. Young John's great contribution to the system was to divide the stock books into three volumes, rather than the former two, so that more people could work on them at once.

The entire system was manual, but it told people all they wanted to know about every item in stock: its date of arrival, all the documentation (so they could go to the accounts people armed with delivery docket and invoice details), the in-store cost, the selling prices that had been set, how many bales or cartons were left in stock. Unless somebody made a mistake, the stock book told exactly how business was going in every line, what the profit margins were, and the total cost of goods in stock.

One year, in an excess of enthusiasm, John Reid decided on a new method of stocktaking. The way it had always been done was to take the stock books down to the basement, in 'this unbelievable old building in Little Collins Street'. There, somebody would call out the figures from the book, while somebody else verified that the goods were there. This task completed, anything else was ignored and left undisturbed. The new approach was to take note not of what was in the book but what was in the basement.

Fibrolite pipes ready to be installed at Bogor, Indonesia, under the Colombo Plan, to expand and improve the town's forty-year-old water supply system. 'Young John' played a major role in setting up the company's Indonesian operation. One of its first ventures overseas, the move gave the company 'a window on the world'.

John B. Reid (centre), with
South Australian Premier
Sir Thomas Playford (left)
and John T. (Jock) Reid, at
the opening of the pipe plant
at Elizabeth in 1961.
After the Group acquired
Wunderlich's half-share in
the Asbestolite plant,
'Young John' became James
Hardie's first State Manager
in South Australia. He filled
the role from 1960 to 1965.

This revealed a large accumulation of odds and ends, perhaps going back half
a century or so. These included items that had long been written out of the books
or samples that had never been in the books. Among the more interesting items
were multiple layers of thick buffalo hide made into various shapes and sizes to
cushion the sudden stop of flying shuttles in looms. The change in stocktaking
procedure led to a cleaning out of all the surplus stock and freed a lot of valuable
space.

During his time on the stock books, Reid had his first experience of selling,
dealing with people who actually walked into the office and asked if they could buy
some of this or that. Based on this, he was told to go out and sell shellac. 'I didn't
even know what you did with a customer,' he recalled more than thirty years later.
'There was no counselling, as they call it today, no instruction manual, nothing.'
He was just told to 'go out with Keith Ready and sell shellac'. Their first call was
to a firm in Carlton known to use shellac on the wooden lavatory seats it made.
The owner, whom Reid remembered as 'twelve feet tall and three feet wide over
a bulging girth', asked him if he was 'any relative of that old bastard Andrew Reid'.

Before long, Reid was provided with a company car, a Hillman Minx with more
than 100 000 miles behind it. He and his wife were both quite pleased about that,
for until then they had had no personal transport at all. He lost a little face in the
short term, however, for the first night he took the car home it became bogged in
the earth floor of the garage he was still building and he had to call a tow truck to
pull it out.

Since the company gave no sales training at all to its salesmen, Reid took himself off to the Australian Institute of Management for a ten-week evening course, where he learned much about the art from Frank Mitchell. He and some of his contemporaries persuaded George Jackson, Managing Director of Hardie Trading, that the company would benefit from an in-house sales course, preceded by a course on the company's history, attitudes, philosophy and range of business, a knowledge of which was vital in the Frank Mitchell method of selling. The sessions were at night, and anybody who worked for the company could come. The series had a good effect on morale, for people met and talked and learned much about the company. John Reid spoke on the impact of the law on business.

On enquiring of his elders if he was likely to be moved from Melbourne and being told that he was not, he went ahead and bought a new house. Soon after that, Thyne Reid suggested it would be a good idea for him to move to Sydney, 'to get some experience', in a very general sense. But in a piece of typical Thyne Reid lack of attention to non-engineering detail, he made no further arrangements.

John Reid arrived in Sydney to find that nobody wanted to know about him, even less so if it meant having him charged to their payroll. Getting on somebody's payroll became a matter of some urgency to a young man with a wife and one daughter eighteen months and another brand new, in the throes of moving from Melbourne to Sydney. Thyne suggested he could go to Hardie Rubber to get some experience, and that he could go on the Hardie Holdings payroll.

He found quite strong resistance to this idea from Chisholm Cameron, who did not want to share his sole position on the Hardie Holdings payroll with anyone, least of all the Chairman's nephew. But John Reid insisted not only on getting on the Hardie Holdings payroll, but also on continuity of the superannuation benefits to which he had been entitled at Hardie Trading. The latter had to be arranged through James Hardie & Coy Pty Ltd with Don Walker, who showed no more enthusiasm than anyone else.

Although Reid was on Hardie Holdings payroll, he would not be working for that company. He therefore suggested he should keep an account of the time he worked for the various companies in the Group so they could be charged for it.

Until 1960, the joint James Hardie–Wunderlich company that made fibro-cement in South Australia sold it as 'Asbestolite'. This arrangement meant that Fibrolite could not be advertised nationally.

189

THE CHEERFUL YEARS

'They were cheerful years, those I spent in South Australia', John B. Reid recalled in 1987. Until about the time I went there, South Australia did not really figure in Hardie thinking very much. Because the plant there was a joint Hardie–Wunderlich operation, South Australia was a sort of truce area.

'We also had the great advantage of being a long way from head office in those days of less rapid transport and communications. I do remember, though, distinct signals of disapproval from head office when I tried to impress the Premier, Sir Thomas Playford, by chartering a tiny Auster aircraft to fly him over a Waikerie irrigation project for which we had supplied pipes. I never really found out whether the disapproval was on the grounds of cost or taking the risk of losing one of Australia's best-known Premiers.'

Cameron suddenly became much more agreeable. As things turned out, Reid did spend most of his time for a year or two with Hardie Rubber at Paddington and Auburn, just as Thyne had suggested. An unholy row cropped up every three months between Cameron and Scholes, Managing Director of Hardie Rubber, over how much his company should be charged for the privilege of educating young John. Hardie Rubber had never been a great profit earner, and had to be wary of such extravagances.

John Reid broke out of that situation by persuading Thyne Reid and Jonah Adamson that Hardies needed a legal officer. We can assess the real need from the fact that once John moved on the company did without a legal officer for the next thirty years. He left that job in 1960 to become the first State Manager in South Australia for James Hardie. This position became available when James Hardie acquired Wunderlich's half-share in the South Australian fibro-cement operation hurriedly set up during the Second World War.

The shared company had always been a problem, for various reasons. The name Asbestolite was used only in South Australia, which complicated any attempt at national promotion of product names. Because Wunderlichs competed with Hardies in other states, Hardies were reluctant to pass on Hardie technology to the Adelaide plant, even though Wunderlich people were not so much as allowed to walk through it. Once Hardies had bought out the Wunderlich interest, and also decided to make Fibrolite pipes in South Australia, the company set up a full-scale branch there, one of its major initial tasks being to make the Hardie name, and its numerous product names, known there, almost from scratch.

In 1965, not long after Thyne Reid died, John Boyd Reid moved back to Sydney as Marketing Manager of Hardies building products. His father, John Thyne (Jock) Reid, who had become Chairman of the fibro-cement side of the business on Thyne's death, continued to live in Melbourne, the major centre of activity of Hardie Trading Limited, of which he was also Chairman. By then, John Boyd Reid had also become deeply involved in a fibro-cement pipe and sheet factory the company set up in Malaysia, run by a Malaysian public company of which he was to become Chairman.

CHAPTER THIRTY-EIGHT

A VERY GOOD
BUSINESS INDEED

If James Hardie had been able to study the accounts of James Hardie Asbestos Limited while Jock Reid was Chairman, he would have seen that the company had become 'a very good business indeed'. It had grown beyond his wildest dreams. The scale of it would no doubt have terrified him and made his nights even more 'hideous for want of sleep'.

This motif from the 1965 Annual Report shows the range of the company's products.

After a one for four cash issue of shares at par in 1964–65, all the company's considerable expansion was financed from internal sources. Other share issues during his term, in 1969 and 1973, were bonus issues that did not involve any call on the shareholders for cash.

Earnings per share were high all through the Jock Reid era, starting at 28.5 cents in 1965, falling to a low for his term of 26.4 cents in 1968, then rising steadily to a high of 39.5 cents in 1973. Such earnings covered the dividend by a ratio of about three to one in the early years, rising to almost four to one at the end of the period. For the first five years the dividend was steady at the established rate of 10 per cent, even after the 25 per cent lift in capital from the bonus issue of 1966. Then it rose to 12.5 per cent, where it stayed for the rest of the Jock Reid era, even though the amount needed to cover it rose steadily with the 1969 and 1973 bonus increases in capital.

Keeping such a large part of profits in the business helped Hardies' impressive financial performance. Shareholders' funds, $19 726 000 in 1965, at the start of the Jock Reid era, had risen to $75 285 744 by 1973, the end of the era, only $2 100 000 of the increase having come from the shareholders as cash contributions. Shareholders' funds had risen by a ratio of 3.8 to 1, profits by a ratio of 3.1 to 1. It was a creditable performance, given the general tightening up of business conditions in Australia between 1965 and 1973.

The company made no secret of the fact that it provided for depreciation at higher rates than those allowed by the taxation department. This meant that its published profits were less than those calculated for tax purposes. The shareholders' funds would have been even higher if profits had been based on the tax-approved depreciation rates. The company's approach to calculating its profits and to finance in general certainly seems to have been conservative.

From the company's earliest days, the shareholders had rarely been called upon for cash. We can trace its capital development from its formation in 1936, expressing all amounts in dollars, for ease of comparison. The original paid-up capital was $979 200. This was increased in 1937 to $994 200 by the issue for cash of $15 000 in shares.

This was the paid-up capital of the company when Thyne Reid succeeded Andrew Reid, in 1939. It was increased several times during his period of control, but mainly by bonus issues and issues to the owners of assets it acquired. Paid-up capital did not alter at all until 1948, when a one for two bonus issue from tax-free profits raised it to $1 491 226. A minor cash issue of $39 800 later in the year brought it to $1 531 026. A further bonus issue of one for two in 1951, from an asset revaluation, raised it to $2 296 454. This was rounded off to $2 300 000 by an issue of $3546 for cash.

Another bonus issue in 1954, this time one for ten, from tax-free reserves, raised the paid-up capital to $2 530 000. This was quickly followed, in 1955, by another one for two bonus, from an asset revaluation, which brought the paid-up capital to $3 795 000. Capital increased again in 1956, to $3 995 000, with the issue of $200 000 in shares for cash at par to the company's staff assurance and retirement fund.

The early 1950s were years of rapid inflation, and the two asset revaluations served to dilute any appeal the company might have had to corporate raiders on the lookout for companies with undervalued assets. They also provided the shareholders with tax-free capital profits. Still another bonus issue from an asset revaluation was to come in 1959. By then corporate raiders were well and truly active.

In the meantime, however, the company had for the first time since its initial issue used shares to buy assets. In 1959 it issued $366 310 to acquire Better Brakes Holdings Ltd, and $80 000 for further distribution outlets for brake linings. Then, later in 1959, came the one for two asset revaluation issue of $2 220 654, which brought the paid-up capital to $6 661 964.

The company's paid-up capital was unchanged for the next five years, until 1964, when for the first time since the first issue, in 1936, shareholders contributed other than token amounts of cash. A one for four issue at par raised $1 738 036. In calculating each shareholder's entitlement, fractions were ignored, and the resulting surplus of shares, $72 546 (included in the $1 738 036), was issued to the staff assurance and retirement fund at par. All this brought the paid-up capital of the company to $8 400 000, and this was what it was when Jock Reid became Chairman.

He asked the shareholders for $2 100 000 in cash in 1965, with a one for four issue at par, making the paid-up capital $10 500 000. This was relatively steady until 1969–70, when $1 shares were issued at $5 to acquire Hardie Holdings Limited. The share premium reserve so created was used for a one for four bonus issue, with fractions again allocated to the staff assurance and retirement fund, along with a further 273 248 shares, all for cash at par. After all these steps, the paid-up capital of James Hardie Asbestos Limited was $14 600 000.

A one for four bonus issue, involving 3 698 062 shares, was made in 1972–73. Also issued during that year were 197 100 shares to Trustees, 'for the benefit of employees of the Company and its subsidiaries', at a premium of $3.05, and 1213 shares arising from fractions from the bonus issue to the staff assurance and retirement fund for cash at par. This brought the paid-up capital to $18 496 375, at which figure it stood when Jock Reid retired as Chairman.

JAMES HARDIE
PROJECT 72

In 1972 James Hardie & Coy Pty Ltd, the Group's fibro-cement manufacturing company, sponsored the James Hardie Project 72, a development study of the town of Sunbury, near Melbourne.

The study, by architects and planners, was designed to show how a metropolitan fringe area or a rural town might be properly planned for big population growth. It used consultants in architecture, market research, traffic and movement, economics, demography, sociology, landscaping, conservation, ecology, recreation and pollution control.

The comprehensive plan they developed was presented to the Twenty-first Australian Convention of the Royal Australian Institute of Architects.

Opposite: A selection of annual reports from the years 1963-1974.

CHAPTER THIRTY-NINE

THE JOCK REID STYLE

T hose who knew Jock Reid remember him as a calm, gentle man who was very sensitive to other people's needs and feelings. At the same time, he was a man of great inner strength, a man who would not be deterred from what he thought was right. In his time as Chairman of Hardie Holdings Limited, from 1945 to 1973, and of James Hardie Asbestos Limited, from 1965 to 1973, he further enhanced the good standing Hardies already had in the business community.

A widely held view was that if Jock Reid said it was so, then it must be so. His word was his bond, and he expected it to be accepted as such. On one occasion, when the company's bankers asked for guarantees from the parent company for advances to one of its subsidiaries, he refused point blank to give them, on the ground that there should be no need for such formality between people who trusted each other, and the bank accepted this. On another occasion, when a bank did persuade one of his relatives to hand over some shares as collateral, he insisted that the relative concerned go and get them back, because the Reids did not give collateral. Once again the bank complied.

For all his gentle calmness, he had an acute commercial mind. He was always keen to ensure that whatever the company did led to a profit. Nor would he deviate

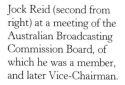

Jock Reid (second from right) at a meeting of the Australian Broadcasting Commission Board, of which he was a member, and later Vice-Chairman.

from a course he had set himself if he believed it to be right, no matter who opposed him.

One example of this cropped up when James Hardie Asbestos Limited set out to take over Hardie Holdings Limited, which was in fact one of its own major shareholders. Hardie Holdings Limited owned 46.2 per cent of the shares in James Hardie Asbestos Limited and 22.4 per cent of the shares in Hardie Trading Ltd, an arrangement that left the group rather exposed to corporate raiders. One result of the proposed takeover would be that James Hardie Asbestos Limited, seen within the group as 'Sydney', would come to own 22.4 per cent of Hardie Holdings Limited, seen within the group as 'Melbourne'.

Just the thought of such an event brought out all the old Sydney–Melbourne and fibro–trading rivalries. The Hardie Holdings Limited board was not at all enthusiastic about the idea, and Jock Reid was under great pressure from his fellow directors not to go ahead with the move. But he believed it to be right, and nothing would deter him from it.

Jock Reid at the School of Architecture at the University of Melbourne, 1968. The company endowed the James Hardie Lecture Theatre at the University.

Both before and after his retirement from James Hardie, Jock Reid was deeply involved in many community activities. He was for many years a Commissioner of the Australian Broadcasting Commission, of which he was Vice-Chairman from 1967 to 1971. He gave freely of his time and concern to the Melbourne and Metropolitan Young Men's Christian Association. He served the Presbyterian Church of Victoria, the Conservatorium of Music at Melbourne University and the Baker Institute of Medical Research. He was a Board Member and for a time President of St George's Hospital in Melbourne. He was President of the Victorian College of the Arts from its foundation until he stepped down in 1976. He gave long service to the Rotary Club of Melbourne, which he joined in 1939 and of which he was President in 1953–54.

In 1974, just after he retired as Chairman of the Hardie companies, Jock Reid was created a Knight Bachelor for his services to the community and to the arts. In 1971, he had been made a Companion of the Order of St Michael and St George. He was awarded the Doctor of Laws degree of the University of Melbourne and the Doctor of Arts and Sciences degree of the Victorian Institute of Colleges. Sir John Reid died in Melbourne in February 1985.

PART FIVE

ENTREPRENEURS

CHAPTER FORTY

A FUTURE
FOR FIBRE CEMENT

In his first Annual Report, for the year to 30 March 1974, John B. Reid enthused about the future of fibre cement.

Rising living standards and increasing costs for an average house would not reduce the role of Hardie building products in housing, he said. On the contrary, new houses used even more of them than before, sometimes in unexpected places. Hardie marketing people had continued to seek out housing uses for fibre cement where it was not only suitable but also best for the job. This also applied to commercial, high-rise and home unit applications.

Super Six roofing was in steady demand for domestic, industrial and commercial roofing, but iron and aluminium roofing in long lengths were making inroads into its traditional markets. The popularity of Super Six as free-standing fencing was rising rapidly in all states, particularly in Western Australia. Hardiflex and flat-sheet products had sustained their growth in recent years. Current designs for houses and other dwellings made them very suitable for inside and outside use. Compressed sheets were finding increasing uses as impervious flooring for verandahs and bathrooms and as structural components in balustrades and screening. These were good examples of the use of engineered fibre cement in the building industry.

The Pipe Division, too, was expanding its markets. In newly developed urban and rural areas, water supply and sewerage systems were being designed and laid down in Fibrolite pipes. In the past year, with the drive towards greater productivity in grazing and pastoral areas, as well as in the more intensive cultivation of fruit, vegetables and other crops, the market in irrigation had grown.

Pipes of larger dimension were being used in slurry and effluent lines for industry, notably over longer distances and in difficult conditions and isolated locations. In water supply systems for the capital cities, Fibrolite pressure pipe was being used more and more. Pipe production capacity was being increased in Western Australia and South Australia. In Queensland, a lease of 29 hectares had been arranged at Wacol, and a new buildings products factory was being planned, to begin production there in 1976.

Still, there were problems. The period was one of acute worldwide economic instability, brought on by the energy crisis', the result of escalating oil prices. In Australia, politics added to the economic instability, as the Whitlam government sought to cope not only with those economic problems but also with its own internal strains.

Some of the current problems had a major impact on the fibre cement industry.

One of the first metric fibre cement pipes produced at Camellia, New South Wales. The changeover — in January 1974 for building products, in April for pipes — was made with few problems, owing to a great deal of preparatory work by many Hardie people, who designed and produced explanatory publications and held numerous meetings with designers, suppliers and users of Hardie products. The Metric Conversion Board congratulated the Group on the success of the conversion process.

JOHN B. REID, Chairman of the Group since 1973.

Asbestos, both imported and locally produced, was in short supply, and prices had risen 25 per cent in one year. Cellulose pulp, which was taking over the role of asbestos in fibre cement, was in very short supply because of a heavy world demand for paper products, and prices had risen 60 per cent.

Large quantities of both asbestos and cellulose pulp were imported, and sea freights had risen by 30 per cent. Shipping from the east coast of North America was difficult and subject to long delays. West coast conditions were not so bad, but they were still serious. In its attempts to thwart inflation, the government had encouraged imports, with the result that Australian ports, notably Sydney, were subject to such unprecedented congestion that Hardies were moving raw materials by road to supply some factories.

The costs of asbestos rose again in 1975, by 40 per cent, mainly because two large Canadian producers had serious production losses, one caused by fire and one by subsidence in its quarry. Further rises of 8 to 10 per cent were expected within the next six months.

Although the building industry was declining, sales of fibre cement products increased during 1975. Fewer new houses were being built, but more people were extending and renovating their houses, and this kept up the demand for Hardie products. Two new products had proved successful, Hardigrain and Hardiplank Woodgrain. Hardigrain found both internal and external uses in industrial, commercial and school buildings. Hardiplank Woodgrain was designed as an external wall cladding and for gable ends, fences and screens.

Exports increased, notably of decorated fibre cement sheets to Japan. New areas, including the Middle East, were being explored for export prospects, but

Hardie 750 mm diameter pipe and compressed sheets were used for this prototype Marina at Southport, on the Gold Coast, Queensland. The pipes provide the floats for the pontoon.

Hardie corrugated fibre cement sheets lend themselves to distinctive use for fascias, sunhoods and canopies. The Hub building, the central administration area at Griffith University, Mt Gravatt (Brisbane), is a striking example.

Harry Hudson joined James Hardie & Coy. Pty. Limited in 1955 and has held various positions within this Division, culminating in his present position as Executive General Manager of the Fibre Cement Division. He became a Director of James Hardie Industries Limited in 1978, holds Directorships with James Hardie & Coy. Pty Limited and James Hardie Impey Limited. He was recently made President of James Hardie Building Products Inc. and a Director of James Hardie Industries Inc. in the USA.

rising domestic costs and competition from alternative products made export development difficult. Exports also helped the Pipe Division, which had kept up a steady volume of sales, an increase in public sector activity offsetting the downturn in irrigation, drainage and domestic building demand.

Sales continued to grow in 1976. While most fibre cement products performed well, corrugated sheets for fencing did particularly well, helped by the introduction of coloured fencing sheets in Western Australia.

The new $10 000 000 building products factory at Wacol in Queensland was opened by the Premier, Joh (later Sir Joh) Bjelke-Petersen, on 8 April 1976. It was completed on time and within budget, a major achievement at a time of 15 per cent inflation. This, John B. Reid noted in his Annual Report, was a credit to the Queensland management, their advisers and contractors. The plant created 250 new production jobs.

Asbestos supply was a problem during 1976, when a seven-month strike stopped production at several large mines in Canada. Fortunately, some Canadian mines were not affected, and because of the company's good relations with them it was able to get enough fibre for its needs. The average cost of fibre, however, rose by another 20 per cent.

Industrial troubles, including overtime bans and stoppages, restricted output from Hardie plants during the year. Greater efforts were being made to improve communications amongst all the Group's employees, in the hope of overcoming such problems, the Chairman said in his Annual Report.

Hardies confirmed its stated faith in the future of fibre cement in Australia

Large-diameter Hardie pipes laid out ahead of trench-digging and pipe-laying machinery.

200

FROM RESEARCH LABORATORY TO MANAGING DIRECTOR'S OFFICE

Ted Heath, who was Managing Director of James Hardie Asbestos Limited from 1971 until 1978, joined the company in 1939 at the research laboratory at Camellia.

In 1947 Thyne Reid chose Ted Heath to accompany him on an overseas tour in search of information about the autoclave system of curing, which Reid correctly believed was the key to the full development of the fibre cement pipe industry in Australia. In later years Heath made several prolonged visits to the United States, seeking knowledge on such diverse topics as pipe-manufacturing techniques, machine design and asbestos substitutes.

In 1950, in company with Frank Page, Heath travel-

Ted Heath joined Hardies at the research laboratory in Camellia in 1939 and retired as Managing Director in 1978.

led extensively, making a technical survey of all the major fibre cement manufacturers of the Western world. Their visits led to long-term agreements with leading American and British fibre cement manufacturers for the exchange of technical information. Heath played a leading part in the early development of the idea of electrolytic separation of pipes from their mandrels, a technique that improved both productivity and pipe quality and was eventually adopted by the fibre cement pipe industry around the world.

His interests gradually switched to marketing, and in 1952 he moved from Camellia to York Street as Pipe Sales Manager for New South Wales. The switch made sense, because the art of selling fibre cement pipes at that time lay in convincing technical people of their capabilities. In 1960 Heath became Federal Pipe Sales Manager.

In 1964 Heath worked with John B. Reid on a feasibility study of fibre cement manufacture in Malaysia, as a result of which James Hardie took part in setting up United Asbestos Cement Berhad to make fibre cement building materials and pipes in Malaysia. He became a Director of the Malaysian company in 1965.

Ted Heath became a member of the Executive Committee of James Hardie & Coy Pty Limited, the fibre cement manufacturing and marketing company in the James Hardie Group, in 1965. In 1968 he became a Director of that company, and in the next year its Chief Executive Officer and a Director of James Hardie Asbestos Limited. In 1971 he became Chairman of James Hardie & Coy Pty Ltd and Managing Director of James Hardie Asbestos Limited.

Ted Heath retired from all his positions with Hardies, on medical advice, in 1978. The Annual Report for that year said: 'His influence on the Group's growth and development has been incalculable, and his cheerful human understanding of people won him great loyalty and affection.'

when, on 30 May 1977, the company notified the Stock Exchange that it had agreed to buy the fibre cement division of Wunderlich Limited, for about $19 million in cash. The assets included, all of which were in New South Wales, Victoria and Queensland, were all plant, equipment, stock and some land. The exact price would depend on stocks at the date of transfer. All Wunderlich employees who wished to do so would become Hardie employees.

The move would result in a stronger industry, with greater scope for efficiencies of scale, technological development and innovations in new products and appli-

Above: Moulded panels and Hardiflex were used under these walkways at Woden College of Technical and Further Education in Canberra.

Right: The fascias, spandrel panels and soffits of this contemporary Queensland home are made from Hardiflex flat sheets.

cations. There would be no question of monopoly, for competition in the cladding market would continue to come from a wide range of other building materials, John B. Reid said. The Trade Practices Commission agreed, and on 29 June 1977 it approved the acquisition.

The outlook for fibre cement continued to be good, in spite of the economic difficulties and the lack of new construction projects in the building industry. Construction in the capital cities was for the most part limited to the completion of projects started in earlier years. Office space was in over supply.

In the housing industry, the period was one of growth in renovations and handyman activity. The number of new houses being built was increasing, and Hardies joined with various project builders in promoting new houses that featured fibre cement in composite construction. Demand for corrugated sheets for fencing continued to grow, as well as for their traditional use in roofing. Compressed fibre cement was also gaining wider acceptance for decking, and for laundry and bathroom flooring. New styles of textured cladding sheets introduced in recent years were well accepted, and sales were growing. Export sales continued to be difficult, but Japan was still taking worthwhile quantities of decorated boards, for use mainly in road tunnel linings, and Hong Kong was taking plain compressed sheets for the same purpose.

Work began during 1976 on a new pipe plant at Moss Vale, in the Southern Highlands of New South Wales. The State government and the Shire of Wingecarribee had both co-operated fully to enable the project to develop rapidly. Production of asbestos cement pipe was scheduled to begin at the end of 1978, when pipes up to 750 mm in diameter would be made in one of the most modern plants in the world. One of the first tasks on the site was to plant 2500 trees, so that the factory would merge into its rural setting.

Hardie natural grey shingles blend well into the rural setting of this Western Australian house.

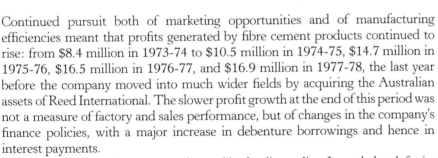

Continued pursuit both of marketing opportunities and of manufacturing efficiencies meant that profits generated by fibre cement products continued to rise: from $8.4 million in 1973-74 to $10.5 million in 1974-75, $14.7 million in 1975-76, $16.5 million in 1976-77, and $16.9 million in 1977-78, the last year before the company moved into much wider fields by acquiring the Australian assets of Reed International. The slower profit growth at the end of this period was not a measure of factory and sales performance, but of changes in the company's finance policies, with a major increase in debenture borrowings and hence in interest payments.

During 1975-76, the company changed its funding policy. It needed cash for its new projects at Wacol in Queensland, Moss Vale in New South Wales, and Tangerang in Indonesia, for new equipment at existing plants, and for increased working capital needed as the result of inflation, mainly for raw materials and finished stocks.

In Australia, the company raised $10 million by a debenture issue on the market. In the United States, P. T. James Hardie Indonesia raised a consortium loan of US$11 million, which was guaranteed by the parent company. In the next year, 1976-77, the company borrowed again, mainly for the Moss Vale pipe plant

Hardiplank Stucco was used as exterior cladding on this house in New South Wales.

The Wacol fibre cement products factory near Brisbane.

and for increased working capital. In 1977-78, it issued another $14 million in debenture stock. By 31 March 1978, the Group's total long-term borrowings had risen to $50 million, almost double the $26 million of the previous year. Interest charges were $6 million a year, enough to warrant a comment in the Annual Report and the financial press.

Shareholders' funds, however, also rose steadily during this period, from $100.2 million at 31 March 1975 to $165.9 million at 31 March 1978, even though the shareholders were not at any stage asked to contribute. Paid-up capital rose in only the last of those four years, from $24.6 million to $31.0 million, the increase being due to shares issued for the acquisition of Gay-Dor Plastics Ltd. Unappropriated profits rose from $29.4 million at 31 March 1975 to $62.5 million at 31 March 1978. Most of the rest of the increase in shareholders' funds was due to the increase in the assets revaluation reserve, which rose from $25.4 million at 31 March 1974 to $48.7 million at 31 March 1978.

CHAPTER FORTY-ONE

THE REED ACQUISITION: NEW FIELDS, NEW HORIZONS

One day in 1978, an alert research assistant at Sydney stockbrokers Ord Minnett, poring over the pink-paged London *Financial Times*, read about talk of trouble in the giant paper and publishing conglomerate Reed International. Reed might be about to sell some of its overseas assets, the newspaper report hinted. Nobody could have guessed at that stage that the research assistant was about to set in train events that would change the whole course of Hardie's future.

Reed's Australian interests were soon the subject of much discussion among Ord Minnett partners. Perhaps they might be among those Reed was willing to sell. One of the partners, Gilles Kryger, was London bound anyway, so while he was there he enquired through 'various sources'. Yes, it seemed, Reed might be willing to sell all its Australian assets. Kryger arrived back in Australia with that piece of news on 13 August.

Ord Minnett, working with investment consultant Keith Halkerston, began to make a list of Australian companies that might bid. They looked among those they thought big enough to handle the $65 million or so likely to be involved, and with a similar business mix to Reed. No one company ideally fitted that specification, but James Hardie came out on top of the list.

Three days after Kryger arrived back from London, Ord Minnett sought an interview with Hardie's Managing Director, David Macfarlane, and its Finance Director, Fred Loneragan. Gilles Kryger, Keith Halkerston and Ord partner David Nicol arrived at Hardie headquarters to put the proposition. Macfarlane later recalled that his first reaction was caution and trepidation, for a lot of people had come to Hardies with a range of propositions in recent years. But he soon found himself asking Chairman John B. Reid, 'How do you feel about $64 million?'

Over the next ten days, Macfarlane and his team looked closely at the Reed proposition. For all their faith in the future of fibre cement, they saw clearly that it had nearly reached its full potential. It would very likely go on indefinitely, but it was not very likely to grow much faster than the rate of national growth. Since their Wunderlich acquisition, Hardies had most of the Australian market for fibre cement, and demand had flattened out.

Fibre cement faced intense competition from other cladding, roofing and piping materials. New developments in other building materials could well decrease the demand for fibre cement, and Hardies could not realistically look to significant export markets for it. On the supply side, even though the use of

James Hardie's Deputy Managing Director Fred Loneragan, together with Managing Director David Macfarlane, played a major role in the negotiations that led to the Reed acquisition.

cellulose was increasing, it still depended, to a degree, on asbestos fibre, most of which was imported. Fibre had been in short supply, and its price had risen faster than prices in general. Its supply was vulnerable to all sorts of hazards. Public opion was also a consideration, on health grounds.

The clear solution was to diversify, but the problem was to find something to offer comparable returns per share, be compatible with the existing business, and big enough. Reed seemed to fill the bill. Its latest annual report showed its earnings as 28.5 cents on its 50 cent shares, compared to Hardies 53 cents on their $1 shares. Much of its business was in building products, markets James Hardie people knew well. The rest would give a measure of diversification. Many of the firms Reed owned were in consumer markets that Hardie Directors saw as having good growth potential. Several had interesting offshore manufacturing or distributing activities, or Australian export trade.

Halkerston and Ords were appointed advisers for the project. Halkerston and David Macfarlane met in London, where on 12 September they called on Reed International's Finance Director David Cormie and made a direct approach. They were soon back in Sydney, where, as Kryger put it, 'A hell of a lot more work had to be done'. Ten days later, Halkerston, Macfarlane and Loneragan were in London again, ready to work out the details with Reed. This took from 29 September to 5 October. On 6 October the team headed back to Australia with the deal in their bags.

Jim Brookes joined the Group in 1978 on the acquisition of RCI Limited. He held various general management positions during the period 1973–1980 with RCI Limited. He has been Executive General Manager of James Hardie Building Products Pty Ltd since 1980, and Director of James Hardie Industries Limited since 1981.

Inspecting samples of a new colour range of Fowler bathroomware in the early 1980s. Hardies acquired Fowler Ware in 1979, to expand the share of the bathroomware market they acquired with the Reed interest.

A MANAGING DIRECTOR FOR A NEW ERA

David Macfarlane, who as Managing Director of James Hardie Industries Limited was to play a major role in bringing the Group into a new era of diversification, joined it in January 1958 after an earlier career with pump-makers Kelly & Lewis.

Macfarlane was born in 1930 in China, where his mother was a missionary, his father an engineer. He had been sent away to school in Edinburgh for a couple of years, but got most of his education at Brighton Grammar School, after the family moved to Melbourne. He and his family managed to get out of China on the last ship to leave before the Japanese took over the area where they had lived.

Young Macfarlane found work as an apprentice fitter in the Springvale plant of pump-makers Kelly & Lewis and began to study for his Diploma of Mechanical Engineering at night. Once he had finished his apprenticeship, which included stints in the drawing office and in estimating, Kelly & Lewis sent him to the Western Australian coalmining town of Collie to install pumps. The move cut across his studies, because of differing state standards, and he never did finish his diploma. Macfarlane later moved to Perth as State Manager for Kelly & Lewis, but found himself out of a job when the firm wound down its Western Australian operation. He spent a year running a dairy farm his father-in-law had brought in Victoria, but decided he was not meant for life on the land.

He saw a Hardie advertisement for a Technical Sales Representative for Fibrolite pipes, applied, convinced the company his experience of water and its movement with Kelly & Lewis was an appropriate qualification, and got the job. His early contacts were mainly with consulting engineers working on water reticulation schemes, as the use of Fibrolite pipes for sewerage and irrigation was still in the future. At that stage the Brooklyn plant in Melbourne was making pipes up to 20 centimetres in diameter and bringing larger sizes from Camellia. Brooklyn was later equipped with a bigger machine that supplied larger sizes for both Victoria and South Australia.

In 1961 Macfarlane went as Pipe Sales Manager to South Australia, where the future Chairman, John B. Reid, was State Manager. Macfarlane sold pipes made in Victoria until the first pipe machine, a Mazza, was installed in the new Fibrolite pipe plant at Elizabeth. It produced mainly 10 centimetre and 15 centimetre diameter pipes at first, but was gradually worked up to 50 centimetres.

As Managing Director, David Macfarlane was to play a major role in bringing the Group into a new era of diversification.

Macfarlane became Acting Manager for South Australia when John B. Reid moved back to Sydney as Federal Building Products Sales Manager. By then, however, Macfarlane was General Manager Designate for the Malaysian venture, in which Hardies had a major role, including overseeing construction and managing the operation. He lived in Kuala Lumpur and travelled once a week to the factory at Ipoh, where Pat Collins was Factory Manager.

Late in 1969 the Group brought Macfarlane back to Australia as Manager of Product Planning and Development, which was really a holding post. He became Marketing Manager Pipes and, in 1973, a Director of James Hardie & Coy Pty Ltd, the fibre cement manufacturing and marketing company.

He soon became Operations Manager of that company and later its Chief Executive Officer, directly responsible to Ted Heath, who was Managing Director of James Hardie Asbestos Limited, the Group's holding company. Macfarlane also became involved in Hardie Extrusions and Hardie – Ferodo. He became a Director of James Hardie Asbestos Limited in 1975 and its Managing Director in 1978.

Fowler's Pottery at
Camperdown. From the
Illustrated Sydney News,
15 October 1865.

On Friday 13 October 1978, newspapers throughout Australia carried the
news that James Hardie Asbestos Limited had taken the biggest step in its ninety-
year history when it handed over a cheque for $52.1 million for Reed International
Ltd's 80.5 per cent share in Reed Consolidated Industries Limited. It would now
make a similar offer, of $2.60 a share, to the minority shareholders, bringing the
total cost of the acquisition to around $65 million. This offer was required by
Stock Exchange rules, but was also in keeping with Hardies' desire to own the
Reed subsidiary outright. As an alternative to the straight cash deal, Hardies made
a cash and share offer, pitched at the institutions that controlled most of the
Australian-held shares: three James Hardie shares and $1 cash for every five Reed
Consolidated shares, which were worth $2.81 on the then current price of Hardie
shares, $4.35. Reed's directors unanimously recommended the offer to minority
shareholders.

The deal would be financed by borrowings, cash flow and a two-for-nine
$24.13 million share issue, with the $1 shares issued at $3.50. After the cash issue,
which would involve 7 million shares, Hardie capital would be $37.9 million. A
further 2.88 million shares were issued in respect of the stock units in Reed
Consolidated Industries which had been held by the public. Several new
institutions became Hardie shareholders as a result of the increased shares on
issue. Hardies' traditional broker, J. B. Were and Son, joined with Ord Minnett in
a joint arrangement to raise $30 million in debentures and underwrite the share

issue. As a bridging measure, Hardies asked for, and got, temporary accommodation of $50 million from the ANZ Bank.

The $65 million acquisition was at the time by far the biggest takeover of a listed company ever made in Australia. It gave Hardies control over tangible assets of up to $138 million and extra annual sales of more than $224 million. The process of acquiring Reed International's 81 per cent of RCI had taken between four and six weeks before it was publicly announced and the offer made for the public shareholding.

RCI's parents were the large Reed Paper Group and International Publishing Corporation (IPC), the world's biggest newspaper and magazine publisher. Each had owned various businesses in Australia. RCI, the Australian subsidiary, had taken these over from its parent companies at various times, the most recent case having been Reed Publishing and Leisure (RPL), which it had acquired in 1973.

RCI had been formed in 1960, but some of the firms it owned had a much longer history. The Spicer paper interests dated from the 1870s, the packaging companies from the 1880s. RCI had 40 per cent of its funds in paper and packaging firms, which made and sold paper products throughout Australia. Wilson Fabrics, which RCI acquired in 1966, had been started fifty years ago by an Australian, Arthur G. Wilson. RCI had also acquired Ashleys, a New Zealand wallpaper manufacturer. It had fabric distribution, stationery manufacturing, publishing and mail order interests in New Zealand.

Enoch Fowler, founder of Fowler's Pottery.

In building materials, RCI interests included Iplex, which made a wide range of plastic pipes and fittings and had recently begun to make a new wall-cladding product by the Celuform process. RCI had brought together Twyfords (in Victoria) and Elderware (in New South Wales) to form Reed Bathroomware, which made various bathroom products. Other building subsidiaries included Renhurst, which made foil insulation in Melbourne. Partly owned interests included Iplex Asia, in Singapore, and two Polycell companies in Australia and New Zealand.

RCI's most recent overseas acquisition had been in drip and trickle irrigation. It had a factory in San Diego in California and sales subsidiaries in France, Italy, Jordan, the United Arab Emirates and Australia. Irrigation was the only Reed business John B. Reid admitted to having reservations about keeping. It had lost over $1 million in 1977. James Hardie would, however, listen 'very carefully' to the opinion of Reed executives before deciding its future.

Soon after the Reed acquisition, Reid and Macfarlane went to see the senior managers of the major Reed subsidiaries. They had acquired the group, they explained, because it had competent managers and was producing a return comparable with their own. 'They clearly did not believe us,' Reid recalled a few years later. Some even became a little restive at what they saw as Hardies' lack of concern and had to be reassured that they really were being left alone to get on with managing their part of the newly enlarged group. Most of them did just that, and only a handful left as a result of the Hardie acquisition.

In the 1979 Annual Report, the Hardie Board restated its philosophy on the future of the RCI acquisition: 'The businesses, including those which have experienced some difficulty in recent times, are good businesses. They will be retained, strengthened and developed to grow further.' This view was to be modified with experience, but it was firmly held at the time.

WILSON BEGAN WITH MOTOR TRIMMING

The story of Arthur G. Wilson Pty Limited, which became part of the James Hardie Group with the Reed acquisition in 1978, began in 1926, when Arthur Wilson began importing and distributing accessories for the motor-trimming trade and canvas for shipping. In those days, many cars had soft 'canvas' tops.

By 1939, the company had expanded into soft furnishings and upholstery fabrics. It added wallpapers after the Second World War and by 1966 was the leading Australian distributor of both furnishings and wallpapers. Various takeovers and company formations followed, and the group grew strongly, setting up warehouses and sales offices in all states.

Once in the Hardie Group, Wilson diversified into vinyl floor coverings and hand-printed fabrics and wall coverings. It became Australia's leading supplier of wall coverings, furnishing fabrics and vinyl floor coverings, selling to retailers, interior designers, furniture manufacturers, upholsterers and commercial and institutional bodies.

An advanced computer system installed in the early 1980s made it possible to centralise warehousing in Sydney, with sales offices and showrooms in all major cities.

Printing Wilson wallpaper by the silk-screen method. Wilson was acquired along with the Reed group.

The 1979 Report also noted the harmony and co-operation that had prevailed during the period of acquisition in the Board's relations with both Reed International Limited and with the Australian board and management. Hardies' initial view that RCI was a well-managed business was confirmed on closer acquaintance. Two problem areas, Reed Irrigation Systems in California and Ashley Wallpaper in New Zealand, turned from loss to profit in 1979.

The Reed acquisition began a period of intense activity for the James Hardie Group. Several Reed companies had about 10 per cent of their markets, a worthwhile start but not enough for a company that enjoyed such a dominant market position as James Hardie. Further acquisitions of similar companies showed the Group's determination to increase its market share quickly to the 25 per cent or so it regarded as worthwhile, rather than build it up gradually, a process that could take decades.

One case in point was the acquisition in 1979 of Adelaide publisher Rigby Limited, through RCI, at a cost of $2.3 million. In 1980, the Group added Fowler Ware to its stable to complement the Reed Bathroomware acquired from RCI. Fowler's history went back further than any other unit of the Group, for it had started business at Camperdown, in Sydney, in 1837. Other acquisitions in a similar vein included Brisbane envelope manufacturers Besley & Pike, Cameron Irrigation, KGC Magnetic Tape, Rockware Plastics, Fire Fighting Enterprises Ltd, Irwell Pty Limited, and the Pope Irrigation and Garden Products Division of Simpson Holdings. James Hardie Industries Limited also became involved in various joint ventures, which took it into both familiar and unfamiliar fields.

CHAPTER FORTY-TWO

EXPANSION IN PUBLISHING AND LEISURE

With the Reed acquisition, Hardies had moved into publishing and the leisure industry on a major scale. In the next few years, the Group acquired further well-established firms and became involved in joint ventures that helped balance its Publishing and Leisure Division. It came to have about 30 per cent of the book-publishing business in Australia, and was one of the few Australian book publishers that were Australian owned.

Publishing and leisure companies acquired in the Reed deal included RPL Limited, Paul Hamlyn Pty Limited, Books for Pleasure Pty Limited, Summit Records Pty Limited and Hanna-Barbera Pty Limited. The publishing companies had traded generally as The Hamlyn Group. The book imprints involved included Summit, Lansdowne, Ure Smith, Books for Pleasure and Universal Books. Partworks included the New Zealand Heritage series and the Filipino Heritage encyclopaedic 10 volume history set. The companies also published maps, guides and street directories.

Hanna-Barbera Pty Limited, of which Hardies acquired 51 per cent in the Reed deal, made live and animated films, mainly for television, and mainly for United States television networks. These included 'Popeye', 'The Flintstones', and 'Casper'. Its major achievement during the year in which Hardies acquired it was the sale of an 18 hour animated film series to a United States television network. It had contracts for further such works. A joint-venture project, 'This Fabulous Century', dealing with Australian history in the twentieth century and hosted by Peter Luck, won high ratings on Australian television. Hanna-Barbera was later involved in the Australian mini-series 'Against the Wind' and a second Peter Luck series, 'The Australians'.

In February 1979 the old-established Adelaide firm of Rigby Limited also became a Hardie subsidiary when the Reed Division acquired 53 per cent of its shares. The deal began when Reed bought 33.3 per cent of Rigby from Motors Ltd, owned by Rigby Chairman Bill Hayes. It went on to buy another 10 per cent from Hayes' interests, and the 9 per cent owned by the Octopus Group. Hardies went on to acquire the rest of the shares at the same price, $1.30 per ordinary share, making the total cost $2.3 million. Although Rigby had been making losses, it soon become profitable as part of the Hardie Group.

Rigby could trace its history back to 1859, when William Charles Rigby, who had come from England, started a bookshop in Adelaide. The publishing operation that developed from this had since the early 1960s grasped a major part of the thriving Australiana market. Rigby had a range of illustrated Australian

With the Reed acquisition, the Hardie Group became one of Australia's largest publishers.

Heritage books, the successful Dreamtime series of Aboriginal legends, the popular Sketchbook series, a range of sports coaching manuals, and instant 'how to' books. Writer and critic Max Harris meant it as a compliment when he ranked Rigby as Australia's undisputed leader in 'outbackery and bushwhackery'. Rigby Education was also Australia's leading publisher of primary school textbooks and learning programs. It had two highly successful projects, *Reading Rigby* and *Moving Into Maths*. Both included material for teachers as well as pupils, with such modern aids as audio-visuals, flip charts and audio cassettes.

The Rigby acquisition led to a change of name for The Hamlyn Group, which became The Rigby Group. Hamlyn Trade Books became Lansdowne Press, Hamlyn House (a direct marketing activity) became Rigby House, and the Special Projects section became Heritage Publications. Hamlyn House, the direct marketing activity, had started in 1968 with a range of recipe cards that gave buyers step-by-step instructions on how to cook dishes from a wide range of countries. Its success led Hamlyn to continue the idea, enlarging the range to a full series of such cards, with step-by-step guides to such things as knitting and gardening, as well as cooking. In 1977 Hamlyn acquired the activities of Heron books, which not only expanded its range of books but also added a new product, the Bullworker fitness and muscle builder. It also launched *Geo*, a geographical magazine designed to take readers on photographic visits throughout Australia and New Zealand, covering some of the most out-of-the-way villages and remote places.

In 1981 Hardies acquired KGC Magnetic Tapes Pty Ltd, one of Australia's largest audio tape duplicators. This gave it an entry into the growing market for video cassette duplicating and supported its educational publishing. In the following year it formed Rigby-CIC Video Pty Limited, a 50-50 joint venture with Cinema International Corporation of the United States. The new business had sole Australian distribution rights for the video films of Paramount and Universal Studios from the United States and Hanna-Barbera from Australia. It quickly established itself as a market leader, with a good range of quality products and vigorous marketing.

In 1983 James Hardie and Taft Broadcasting Company, of the United States, formed a joint-venture company, Taft Hardie Group Pty Limited, to capitalise on the combination of Taft's skills in broadcasting and entertainment in the United States and Hardies' knowledge of the Australian market. Hardie and Taft had enjoyed a happy association for years through Hanna-Barbera Pty Limited. At that stage, Hanna-Barbera was going through a disappointing year, but it had high expectations of its latest television mini-series, 'Return to Eden'.

The relationship between Hardies and Tafts was rearranged in July 1983, when Hardies sold Taft 2 per cent of Hanna-Barbera Pty Ltd, switching the controlling 51 per cent from Hardies to Tafts. Hardies then sold to this company, now called Taft Hardie Group Pty Limited, its KGC Magnetic Tapes business and its investment in Rigby-CIC Video, all of which left Hardies with 49 per cent of combined businesses. Taft's specialist expertise in the entertainment markets and worldwide sales network were working well, to the benefit of the new businesses.

During 1983-84, the Lansdowne and Rigby marketing, administration and distribution departments were combined. One of Lansdowne's 1983 publications, *The Complete Works of Banjo Paterson*, was an all-time Australian bestseller.

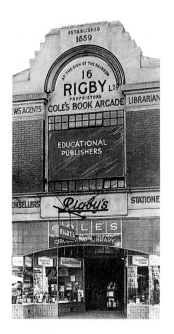

The Hardie Group acquired the long-established Adelaide publishing firm of Rigby in 1979 expanding the share of the Australian publishing market it had acquired through the Reed takeover.

Magazines such as *Geo* and *Nature and Health,* which the Division published, were making good profits.

In January 1985, Hardies put all their publishing business assets into a new 50-50 partnership agreement with the well known and highly successful publisher Kevin Weldon, in a new company, Weldon Hardie Pty Ltd. Weldon had been Managing Director of Hamlyn Publishing but had left in 1979 to set up his own publishing company. Its successes had included the *Macquarie Dictionary, A Day in the Life of Australia, The Victorians, Aussies at Play,* and *Above Sydney.*

Weldon's expertise was in concentrating on a few large-scale projects, which meant they could be given adequate marketing attention. He initiated each project, then arranged for the writing and illustrating to be done. He had also used the technique with notable success in the United States and Singapore markets. He had other projects in hand at the time he began his association with Hardies, including one with the Government of China, celebrating the fiftieth anniversary of the Long March, and another in the United States, the first picture book on high technology.

Weldon said at the time that he admired every Australian publisher. Australia produced the best books, he said. They were well designed, well written and reasonably priced, all with a small market of only 15 million people.

Under Weldon's leadership, Weldon-Hardie set about rationalising its book operations under the Lansdowne and Rigby imprints, notably in distribution.

The biggest and longest wooden roller coaster in Australia under construction at Australia's Wonderland, a theme park near Sydney. James Hardie Industries Limited is a partner in the venture that built the park, which opened in 1985.

213

Above: The film crew on location making 'Return to Eden' for Hanna–Barbera Live Action.

Right: The Taft–CIC videotape range specialises in family entertainment.

Stocks were reduced and new relationships for retailing books developed with Coles and Myers. Rigby Education continued to do well, with an increasing volume of its products being sold in the United States and Britain.

The high hopes held for the Hanna-Barbera television mini-series 'Return to Eden' proved to be well founded. It sold well overseas after scoring high Australian ratings on Network 10. A series of twenty-two hour-long episodes developed from the mini-series followed. Hanna-Barbera also continued to do well in its animation work, with significant growth in 1985-86 from a contract with a major United States television network.

Hanna-Barbera went on to further successes with 'The Last Frontier', with Linda Evans (star of 'Dynasty'), Jack Thompson and Jason Robards among others in an outstanding cast. It was the first Australian mini-series ever to be sold to an American network. In 1985-86 Hanna-Barbera produced the animated films 'Berenstain Bears' and 'The Story Break' for CBS, which were well accepted in the United States as well as in Australia.

In 1983-84 the Group expanded its leisure interests by investing in Australia's Wonderland, an amusement park at Minchinbury, in Sydney's western suburbs. Other investors in the project included Taft Broadcasting, the State Super-annuation Board of New South Wales and Leighton Holdings Limited. The largest amusement park of its kind in the Southern Hemisphere, Australia's Wonderland opened in December 1985, a few weeks ahead of schedule. In spite of poor summer weather, attendances increased steadily. In the May 1986 school holidays, with the help of a heavy promotion campaign, attendances reached record levels, and the gates had to be closed on a number of occasions to guarantee the enjoyment of those already inside.

Sorting incoming mail at the Rigby House Direct Mail organisation.

Explaining the first level of *Rigby Maths,* an
Australia-wide program for all levels of primary school.

FOWLER PREDATES HARDIE

Fowler Ware is the longest surviving brand of all the products made and marketed by James Hardie Industries Limited. It began in 1837, when Enoch Fowler, newly arrived from Ireland with his wife, Jane, started a small pottery in the part of Parramatta Road, Sydney, that is now Broadway.

For the first twenty years, Fowler's main products were rough-glazed stoneware bottles and jars. They had some natural protection from imports in that they were bulky and heavy, and therefore expensive to transport, but they did not lack local competition from other potters. Still, the business prospered, and the Fowler family began to prosper with it. Other products included clay smoking pipes, plant pots and earthenware storage jars. Finding enough suitable clay was a problem and the Fowler pottery moved to various sites in Glebe. In those days it was easier to take the pottery to the clay than to bring the clay to the pottery.

Enoch and Jane's son, Robert, took to the pottery trade to such an extent that, at the age of sixteen, he was able to produce in one day at his wheel a special order of ten gross of ginger beer bottles. Every one of the 1440 bottles had to be thrown and formed by hand.

In the 1850s, Fowler's began to make six-inch-diameter earthenware pipes on a small hand machine that extruded them in a perfectly circular shape, making them less likely to block or to collapse under pressure than the earlier handmade pipes. Pipe production became a major and growing part of Fowler's business. It also created a need for much more clay, which was one of the reasons why, in the 1850s, Enoch Fowler bought a pottery on what is now Parramatta Road, Camperdown, together with a 2 hectare site that included the pottery's associated brickpits. He set out to expand the pottery rapidly, making earthenware drainpipes, edging tiles, stoneware containers of many types, plain bricks, firebricks, chimneypots, laundry tubs and similar products.

When Enoch Fowler died, in 1879, Robert, then thirty-nine, took over. He expanded the range of items made at Camperdown, which came to include stoneware flushing toilet cisterns. As Sydney's sewerage system grew, so did the profits of Fowler's Potteries. Another Robert, son of Robert and grandson of Enoch, took over the business in 1903, when his father had a stroke from which he never fully recovered.

By 1912, the Trustees of the Robert Fowler Estate decided to give up the Camperdown site and move the main pottery in stages to a 7 hectare site in Fitzroy Street, Marrickville. The first part of the move took place in 1914, and for a time the firm had potteries at Camperdown, Marrickville, Bankstown and Longueville. Capital for expansion became a problem, and on 1 May 1919 the enterprise became a public company, R. Fowler Ltd. The Camperdown site stayed with the family but was no longer used as a pottery. The Fowler family continued to be involved in senior management of the firm, with the young Robert as Chairman and Managing Director until his death in 1928. Other Fowlers continued to work in senior jobs until the 1960s, but Fowler control over the firm rapidly declined from the 1930s on.

The Marrickville pottery was well planned for its time and its work force gradually grew to about 400, with clay coming from all over New South Wales. Public works contracts in the 1920s kept it fairly prosperous — it made most of the ceramic tiles for the original Sydney underground stations, for instance. It opened a new plant at Thomastown, in the northern suburbs of Melbourne, in 1927.

But the loss of the clear guiding hand of the younger Robert Fowler, in 1927, plus the onset of the Depression, created economic chaos for the company. The substantial capital sunk into the Victorian venture could not be recouped, and the company did not pay a dividend for years. Cheap imports played havoc with sales of some of the smaller lines, and for some years the firm made major losses. In 1934 the shareholders unhappily agreed to write off 40 per cent of the capital.

Revival came with Fowlerware, a range of blue and white and (as from Christmas 1936) green and white kitchenware, all of it made at Marrickville. But the pottery remained very labour-intensive and this was a major drag on its profitability and competitiveness. The Second World War, postwar prosperity, and the import restrictions of the 1950s kept the pottery going along its established course, but by the late 1960s it was again in trouble, owing to cheap imports and substitute materials, such as plastics.

James Hardie Industries Limited bought Fowler from Manufacturing Resources of Australia, without the Marrickville site, in 1979, for $8.7 million. By then, most of Fowler's sales were in sanitary ware, such as toilet seats and systems, and bathroom items, such as baths and basins.

FRED BESLEY PUTS HIS FAITH IN ENVELOPES

Besley & Pike, the Brisbane envelope maker that became part of the James Hardie Group in 1979, started its business in 1913. In that year Frederick Besley, who had worked in the printing industry in England and South Africa, arrived in Brisbane with his family. He took over a bankrupt printing firm in Fortitude Valley and on 12 February 1914, renamed it the Valley Art Printing Company. It specialised in catalogues and periodicals, and later in direct mail and advertising literature, most of it printed by the letterpress method. In 1919, the firm moved into its own two-storey building at 93 Alfred Street, Fortitude Valley.

Besley knew printing well enough, but not so much about advertising. Doing so much advertising literature led him to bring Bert Pike into the business as a partner in April 1916, and on 10 January 1918 Besley & Pike Limited was registered as a company. Pike left in 1924, but the name continued. Besley soon formed a working relationship with Brisbane consulting accountant George Offner. Company records contain monthly statements of production from as early as 1918, and show that the firm had a well-developed system of cost accounting.

Soon after the First World War, Besley & Pike imported its first two envelope-making machines. One of them fell into the Brisbane River while being unloaded, and it took almost twelve months to get a replacement. The firm grew steadily through the 1920s, with its printing, envelope and agency trade. One good agency was for Ellam's duplicators, which it had held since 1914. But the 1930s Depression brought hard times, and for a long period all employees worked one week on, one week off, to ration the available work. Even then there was often barely enough to go around. To overcome this, the company began to make such stationery lines as exercise books and writing pads. It also developed its importing and agency lines.

In the 1930s, Fred Besley saw clearly that the company's most successful lines were envelopes. It had expanded in this field in 1928, just before the Depression, when it made the first glassine-panelled window-faced envelope in Australia and imported a rotary-envelope making machine, the first of its kind to come to Australia. Late in the 1930s the company installed machinery to make end-opening envelopes, the only such machinery in Queensland and among the first of its kind in Australia.

By the time the Second World War began, Fred Besley had all but decided to concentrate solely on envelopes. The war helped him make up his mind to do so, because of the scarcity of materials for his other operations. Even getting enough for envelopes was difficult. One big problem was that he needed new machinery, and it was impossible to buy. He decided to have two rotary envelope-making machines made in Brisbane, using existing German-made machines as models. The wooden patterns for the castings for these are still carefully preserved at the Brisbane plant. The new machines worked quite well for many years and made hundreds of millions of envelopes.

When Fred Besley died, in 1946, his son, Bob, took over running the firm. His was the task of re-equipping the plant, once a postwar generation of machinery was available. This led to a complete changeover to the more efficient rotary equipment. One new machine, a window patcher, was so new to Australia that the firm prevailed upon its German supplier to persuade an engineer who knew how to operate and maintain it to migrate to Brisbane. He stayed five years before he moved on to America and finally back to Germany, where he became Senior Research Engineer with his company.

Besley & Pike grew steadily, and on 12 December 1957 became a public company. It continued the policy of sales expansion it had begun in 1956 with a new sales office and warehouse in Sydney. In 1959 it opened a sales office and warehouse in Melbourne, and appointed sales agents in Hobart. It opened a sales office and warehouse in Adelaide in 1961, and in Perth in 1962. By now it had outgrown the Valley premises it had occupied since 1919. Late in 1961 it moved into its new single-storey plant in the industrial suburb of Rocklea, 12 kilometres south-west of Brisbane.

The new plant enabled the firm to expand its markets overseas, setting up agency arrangements or direct representation in Fiji, Hong Kong, Singapore, Papua New Guinea, the Solomon Islands, the New Hebrides, Malaysia, Thailand and Laos. All this activity led to an Export Achievement Award in 1968. An envelope-making plant set up in Singapore in 1967 did so well that in 1970 it moved to bigger premises. The Rocklea plant was also extended several times. Fortunately, the firm had allowed ample room.

Besley & Pike made an immediate contribution to the Group's profitability from the time of its acquisition, and it has continued to do so.

CHAPTER FORTY-THREE

AN END
TO ASBESTOS

Machinery for refining the cellulose pulp used in the manufacture of cellulose-reinforced, asbestos-free building materials.

Almost as soon as he became Managing Director, David Macfarlane decided that Hardies should work towards eliminating asbestos from all their products. His fellow Directors readily agreed with him, for asbestos was causing too many problems.

Hardie technical experts had in fact been looking for a suitable replacement fibre, preferably from Australian sources, for years. They had tried such things as bagasse (sugar cane fibre), cotton, seaweed and fibreglass, putting vast amounts of time, effort and money into the project.

They had almost found a solution by accident, in 1960 while searching for something to replace the expensive steel sheets used to separate sheets of fibre cement while they were being autoclaved. Somebody suggested that sheets of fibre cement itself could do this job just as well, and that since they would never leave the plant, they did not need much asbestos content. If they broke, they would simply be replaced. The idea was tried, and found to work well. In 1963, a proportion of cellulose fibre was introduced into the new flat sheet, Hardiflex.

In the early 1970s, Hardies set out to progressively reduce the asbestos content of their fibre cement sheets to zero. Western Australia was chosen as the place where the idea would be tested on a production scale, because it was the largest market for corrugated sheet, which was used just as much for fences as for roofs. Corrugated sheets are subject to greater stresses than flat, so it was important that any replacement fibre should work well in them.

The team that led the project, under the overall direction of Frank Page, was Harry Hudson, Bill Waters as State Manager, John Pether as Research Manager, and Pat Collins as Factory Manager. They were soon making asbestos-free flat sheets, and within a few months, asbestos-free corrugated sheets, too. The summer of 1979-80 was one of the hottest and driest on record in Western Australia, and there were some initial problems with cracking. But these were overcome with better regulation of the moisture content, and the asbestos-free fibre cement sheets were soon the only sheets bearing the Hardiflex brand. The Annual Report for 1980–81 noted that at least 85 per cent of the Group's fibre cement building products would be asbestos free by mid–1982.

Hardiflex II, in which specially treated cellulose took the place of asbestos, became Hardie's general purpose building board in 1980. Another new asbestos-free product, Harditherm 700, a fire resistant insulation board, was developed for use in fire doors and general fire protection in the ship-building industry. The Brake Division introduced metallic disk brake pads. Field tests of asbestos-free

railway brake blocks were undertaken in Australia, the United States and several other countries, and some trial orders were soon received from Australian and overseas railways. The commissioning of a new press in Perth in 1984 to make reinforced fibre cement corrugated sheet was the last link in the program to remove asbestos completely from the Hardie range of building products, although it was still present in pipes.

Hardies had long been experts at opening up asbestos fibre to give greater strength to products containing it and was able to call on its previous knowledge to do the same with cellulose fibre. In previous times, the strength of the sheet had been adjusted by adding as much extra fibre as human judgment deemed to be needed. The factory workers joked that since this was neither a science nor an art, it must be a sport. With cellulose fibre it became very much a science, and the whole process was soon computerised.

Similar techniques to those used for making asbestos-free sheets were used to make asbestos-free non-pressure pipes. Unable to find a way to make pressure pipes from fibre cement without asbestos, Hardies opted to move away from fibre cement into fibreglass for its pressure pipes. It began by using European

The special press at the Welshpool plant in Western Australia for making cellulose-reinforced, asbestos-free fibre cement corrugated sheets.

technology to make 30-centimetre diameter pipes, then used its own knowledge of fibre technology to make smaller pipes, of 15 and 10 centimetres diameter, something the Europeans had not been able to do. The company ceased making pipes containing asbestos in March 1987.

Because of the heavy capital costs of the new plant needed to make asbestos-free corrugated sheets, Hardies' entire corrugated production for Australia and New Zealand was made at the Welshpool plant in Perth from the early 1980s. As well as putting the new technology to work in its own production, Hardies are also licensing its use to overseas fibre cement makers. The secret lies in the way the cellulose fibre is treated and spread through the sheet.

Switching to asbestos-free fibre cement proved to be costly. There was no way of working it out before it was started and not a lot of point to the exercise either, because Macfarlane was determined to do it. As well as the complete support of the Chairman and the other Directors, he also had that of the Miscellaneous Workers Union, of which most Hardie fibre cement workers are members.

CELLULOSE FIBRE

The fibre found to be the most satisfactory substitute for asbestos in fibre cement was cellulose extracted from radiata pine chips by the Kraft pulping process. This process removes about half the original mass of the wood and leaves almost pure cellulose in a form known as 'unbleached softwood Kraft pulp'.

Cellulose is not affected by the alkalinity of the cement, nor does it interfere with the chemistry of the cement. It is capable of withstanding the high temperatures of the autoclave reaction, and is a strong and durable fibre.

The effective use of cellulose in fibre cement calls for an understanding of the bond between the fibres and the calcium silicate hydrate matrix. This understanding, plus a knowledge of the forming process, is the essence of modern fibre cement technology.

Cellulose is a stable polysaccharide, a natural polymer produced by plants along with other organic compounds such as sugars, starches, lignins and tannins.

Cellulose fibre ready for inclusion in asbestos-free building materials.

CHAPTER FORTY-FOUR

HARDIE TRADING COMES HOME

On 3 March 1980 the directors of both James Hardie Industries Limited and Hardie Trading Limited announced that they had agreed on a merger. The two companies had close connections, including two Directors who sat on both boards: John B. Reid, who was Chairman of both companies, and Fred Loneragan. Neither took any part in the negotiations that led to the merger proposal, but both supported it.

Hardie Trading Limited had had a separate existence since 1926, when the original company's trading and fibro-cement interests were separated. It had taken on a distinct Melbourne orientation, with its trading in all states and New Zealand controlled from head offices first in Little Collins Street, later in St Kilda Road. James Hardie executives in Sydney, concerned mainly with making and marketing fibre cement building products, and Hardie Trading executives in Melbourne concerned mostly with buying and selling, developed a considerable antipathy for each other.

The fact that such feelings had passed into history with various retirements was at least a factor in making the proposed merger seem attractive. David Macfarlane, Managing Director of James Hardie Industries, and Bill Butterss, Managing Director of Hardie Trading, had known each other for a long time, and were on good terms. They had often talked about the benefit of merging the two companies.

James Hardie Industries Limited already held 22.6 per cent of Hardie Trading Limited shares. For the other 77.4 per cent, it offered one James Hardie share plus $2.40 in cash for every two Hardie Trading Shares. Based on the last sale prices at the close of trading on 27 February 1980 of $3.68 for James Hardie on the Sydney Stock Exchange, the offer was worth $3.04 for each Hardie Trading share, a premium of $1.09 (56 per cent) for Hardie Trading shareholders. They would get the same dividend income after the merger as before, based on dividends of 8.75 cents per share for Hardie Trading and 17.5 cents per share for James Hardie, with the $1.20 a share in cash as a bonus. By reinvesting this, they could increase their income substantially. They could also expect an increasing return on their investment in the merged company, the joint statement said, for it was James Hardie policy to increase dividend income steadily in line with increasing profits and with the added objective of improving the dividend pay-out ratio.

James Hardie shareholders, who did not have to be wooed, could nevertheless take comfort from their Directors' belief that profits from the Hardie Trading businesses would continue to grow and that the merger would increase earnings per share in the enlarged group.

ICS equipment at the Coats Paton textile yarn plant in Victoria, supplied by the Trading Division. This high-technology equipment is used to match and control colour.

Australian United Corporation Limited had provided independent advice to Hardie Trading that in their opinion the merger terms were fair and reasonable and to the benefit of Hardie Trading shareholders. Hardie Trading directors intended to recommend that shareholders accept the proposed offer by James Hardie Industries, and they all intended to do so for shares they owned or controlled. James Hardie was being advised by David Block and Associates Pty Limited, who had confirmed that in their opinion completion of the merger on the terms proposed would be in the best interests of James Hardie shareholders. Many Hardie Trading businesses complemented James Hardie activities, which had been greatly widened with the Reed acquisition only eighteen months before, in October 1978. The total cost of the acquisition was $31.2 million. Hardie Trading had annual sales of over $80 million and profit of over $4 million.

The enlarged group was very strong in the building products markets. James Hardie Industries already had fibre cement building materials and pipes, plastic pipes and fittings, bathroom ware, wall coverings and fabrics. Hardie Trading would add paints and chemicals, electrical switchgear, laundry and dry-cleaning equipment, and water filters and softeners.

Hardie Trading's position as a supplier of Spartan automotive finishes and Re-po car care products was complementary to James Hardie's brake lining business. Hardie Trading was a major importer of a diverse range of raw materials for Australian industry. Both companies had trading activities overseas, mainly in New Zealand and South-East Asia.

A Freshmatic domestic water-treatment unit made by Commando Water Treatment of Adelaide.

A Ring Grip product at the time of the acquisition of Hardie Trading, the 'Portapal', a tool and utility tidy for housewife and handyman, had a built-in extension cord and two power outlets.

Part of the Spartan range of
Re-po car care products.

Hardie Trading had grown strongly in recent years, both in activities and earnings. Each of its operating divisions had capable and experienced managers, who had played a major part in these results. The merger would create a group of considerable size and financial strength, and this would mean greater opportunities for the employees of both companies. The superannuation and other rights of Hardie Trading employees would be preserved.

HARDIE TRADING LIMITED

(from a brochure published just before the merger)

Registered Office:
594 St Kilda Road, Melbourne 3004
Victoria Australia
Branches throughout Australia and overseas in New Zealand and Singapore

IMPORTING AND MERCHANDISING DIVISION

Acts as distributor of Hardie manufactured goods and many products made
by other Australian companies, including:

Chemicals	Fibreglass
Textile yarns	Audio-visual supplies
Plastic compounds	Equipment for textiles, foundry
Cellulose film	and record industries

Imported products include:

Carbon electrodes for smelting

Accelerators for rubber industry

Bentones for paints, inks and adhesives

Pyrethrum – insecticide

Textile machinery and accessories

Ultra-violet absorbers, flame retardants and other additives for plastics

Resins for plastic injection moulding

Mimosa extract for tanning leathers

Yarns and fibres for textiles

PLASTICS DIVISION

PVC Record-pressing compound

Plastic moulding compounds

Activity plastics (compounding and

master batch colouring of plastic polymers – reclamation of plastic film scrap)

INDUSTRIAL ENGINEERING DIVISION

Hardilec, the Electrical Division's original equipment and marketing group, supplied 42-pin jumpers for inter-car connection of electrical and control circuits for the New South Wales Rail Authority's inter-city XPT and for other rail authorities.

Subsidiary companies include:

Horscroft Engineering Pty Ltd

Commercial laundry, dry-cleaning and textile equipment

Dry-cleaning soaps and spotters

Commando Water Treatment Ltd

Domestic water softness and filters

Water treatment equipment for industrial applications

Bloomer Boiler Co.

Boilers for industry

Horner & Coutts Pty Ltd

Repetition and fabrication engineers

Johnson hide-strippers

Airshield Manufacturing Pty Ltd

Wind deflectors for trucks and caravans

PAINTS AND CHEMICAL DIVISION

Spartan Paints Pty Ltd

Automotive lacquers, enamels, putties, fillers etc

Industrial finishes for furniture sheet metal etc

Architectural and specialty paint systems

Sophisticated coatings for shipping, harbour installations and the aviation industry

Spartan Chemical Company

Sanitation and industrial cleaning chemicals

Floor polishes, germicidal cleaners and all-purpose cleaners

Industrial Adhesives

Hardie Trading has produced industrial adhesives for thirty years, particularly hot-melt adhesives

Dura-Bond – widely used for laminating and packaging

Re-Po Manufacturing Company

Car care products renowned for forty years, including:

Re-po deluxe liquid car polish

Re-po auto cream

Re-po polish and cleaner

Re-po rubbing compound

Colours and Chemicals Pty Ltd

Resins and driers for the ink and paint industries

Polyester resins for boat building and other users of reinforced plastic

ELECTRICAL AND ELECTRONICS DIVISION

Familiar brands for industrial, commercial and domestic
applications, including:

Wilco
Industrial switch and switch-plug
combinations, circuit breakers,
domestic insulated switch and
fuse boards

Pierlite
Fluorescent lighting accessories
Desk lamps, domestic automotive,
special, industrial and street
lighting

Acme
Electronic – radio frequency and
audio connectors and co-axial
cables

Ring-Grip
Domestic electrical accessories,
handyman products, industrial
switch and switch-plug
combinations

Airflow
Domestic exhaust fans and torkflow
subfractional motors

Rayflow
Domestic strip-heaters

STATISTICS

Sales for the year ended June 1979	$80 million
Profit	$5.9 million
Assets	$63 million
Number of employees	1750

CHAPTER FORTY-FIVE

MANAGING
GROUP FINANCES

The need to finance the Reed and Hardie Trading acquisitions, and the steady program of other acquisitions, brought with it a need for steadily increasing funds. Added to this need was the impact of growth and inflation on the Group's many established businesses.

In his 1978-79 Annual Report, the Chairman confirmed the Board's policy of increasing future dividends by issuing bonus shares from time to time as profits and cash flow permitted. The Chairman noted, however, that on this occasion, the Board felt that any issue of bonus shares, so soon after the recent cash issue made to finance the RCI acquisition, could adversely affect the market price of the company's shares.

In spite of the need to finance the newly-acquired Reed businesses, the company clearly had the ability to pay more in dividends without undue strain on cash and without unduly increasing the payout ratio. It therefore increased the dividend for the year from the established 12.5 per cent to 17.5 per cent, and forecast that this rate could be repeated in 1979-80.

Shareholders did not have long to wait for their bonus shares, after all. They came in a one-for-three issue in the next year, 1979-80. In the same year, the Board recommended a final dividend of 10 cents a share on the enlarged capital and said that it could keep up this rate, hardly a rash promise in the light of earnings of 66.5 cents a share. After adjusting for the bonus issue, the 1979-80 dividend was an effective increase of 26.2 per cent over the previous year's. A dividend of 20 per cent in 1980-81 would be an effective increase of 20.8 per cent over that for 1979-80.

The Board set management the target of reducing the Group's total net borrowings, which were $145.2 million at 31 March 1979. By 31 March 1980, they were down to $131.8 million. This was done despite the cost of acquisitions made during the year — which included Fowler, Besley & Pike, Cameron Irrigation, Glaskraft and a 20 per cent interest in Hardie Extrusions — and the borrowings taken over or incurred through those acquisitions. It was the result of cash flow from increasing sales and profits and of rigorous control of stocks and expenditure on capital works, none of which had impaired the Group's ability to develop its businesses.

The reduction in debt and a revaluation of certain assets brought the debt equity ratio down during 1979-80 from 71.9 per cent to 54.7 per cent. By the end of 1980-81, however, borrowings were up again, to $178 million, owing to a variety of factors. One was the cost of acquisitions and the borrowings the Group assumed along with the businesses concerned, including Hardie Trading Limited, J. Fielding Holdings Limited, and the 40 per cent Turner & Newall interest in Hardie-Ferodo Pty Limited. Another factor had been the need for extra working capital and investment in fixed assets for Group businesses that increased their commercial activity during the year. Inflation was also a factor.

The rate of increase in the Group's borrowings over the past four years, the Annual Report noted, had to be taken in the context of the increase in the value of the assets that supported them and the increase in the Group's earning power over the same period. Its balance sheet ratios were still strong, with external liabilities equal to only 52 per cent of tangible assets. Spending on fixed assets during the year had been $27 million. This was partly because the Group was now larger, but also because of the investment needed to convert its fibre cement plants to make asbestos-free building products.

This increased need for funds had made it desirable to spread the maturity dates of a range of borrowings and to dampen the effects of volatile interest and exchange rates. The Board therefore issued $25 million in promissory notes to financial institutions to help fund its short-term working capital needs. It also issued $50 million in convertible notes to shareholders to raise funds for longer-term needs, mainly plant and machinery.

At the same time, the Board also proposed an increase in the authorised capital from $80 million to $150 million. It had last been increased in 1978. Issued capital at the time of the proposed increase was $65.4 million.

The increase in profits in 1981-82 led to a further one-for-four bonus issue, and an increase in the dividend rate to 22 per cent. Borrowings increased again in that year, from $177 million to $200 million. Much of the increase again went to fund Group acquisitions, which included Robinhood Industries Limited and Rockware Plastics (Australia) Limited. The interest on these borrowings would be more than offset by the present and projected earnings of the businesses acquired, the Annual Report said. This earnings test was vigorously applied when deciding whether to make new acquisitions.

David Say CA, FCA, Dip.BA, MBCS became Finance Director of James Hardie Industries Limited in 1980. He joined the Group in 1978 at the time of the Reed acquisition. He held various positions with RCI between 1973 and 1980, including Group Finance Manager and Finance Director.

CHAPTER FORTY-SIX

EXPANDING INTERESTS IN NEW ZEALAND

An advertisement for Hardies' building products, including Hardiflex and Hardiplank, in New Zealand.

The James Hardie Group expanded its long-standing interests in New Zealand even further in 1981, when on 1 September it joined with Phillipps & Impey Limited to form James Hardie Impey Limited, a company with net tangible assets of over $34 million. The new company would supply the building industry with cladding materials, pipes, wallpapers and fabrics, paints and decorating accessories, electrical switchgear and fans.

Phillipps & Impey's English-born founder, William Phillipps, started one of its antecedent businesses in 1854 in Auckland, thirty-four years before James Hardie set up his business in Melbourne. In 1911 William Phillipps and Son joined with Impey Limited to form Phillipps & Impey Limited. Its shares first went on sale on the Auckland Stock Exchange in 1913, making it one of New Zealand's oldest listed companies.

By 1981 Phillipps & Impey Limited had grown into one of New Zealand's most highly respected and best-known firms. It made Samson and Gold-X paints and stains; supplied builders' and plumbers' hardware, wall coverings and glass to contractors; retailed wall coverings and home decorative supplies. It jointly owned, with James Hardie Industries, Polycell Products, makers of home handyman products. From its first single shop in the Queen's Arcade, Auckland, Phillipps & Impey had built a national network of twenty-eight retail paint and paper outlets, a hardware division and nine glass depots. It also owned the Alexander Clark wallpaper and fabric showrooms in Palmerston North.

To establish James Hardie Impey Limited, Phillipps & Impey Limited first acquired James Hardie's shares in four New Zealand companies: James Hardie & Coy Pty Limited (with its subsidiaries, Ring Grip Electrical Limited and Utility Castings Limited), Hardie Trading Limited, Wilson Fabrics & Wallcoverings (NZ) Limited (previously E. H. Lund Limited), and the 51 per cent of Polycell Products Limited it did not already own. These four companies' activities included manufacturing fibre cement building products and pipes, cast iron fittings and valves, importing machinery and industrial equipment, and distributing decorative furnishings and car-care products. They added to Phillipps & Impey's already wide range of activities, which included manufacturing paints and stains, wholesaling building and plumbing hardware, and selling wall covering, decorative and handyman products.

In return for those businesses, Phillipps & Impey Limited, which changed its name to James Hardie Impey Limited, issued 15 572 825 ordinary 50 cent shares to James Hardie Industries Limited. The next stage was the purchase by James

Hardie Industries Limited of 71.75 per cent of the issued capital of the regrouped company. The New Zealand transactions were actually completed by Hardie Holdings (NZ) Limited, a wholly owned subsidiary of James Hardie Industries Limited, formed to hold the Group's shareholding in James Hardie Impey Limited. The 28.25 per cent of Phillipps & Impey Limited not owned by James Hardie Industries Limited was held by the New Zealand public and quoted on New Zealand stock exchanges.

Spencer Browning, Chief Executive Officer and Deputy Chairman of James Hardie Impey Limited, described the new company as 'an enlarged P & I, with increased financial strength, opportunities to reach new markets and more technical expertise'. No staff were made redundant when the new company was formed. One immediate product of the merger was useful marketing and technical links between Spartan, Samson and Gold-X surface finishes.

James Hardie Impey Limited had a good 1982-83, its first full year as part of the Group. In spite of the government's freeze regulations and a deterioration in business activity in the second half, sales and profits rose over the previous year, largely as a result of considerably increased turnover and better cost control. Production capacity in fibre cement building products was expanded, and a plastics plant was built. The retail chain performed well, and two new units were added to it: the Paint Pot Limited, of Levin, and the major assets of John Trewavas Limited, Dannevirke.

In his 1983-84 Chairman's Review, John B. Reid noted that the creation of James Hardie Impey Limited in New Zealand had given that company the size and range of activities to parallel the Group's development in Australia. It was progressing very well and, together with the Australian divisions of the company,

Spencer Browning joined Phillipps and Impey Limited in 1961, became a Director in 1963, Managing Director in 1967 and Chairman in 1979. He became Managing Director of James Hardie Impey Limited in 1981. On his retirement as Managing Director in 1985 he became Chairman of Directors.

The roofs and walls of the Kapuni urea plant at Taranaki in New Zealand, were sheeted with Hardies' Super Six. Fibrolite pressure pipes (250 mm diameter) were used to supply water for the plant, which converts natural gas into urea fertiliser. The volcano in the background is Mt Egmont.

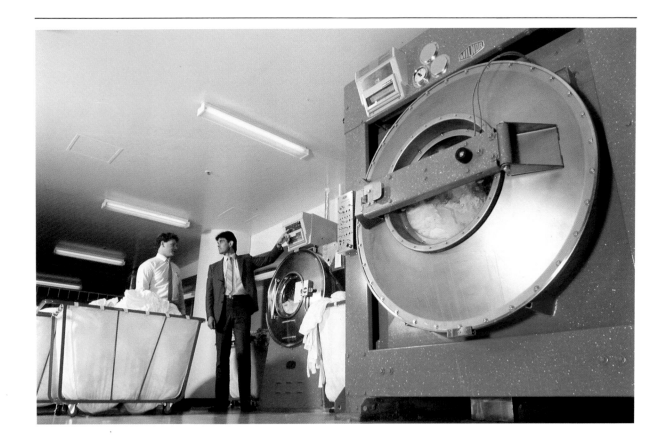

Staff from Hardie Trading in New Zealand supervise the installation of a 100 kilogram industrial washing machine, one of twenty at the new Regent Hotel in Auckland.

gave the opportunity to maximise business prospects under the Closer Economic Relations agreement between Australia and New Zealand. James Hardie Impey Limited sales increased marginally in that year, but operating profits after tax declined, mainly as a result of a number of non-recurring costs, together with the costs of funding capital expenditure for major development projects in the fibre cement, plastics and envelope businesses.

The complete building products range in New Zealand was produced without asbestos from September 1983. New machinery for producing fibre cement sheet was commissioned on schedule during the year. Production also began in September 1983, on schedule, of a comprehensive range of polyvinyl chloride sewer, drainage, soil and vent fittings. Mouldings for James Hardie Electrical and other members of the Group formed part of the regular workload, and extra injection moulders and a pipe extruder were soon being installed.

The good news continued during 1984-85, with James Hardie Industries' Managing Director David Macfarlane reporting favourable trading conditions and a significantly improved level of both sales and operating profit. Market conditions in most areas had been buoyant, with more new houses being built and many home renovations taking place. Performance had been uniformly good, with some significant areas of improvement resulting from effective management of people and resources and the development expenditure previously committed. It had also been a year of consolidation, with the realisation of the benefits forecast in 1981 when James Hardie Impey Limited was formed. Even so, major emphasis was being given to better use of funds employed, because finance costs had risen sharply. During the year, James Hardie Impey Limited acquired Jas Robertson Limited, makers of acrylic sanitary ware and spa pools, and Noel Products Limited, distributors of bathroom ware, spa pools and plumbing supplies. Both were making a very satisfactory contribution to profit.

On 29 April 1986 James Hardie Industries Limited, through its wholly owned New Zealand subsidiary, Hardie Holdings (NZ) Limited, made a takeover offer for the 28.25 per cent of publicly quoted James Hardie Impey Limited shares it did not already own. The offer would cost about $25 million. Full ownership would help the Group achieve an immediate increase in profitability, because it would be able to raise funds on better terms, John B. Reid observed in his Chairman's Review for 1985-86. In the longer term, using James Hardie Impey to provide product at competitive prices for export would greatly assist in the development of the United States fibre cement market.

The new office building of James Hardie & Coy Pty Limited at Penrose, Auckland, in the early 1980s.

The offer, which provided share and cash alternatives, was declared unconditional on 29 May 1986, when acceptances exceeded the New Zealand Companies Act implementation levels for compulsory purchase of the remaining shares. James Hardie Impey Limited shares were removed from the quotation list of the New Zealand Stock Exchange and James Hardie Industries Limited shares were quoted instead. On 12 June 1986 James Hardie Industries Limited issued 3 837 647 ordinary shares pursuant to the offer, and James Hardie Impey Limited became a wholly owned member of the James Hardie Group.

Hardies' Roofing Shingles on a home at Wanaka,
South Island.

CHAPTER FORTY-SEVEN

SHORT
SHARP SHOCK

For the first time in many years, James Hardie Industries' Annual Report in 1982-83 reported a fall in profits, even though sales, at $1015 million, passed the billion dollar mark for the first time. Profit before interest and tax was down from $99.6 million in the previous year to $90.9 million. The after-tax and after-interest but before-extraordinaries profit was down from $41.1 million to $32.2 million.

Much of the bad news was from the Group's fibre cement and building products activities. Building products had retained their market shares, but dwelling construction was at its lowest level for twenty years, and the markets had shrunk. Three plants had been closed and their operations merged with others. Fibre cement pipe sales were down, in line with the industry trend, and production had ceased in Victoria.

In Indonesia, several national water supply projects were either cancelled or postponed, and pipe sales fell. This, plus devaluation of the rupiah, meant that Indonesia did not contribute at all to Group profit during 1982-83.

The Group had launched a major rationalisation program of its fibre cement activities, closing down several unprofitable operations at a cost of about $15 million, and reducing its workforce by 2000 to about 13 000. An early retirement scheme was introduced for those made redundant and for those who were not eligible for this, every effort was made to find alternative employment.

Sales were down in Hardie bathroom products. Wilson had a very difficult year. Hardie Trading sales of industrial products reflected the low level of economic activity generally. Paints and chemicals suffered, along with the rest of the paint market. Horscroft's manufacturing operations were closed. Sales of brake materials to the automotive industry were down. Stationery and flexible packaging showed disappointing performances. The publishing companies suffered from the depressed retail market, and demand for animation was disappointing.

Some parts of the Group, however, did well. Hardie Iplex Plastics increased its market share, as did Renhurst and Duraform construction products. Hardie-System Built sales grew strongly. Polycell did well with an expanded product range. Commando Water Treatments improved its performance. Electrical and Electronics also performed well. Paper and Packaging had a good year, with excellent results from paper merchanting, moulded plastic packaging and fibreboard containers. Video sales and profits grew strongly. Sales growth continued in irrigation, but profits were down largely because of difficult trading conditions in the Middle East and the United States. One particularly bright spot was New Zealand, where James Hardie Impey had a most satisfactory year. Production capacity in fibre cement building products was being expanded there, and a plastics plant was under construction.

The Group had acquired five businesses during the year. Among them were the Rain Spray group and Antel, both of which made and marketed sprinklers complementary to the Group's existing range. Another was the Corrugated Paper Group, which specialised in short-run manufacturing of corrugated boxes and distributed packaging materials in New South Wales. It was acquired by James Hardie Containers, in which James Hardie Industries Limited had a 60 per cent interest. The James Hardie Paper and Packaging Division acquired two businesses: Medical Plastics, a specialist producer of disposable medical products, which strengthened its product range in that field, and Protopak, a specialist manufacturer of plastic and other flexible packaging materials, which would strengthen its New South Wales operations.

In spite of the downturn in profit, the Group continued its dividend rate of 22 per cent. The one-for-four bonus issue during the year meant that the total dividend for the year was up by 11 per cent. The Group's total borrowings continued to increase during 1982-83. Of the $55 million borrowed during the year, $5 million was spent on acquisitions, $15 million in the closure and rationalisation campaign, $9 million on reducing creditors, and $17 million to increase cash on deposit by the company. The Group invested $47 million in fixed assets, an increase of $4 million over the previous year. During the year, it placed 8 million shares direct with investors at $3.90 each, to raise a net $30.8 million. The economic downturn, which started sharply in the middle of 1982, lasted just over twelve months. The recovery started almost as sharply when, led by the United States and Japan, the world economy began to improve.

Keith Davenport became a non-executive Director of James Hardie Industries Limited at the time of the Reed acquisition. He held various positions with International Publishing Corporation Limited and Reed International Limited during the period 1960–79.

When the South Australian outback town of Leigh Creek had to be created anew because the old town was found to be sitting on coal deposits, various Hardie products were used in the construction process. They include Villaboard, Hardiflex, Hardiplank, Hardies' pressure and drainage pipes, Hardies' UPVC sewer pipes and Renhurst foil insulation.

Alexander Thyne Reid, a grandson of former Chairman Andrew Reid, became a non-executive Director of James Hardie Industries Limited in 1973. His main interests are rural. He is Chairman of the Post Graduate Foundation in Veterinary Science, a member of various Committees of the National Farmers' Federation and on the Management Committee of Outward Bound Australia.

In Australia, funds for housing rose significantly, and interest rates came down marginally. Wage restraint seemed set to lead to lower inflation. The number of new building projects increased, and this led to a higher demand for James Hardie Group building products.

None of this had much positive effect on Group profits until late in the half year to September 1983. From then, although the improvement was erratic, results were well up on both the previous two six-month periods. Group sales for the year to 31 March 1984 were $1160 million, and operating profit before interest and tax was $98.7 million, almost back to the $99.6 million of 1981-82.

The strong stock markets led the Group to raise $85 million through a one-for-three rights issue at $2.50 per share. These shares, issued at $1.40 under the then market price, included a bonus element of almost 9 per cent for share and note holders. It also gave the Group increased borrowing power, adding to its reputation in Australian and overseas markets as a strong and secure borrower.

The improved result enabled the Group to resume its aim of increasing its earnings per share and dividends. In the eight years to 1982, earnings per share had increased at an average annual compounding rate of 15.8 per cent. The 1982 downturn halted that growth. In spite of the increase in the number of issued shares in the year to 31 March 1984 (from 81.8 million to 123.9 million), the Group was able to maintain the 22 per cent dividend, and expected that earnings per share would start to improve steadily once again. With issued capital now at $123.9 million in an authorised capital of $150 million, the shareholders at the 1984 Annual Meeting agreed to a Director's recommendation that they increase it to $250 million.

An RIS 'Waterbird' irrigation system, similar to the micro-irrigation equipment exported to China.

CHAPTER FORTY-EIGHT

GROWTH IN BUILDING SERVICES

One Hardie Division that grew steadily in the 1980s and increased the Group's gradual move into services, as a balance to manufacturing, was Building Services. It provided owners, builders, managers and tenants of commercial and industrial buildings with fire protection and control, access control, after-hours security and monitoring, and air-conditioning and communications systems.

The whole field was a growth area, something the New South Wales Institute of Technology recognised when it set up a degree course in building services. Several state and national committees were at work developing building services standards. One attraction was the continuing nature of any business won. Once arranged, contracts were likely to continue for the life of the building, so long as the service was satisfactory.

Development of the Division began in June 1983, when the Group acquired Fire Fighting Enterprises (FFE), a company involved in fire protection, communications and building security in Australia, New Zealand and Britain. The Division was expanded by the addition in April 1984 of Access Control Systems (a company specialising in building security through an electronic key system) and in 1985 of Kastle Systems (a unique building security service developed in the United States) and also of a 75 per cent interest in Environ Mechanical Services (specialists in air-conditioning system design and construction, as well as fire protection and services automation).

Fire Fighting Enterprises was formed in 1947 to sell portable fire extinguishers. In the next ten years it set up representation in every state and expanded its product range through licences and agreements with overseas fire protection companies. In 1960 it acquired May Oatway Fire and Alarm and set up a new head office and factory in the Sydney suburb of Ermington. By 1974 it had acquired twenty-nine companies, had established itself in New Zealand and Britain, and developed markets in South-East Asia, the Middle East, Africa and North and South America.

FFE added electrical contracting to its range of services in 1977, when it acquired the K.J. Aldridge Group, one of Australia's major electrical engineering and contracting groups, engaged in the design, installation and maintenance of electrical services. The Aldridge Group included Spencer Electrical, which specialised in the installation of automatic doors and gates and card access control systems in Sydney. It also offered a comprehensive package of electrical maintenance and service to industry, commerce and hospitals.

The Qantas International Centre in Sydney has a computerised event processing and monitoring system designed and installed by FFE. It provides total integration of many sub-systems, allowing one person to control and take action on security, lift control and access control.

In FFE, Hardies acquired an innovative company, which was taking advantage of international technology and applying it to Australian needs. It operated largely as an agent for overseas suppliers, and continually introduced new products, for although Australian fire safety standards were high, the market was limited. It did, however, make in Australia the products that were economically feasible, including fire extinguishers, sprinkler heads, detectors and control panels, at its Sydney and Melbourne plants.

FFE designed, manufactured, installed and commissioned automatic sprinkler systems in multi-storey buildings, warehouses, industrial buildings, shopping centres, hospitals and residential buildings. Its systems included water-pumping equipment and control valves. It had designed and installed fire protection systems in such far-flung locations as the North West Shelf gas project off the coast of Western Australia, the Ranger uranium site in the Northern Territory, LPG depots in Queensland, and the Australian Airlines jet base in Melbourne. It had equipped seagoing tugs to fight fires at sea, such as on offshore platforms or on ships. It had protected draglines, conveyors and the huge trucks used on mining sites. It provided Halon gas systems, which smother fires, to protect many computer rooms, electrical switch rooms and telephone exchanges for both government and commercial customers.

FFE was well placed to supply the new market created when legislation in the mid-1980s required that all buildings more than 25 metres high must have emergency warning and intercom systems. Soon after it became part of the Hardie Group, it developed a microprocessor-controlled emergency warning system to handle speedy and orderly evacuation of threatened areas. The system featured a digitally recorded recognisable voice, such as the building manager's, to give directions to occupants of a building in an emergency. It operated automatically, and had mechanical safeguards that ensured voice quality and complete reliability of operation. A television commercial produced in 1986 increased sales of the system substantially.

Access Control, which the Group acquired in 1984, was formed in 1975 to market a new, unique, Australian-developed system of access control, the MIL key. Based on an apparently simple flat plastic 'key' tab, the MIL system had come to be used widely throughout the world, safeguarding access to office buildings and factories, and to lifts, individual rooms, and secure areas within them.

Access Control had also become Australian agent for the United States Kidde system of access control and event monitoring. It had installed systems for several major banks' computer centres and at the Qantas jet base at Mascot. Together, the two systems gave Access Control the ability to provide security for anything from one-door, self-contained systems up to computer networks covering multi-storey buildings. For industrial premises and prisons, Access Control marketed a guardwire perimeter fence protection system that alerted guards or the gatehouse if an attempt was made to cut the fence, whether from inside or out.

In 1987 Access Control brought to Australia the EyeDentification System, which identifies people by the pattern of their retina, a characteristic that, like their fingerprint, is unique. This level of security is of interest to top-secret establishments such as defence departments, banks' computer centres and sensitive government areas.

Kastle Systems, established in the United States in 1972, began operations in

Australia as part of the Hardie Building Services Division in 1985. It had specialised in security services for multi-tenanted (usually multi-storey) buildings. The Kastle Security System controls after-hours access to a building and to individual offices within it as required, using a dedicated computer system monitored from a central location.

Authorised people carry electronically coded cards to give access to the building, to lifts and to certain offices, or whatever part of the building is required. The cards can also be coded to give access only between certain hours. Each card is unique to the holder, and can be simply deleted from the system if it is lost or not returned when the holder leaves the employer. A telephone near the front door enables visitors, clients or couriers to be admitted to buildings after hours. They simply speak to the central monitoring station, which releases the door. People admitted in this way need not be aware that the monitoring station is in another part of town.

Early Kastle projects in Australia included an office block and shopping centre at Bankstown in western Sydney, the new Maritime Services Board Buildings in Kent Street, and an office building in George Street, Sydney.

The acquisition in July 1985 of a 75 per cent interest in Environ Mechanical Services from Lend Lease Corporation, its original parent company, took the Hardie Building Services Group into the design, construction and maintenance of air-conditioning systems, and further into fire protection and evacuation and alarm systems. Environ projects include the prestigious Riverside Centre in Brisbane, the National Convention Centre in Canberra, and the Gateway Project at Sydney's Circular Quay. It has also had major contracts in the Northern Territory.

It also offers a maintenance package including preventive maintenance and emergency services for its air-conditioning and fire protection systems, and a computer-based monitoring system for building services aimed at maximising their efficiency and saving money.

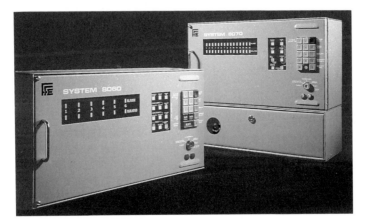

May Oatway fire detection and control panels.

CHAPTER FORTY-NINE

JOHN B. REID: NOT-SO-DOUR DOER

John B. Reid as seen by
Sydney Morning Herald –
cartoonist Colquhoun.

John Boyd Reid, who became Chairman of the Hardie Group when his father retired in 1974, has attracted a steady stream of media attention in his business and public roles.

One business periodical writer described him as 'the dour doer', a straight-backed, Presbyterian Scot, whose principles have been bred into him over generations. Those who know him will say the writer concerned was more fascinated with the play on words than on the real truth of the matter. One who looked up 'dour' in a dictionary found it defined as 'severe, stern, obstinate' and he is certainly none of these.

His colleagues talk of his strength, intelligence, charm, courtesy, consideration and cast-iron integrity. His primary interest in life is work, they say. He is widely seen as being very decisive. His advisers point to the Reed acquisition and the speed and efficiency that made the Reed empire part of the Hardie empire. After a period of negotiations, the deal, documents and all, was finally completed in three days.

'He refuses to compromise on ethical questions,' one Reid admirer was quoted as saying. 'He's totally predictable where principles are involved.' Principles, the same journalist said, had led in 1978 to Reid's resignation as Chairman and as a Director of Mercantile Credits Limited, a position he was the third generation Reid to occupy. In 1978 National Mutual Life Association of Australia managed to acquire 57.8 per cent of Mercantile Credits. It was soon subject to such strong criticism from the press, the Australian Shareholders' Association and Mercantile Credits directors, for not extending its offer to minority shareholders, that it agreed to reduce its holding to 49 per cent. But seven months later, when it had still not done so, Reid resigned rather pointedly, saying directors could not continue in that role unless they were wholeheartedly in accord and able to work harmoniously with principal shareholders.

Reid can be outspoken in a way that seems to contradict his dour image. In 1985, when he was Chairman of Pymble Ladies College on Sydney's Upper North Shore, he said of the government school system that it was 'an intellectual desert'. 'When we recruit young people to our businesses,' he said, 'we have to teach them again how to read, how to write and how to do simple arithmetic.'

Rod Cavalier, the New South Wales Minister for Education, called Reid 'ignorant'. The Chairman of the State's Education Commission, Dr Ralph Rawlinson, said Reid's comments were 'ill-informed and ill-founded', revealed an 'ignorance of education, psychology and geography' and were motivated by an

uninhibited desire to say something sensational to catch media attention. Bob Brown, Federal Member for Charlton and a former teacher, asked Prime Minister Hawke by telegram to remove Reid from the position he then held as Chairman of Australia's Bicentennial Authority. Reid's 'impertinent remarks', he said, were 'grossly offensive to the majority of government schools and teachers'.

In 1982 Federal Opposition Leader Bill Hayden attacked Reid for his alleged participation in bottom-of-the-harbour tax evasion schemes. This came at a time when Reid was appointed to head a Fraser Government enquiry into the public service. Hayden identified Reid with companies sold in 1977 to directors linked with bottom-of-the-harbour promoter Brian Maher. Reid authorised tax commissioner Bill O'Reilly to investigate his business affairs and provide the government with any relevant information. He also issued a statement that said he bitterly resented the unfair and unfounded attack.

Next day, Treasurer John Howard released a letter from O'Reilly that cleared Reid of all Hayden's allegations, but Hayden would not give up, and called for a public enquiry into the sale of the companies concerned. Further information showed that Reid had never had any beneficial interest in the companies and had in no way benefited personally from their sale. He had at one time been a director of Avis, and a trustee for the estate of Eric McIlree, who set up Avis in Australia.

John B. Reid presides over a James Hardie Industries Limited board meeting in 1986. From left, clockwise around the table: W. A. Butterss, J. K. Roberts, D. G. A. Say, J. B. Reid, D. K. Macfarlane, R. J. Wilson, F. D. Loneragan, R. H. Davenport, A. T. Reid, H. A. Hudson, C. J. Brookes.

JOHN B. REID

Outside the James Hardie Group, John B. Reid is a Director of The Broken Hill Proprietary Company Limited, of Bell Resources Limited, and of Abacus Pacific N.V. He was a Director of Qantas Airways Limited 1976–1986 and Vice-Chairman 1981–1986. He is Patron of the Australia Indonesia Business Cooperation Committee (of which he was Foundation President 1971–75), and a Member of the Australia-Japan Business Cooperation Committee.

He is also a Director of World Expo 88, a Member of the International Advisory Board of the Swiss Banking Corporation, an International Counsellor of the United States Conference Board and of the Stanford Research Institute. The Australian Institute of Management awarded him the Sir John Storey Medal in 1986.

In community service roles, John B. Reid is Governor of the Ian Clunies Ross Memorial Foundation, a Member of the Sydney Advisory Committee of the Salvation Army and on its Red Shield Appeal Committee, National Establishment Chairman of the Australian Girl Guides Foundation Limited, and Director of the Institute of Respiratory Medicine. A member of the Council of Pymble Ladies College since 1965, he was Chairman 1975–1982.

John B. Reid has also served the Australian Government as Chairman of the Australian Bicentennial Authority 1979–85, Chairman of the Review of Commonwealth Administration 1982–83, a Member of the Administrative Review Committee 1975–76, and a Member of the Independent Inquiry into Commonwealth Serum Laboratories 1978.

When a Sydney radio station ran a phone-in poll on the issue, callers supported Reid two to one.

In an interview with the *Sydney Morning Herald* Reid said the Hawke Government was the 'best formally educated government we have ever had ... probably the greatest collection of talent that has ever been put together in Canberra'. This was shown by a lot of things they were doing, including their excellent economic performance. Reid was smart enough to see there was no benefit to him, to Hardie shareholders or to Hardie employees in talking down the economy, a practice he saw as being rather too rampant at the time.

It was highly irresponsible, he said, for media people to grab at statistics in search of portents of gloom. There was a risk of that sort of prophecy, particularly by a major newspaper, becoming self-fulfilling. It was not a matter of suppressing information, but of recognising that the economic facts were often rather murky. He spoke of the way the Hawke Government had created a climate of reason, of consensus, of restraint.

Too many people, including some senior business executives, were overly concerned with reducing the government's budget deficit. It was more important for it to formulate longer-term economic guidelines. Only when this was done would official efforts to encourage business (by such means as tax reform, accelerated depreciation and export incentives) make a real contribution to reinforcing the economy.

Arguing about what was going to happen in any one year was almost irrelevant. The key need was for policies to be thought through and be predictable for at least three years. Introducing accelerated depreciation, for instance, then suddenly changing the rules a year or so later, could achieve little. For the government to overcome this by laying down the ground rules for, say, three years, as quite a few western democracies do, would be a major step forward.

The success of the BHP accord was clear evidence of what could be done, Reid said. Productivity at Australia's steel mills was increasing in real terms. That clearly demonstrated that Australian workers were as good as those to be found anywhere. Their popular image of being lazy and not interested in their jobs was plainly just not true.

'Where you have production people who are properly led, you get superb production results. Leading properly means managers who go to the trouble to explain what the company is doing and why it is important to do it well.'

CHAPTER FIFTY

PAPER AND PACKAGING PROSPER

The paper and packaging activities James Hardie acquired as part of Reed Consolidated Industries were destined to become a major part of the Group's activities. They included the long-established paper merchants, Spicers, whose Tudor brand encompassed office, school and household stationery, including envelopes. Among other products were fibreboard cartons, Blowpak plastic bottles and Queen's Slipper playing cards.

From the time of the Reed acquisition, paper merchanting and envelope activities contributed strongly to profits. Paper sales improved with the development of additional supply sources. Improved and expanded stationery manufacturing plant helped the Group become Australia's top producer of envelopes. Plastic packaging benefited from continued investment.

The Group's container activity had plants in Queensland, New South Wales, Victoria and South Australia. The New South Wales plant, at Waterloo, was modernised and re-equipped in 1978; so too was the plant of its South Australian joint venture, Fibreboard Containers. The Victorian joint venture, Corrugated Fibre Containers Pty Limited, found marketing conditions difficult, as did the wholly-owned modern container factory at Strathpine in Queensland. Intense price cutting in both states reduced profitability.

The Reed stationery manufacturing business in New Zealand, Alex Cowan, had a moderately successful year as it became part of the James Hardie Group. There was scope for selective expansion in that difficult market, according to the 1978-79 Annual Report.

Paper merchanting and flexible packaging continued to do well in 1979-80, but the corrugated container companies faced intense competition. The acquisition of Brisbane envelope maker Besley & Pike helped ensure the Group's continued status as Australia's largest envelope manufacturer.

To overcome the problems in its corrugated cardboard container businesses, the Group in 1980 acquired J. Fielding Holdings Limited. That business together with the container businesses acquired from Reed in 1978 were combined with the fibre container businesses of Australian Paper Manufacturers Limited to form a major container company, James Hardie Containers Limited, of which the Group owned 60 per cent. This move gave a considerably expanded market share and enabled an overdue restructuring of the industry in Queensland, South Australia and Victoria. Some plants were closed.

In its flexible packaging operations, the Group relocated its Victorian plants, and this led to write-offs. It expected to maintain and improve its range of existing products and to introduce new flexible packaging techniques to the Australian

Inspecting a copy of the *Manly Daily,* printed on Crofton newsprint supplied by James Hardie Spicers.

market as a result of the link it had established with UCB s.a., a leading chemical, pharmaceutical and packaging company based in Belgium, which would provide advanced technical expertise.

The UCB connection led to the formation in 1981 of a 78 per cent controlled subsidiary, Colin Martyn Packaging Pty Ltd, to operate in flexible packaging. This continued the Colin Martyn business that came into the Group with the Reed acquisition. During 1981 the Group acquired Rockware Plastics (Australia) Limited, whose range of flexible bottles and packages complemented that of Blowpak Pty Limited. The enlarged company won exclusive rights to Combitube, a new type of laminated tube for toothpastes, cosmetics and condiments, which it put on sale in Australia in 1983.

Development of the Paper and Packaging Division by acquisition continued in 1982-83, with the purchase of the plastic film converting company Protopak and the packaging firm Corrugated Paper, both in New South Wales. Spicers had another successful year, with excellent sales growth. Weaknesses in consumer demand and cheap imported stationery from Asia and New Zealand caused some problems for the Group's envelope, exercise book and writing pad business.

By 1983, when *The Name Behind the Names* was published, paper and packaging had become one of the largest operations in James Hardie Industries.

It employed over 3100 people and had annual sales of more than $330 million. Its range of products included corrugated cardboard containers, specialist food wrapping and packaging, envelopes and other stationery, playing cards and plastic containers such as shampoo bottles. Its Western Australia based operation, Paradar, included plastic cattle tags amongst its product range, along with specialist telex and other paper rolls.

Spicers were Australia's largest importer of fine papers, writing and magazine papers, buying from Europe, the United States, Japan and Brazil and trading through a branch network throughout the continent. Its business had expanded considerably since it had become part of James Hardie Industries. It made direct sales to large paper users on a contract basis, and supplied other customers from its own stocks. Spicer stationery was well established in every state. James Hardie Spicers sales exceeded $100 million for the first time in 1984-85, as it continued to enlarge its market share.

In the Group's ninety-ninth year, 1986-87, James Hardie Spicer enjoyed very strong sales growth across its entire product range and this led to an excellent profit. In a market in which local paper mills were unable to meet demand, the international sourcing strengths of James Hardie Spicers played a major role in fulfilling the Australian demand for fine printing and writing papers. There had been some industry rationalisation in fine paper distribution and this too had benefited James Hardie Spicers. It was able to increase its market share significantly, notably in the fast growing coated paper market, and in the more specialised areas that demanded higher quality graphic papers.

Results from the Group's stationery manufacturing businesses were good. So too was the outlook. Major investments in new plant had been completed, and attention was turning to increased market share and product innovation.

By 1987 paper and packaging had become so important to James Hardie Industries Limited that Managing Director David Macfarlane would call Paper Merchanting and Converting one of the Group's 'core activities', along with Building Products and Technology and Services. It had also acquired substantial paper intersts in North America, which we discuss in a later chapter.

CHAPTER FIFTY-ONE

A START TO DIVESTMENT

By 1986, the Group no longer found it acceptable to wait patiently for a turnaround of operations not contributing adequately to profits. The business climate had changed, both in Australia and internationally, and this had a bearing on management's attitude to low-return businesses.

James Hardie Industries Limited was now a changing company in a changing world. The economy was one in which fluctuations occurred more often and more rapidly. Business cycles were shorter and less predictable, making planning harder and the need to be flexible and very adaptable all the more important.

The decision to sell the Indonesian operations was made with those conditions very much in mind. Having recovered from the effects of the devaluation of the rupiah, and helped by rising oil prices, the Indonesian economy for a time had grown, and with it the fortunes of the Hardie fibre cement business. Profits earned by the two Indonesian companies were good in 1980-81 and 1981-82. After that, however, they fell to quite unacceptable levels.

Cardboard containers come off the production line at James Hardie Containers, Brooklyn, Victoria. In 1986 the Group sold its share of James Hardie Containers to Amcor for $65 million which included a capital profit of $37 million.

More important was the Board's view that the Indonesian economy would not recover and profitability would not be restored in a reasonably short time. In August 1985, it therefore sold its 75 per cent interest in the Indonesian operations, incurring the largest single write-off in the company's history. The buyer was P.T. Bakri and Brothers, an Indonesian company, which entered into a technology agreement with the James Hardie Group. The extraordinary loss of $22 350 000 this involved was taken into the 1985-86 accounts.

In 1986 the Group also sold its interest in James Hardie Containers Limited. This company was profitable and had been a good contributor to Group results for some time. Major changes were, however, about to take place in the cardboard box industry. It was poised to integrate vertically into pulp- and paper-making, providing its own materials. The Group's partner, Amcor Limited (formerly Australian Paper Manufacturers Limited), was already a major producer.

Since the field was one in which Hardies did not wish to become more deeply involved, the sensible course seemed to be to sell their share of James Hardie Containers to Amcor. The $65 million received included a capital profit of some $37 million, and enabled a substantial reduction in group borrowings.

During 1986, the Group also sold Renhurst Industries and its investment in the Hooker Corporation. Flexible Packaging operations had a difficult year, and several of the units were closed or sold. Textile marketing activity that had been part of Hardie Trading Limited was sold to a company owned and managed by previous employees, as part of a program to withdraw from this market.

Pets International, of which the Group had owned 90 per cent since the Reed acquisition, was sold early in 1986 to a consortium led by that company's Managing Director, Alan Whelpton, who owned the remaining 10 per cent. In its last year as a James Hardie subsidiary, Pets International contributed soundly to profit, which gave it a good basis for conversion to a franchise operation.

A shipment of goldfish arriving in Sydney from Singapore for Pets International. Part of the Hardie Group since the Reed acquisition in 1978, this company was sold in 1986.

CHAPTER FIFTY-TWO

EXPANDING OPPORTUNITIES
IN NORTH AMERICA

Bill Butterss who joined Hardie Trading in 1948 was Managing Director of Spartan Paints and later became Managing Director of Hardie Trading, succeeding George Jackson. He was a member and later Chairman of the Council of Haileybury College, Brighton and a member of the Health Insurance Commission. He became a Director of James Hardie Industries Limited in 1980 and is President of James Hardie Industries USA Inc., based in California.

I in the mid 1980s, James Hardie Industries Limited began to develop activities in North America, staying within the three areas that had by then developed into its core businesses: Building Products, Paper Merchanting and Converting, and Technology and Services.

It moved into the building products market by exporting 'fiber' cement products from Australia and New Zealand to the West Coast of the United States, with a view to manufacturing there in the not-too-distant future. One product designed for the United States market was Hardishake woodgrain roofing shakes (shingles), made to a style very similar to the Californian redwood shakes so popular in the area. Hardishake had such added advantages as being Class A fire rated when properly installed according to the Hardie instruction manual and being immune to attack by termites, insects and vermin. Other products introduced to the United States include Hardiflex, Hardiplank, and Hardipanel.

Acceptance of Hardishakes was so encouraging, and the company so confident that other fibre cement products would be accepted by the market, that it soon decided to hold its own stocks there, as a prelude to local manufacture. By mid-1987, it had well-advanced plans to build a fibre cement building products plant at Fontana, near Los Angeles. Its products had been certified for a large number of applications by ICBO Evaluation Service Inc., a major building systems appraisal organisation in the United States.

To further its move into the United States building materials market, the Company in June 1987 in separate deals acquired two gypsum wallboard manufacturing businesses, at a cost of about $A100 million ($US71.5 million). The larger of the two firms acquired had a quarry and gypsum manufacturing plant in Nevada, a distribution centre in Los Angeles, and a marketing and distribution organisation in southern California, Arizona and Nevada. The other was a gypsum wallboard manufacturing business in Washington state, which supplied markets in the north-western region of the United States.

The purchase of the two businesses was a major thrust by the company into the United States building materials sector, giving access to internal wallboard markets in the strongly growing western and south-western regions. Both were trading profitably and were expected to make a significant contribution to group sales and profits from the time of acquisition. They would also provide a valuable marketing base for the development of the Company's fibre cement building products in a market that showed major potential for the sale and eventual manufacture of fibre cement roofing shingles, exterior and interior wall cladding and other products.

As a first step in setting up a paper-merchanting network throughout the West Coast of the United States, Hardies in April 1985 acquired the Oregon-based paper-broking operation of Worldwide Paper Factors, a name it soon changed to Paper Products Marketing. A year later, in April 1986, the Group acquired a publicly-quoted United States fine-paper trading company, Nolex Corporation, of California, which traded as Noland Paper Company. Another year later, in April 1987, it acquired La Salle Paper Company, a leading distributor of fine printing and writing papers, with markets throughout southern California and Nevada.

These moves gave the Group a significant paper distributor network on the West Coast of the United States, where its paper operations got off to a good start. In the year to 31 March 1987 Paper Products Marketing benefited from improved market opportunities in paper broking. This, allied with a weaker United States dollar, opened up favourable export opportunities. In the same period, Noland Paper Company sales and profits both met pre-acquisition forecasts. Although the demand for fine paper was down in California, Noland was able to strengthen its overall market position. Its range had been expanded in the printing paper section, a move that would enhance its already strong position in the industrial market.

In its technology and services sector, the Group in 1986 joined with Berkeley Technology to incorporate JHI Berkeley Development Capital Limited as a vehicle for direct investment in small United States companies with high growth potential. Berkeley Technology was already a highly successful provider of development finance in such high-technology fields as computers, communications and medical diagnostic equipment. New products and processes emerging from these companies promised to become important elements of James Hardie's businesses from 1990 on.

Experience gained in the United States was likely to be both rapid and valuable, John B. Reid said in his Chairman's Review for the year to 31 March 1986. The benefit to Australia in the short to medium term would be through profits earned by JHI Berkeley, through marrying Australian inventiveness and new technology to established United States businesses, and vice versa, and by adapting Australian and United States technologies to the needs of the Western Pacific region.

In 1986, John Roberts, a Director of James Hardie Industries Limited, who had been with the Company thirty-three years, moved to Los Angeles as President of James Hardie Industries (USA) Inc. to take charge of its United States investments and to seek new investment opportunities. His experience had been in the building materials side of the Group's business, including its overseas operations in Malaysia and Indonesia. He had for some time lived in Singapore, supervising the Group's investments in the area. One of his early tasks in the United States would be to develop relationships between the companies in which JHI Berkeley had invested and the Group's operations in Australia. He had only been in the United States for a few months when, on 30 August 1986, he died unexpectedly.

His place was taken by Bill Butterss, another James Hardie Industries Limited Director, who had been with Hardies for nearly forty years. He joined Hardie Trading in Melbourne in 1948. His experience with Hardie Trading had a major manufacturing component, for he had for some time been Managing Director of its Spartan Paints subsidiary. He was Managing Director of Hardie Trading Limited when it became a full subsidiary of James Hardie Industries, in 1980. At that stage he became a Director of the parent company.

Hardiplank Lap Siding is made in Australia for the United States market in three finishes: Smooth (top), Woodgrain (centre) and Crosscut (bottom).

The JHI Berkeley Development Capital Limited portfolio was managed by Berkeley Govett & Company Limited, a company quoted on the London Stock Exchange. In May 1987 its founder, Arthur Trueger, who was Chairman and Chief Executive, became a Director of James Hardie Industries Limited, which owned about 20 per cent of Berkeley Govett. Hardies' Managing Director, David Macfarlane, became a Director of Berkeley Govett.

The Group's investment in Berkeley, which cost $65.7 million, had a market value at 31 March 1987 of $85.8 million. JHI Berkeley had invested in ten technology-based United States companies, at a total cost of about $US30 million. In keeping with its prime objective of earning a high financial return, it had sold its investment in one company and part of the investment in another at a profit of 45 per cent on the purchase price.

The Group also had an interest in Wolfensohn Associates, a limited partnership based in New York. It invested in new-technology businesses in their early stages of development, with its prime focus on electronics, computer applications and peripherals, and biotechnology. At 31 March 1987 it had investments in seventeen companies, ranging from 1 per cent to 40 per cent. Several Wolfensohn investments were of special interest to the Hardie Group. In particular, the Hardie-owned Industrial Products Computer Aided Design and medical disposables units had good prospects of developing production relationships with some of the excellent new companies Wolfensohn had identified.

Berkeley and Wolfensohn activities were complementary in two respects. One was that Berkeley operated from a West Coast base, Wolfensohn from an East Coast base, which gave a good coverage of the United States. The other was that Wolfensohn looked out for promising projects in their earliest stages of development, whereas Berkeley generally invested at a much later stage of a company's development, often in the last round of financing before it went public. What the two operations had in common was that they were both expected to provide opportunities of mutual benefit to the Group's businesses in Australia and New Zealand as well as to those in the United States.

In a more direct move into the services sector of the United States market, the group in March 1987 acquired the businesses of All Point Traders Inc., a United States company that markets fire sprinkler systems hardware.

Based in California, Arthur I. Trueger has been a non-executive Director of James Hardie Industries Limited since May 1987. He is the Founder and Executive Chairman of Berkeley Govett and Company Limited. Berkeley Govett manages the Group's invest-ment into west coast companies involved in new technologies and services, with a view to development in the Group's second century of operations.

Hardishake Woodgrain Roofing, which resembles the timber shakes popular in the United States, was developed specifically for the American market. It is made by modern fibre cement technology processes developed and patented in Australia by Hardies.

CHAPTER FIFTY-THREE

APPROACHING A SECOND CENTURY

As James Hardie Industries Limited prepared to enter its second century of business, it was one of Australia's largest industrial companies. Its sales had passed $1500 million in the year to 31 March 1986, then dropped slightly below that figure the next year in line with a rationalisation policy that lifted profit by more than 25 per cent in one year.

Since the Reed acquisition in 1978 the Group had developed and rationalised its many component businesses into three areas: Building Products, Paper Merchanting and Converting, and Technology and Services. It had plants, distribution centres and offices in every Australian state, New Zealand, South East Asia, the United States, Europe and the Middle East. Its assets were distributed 66.0 per cent in Australia, 19.8 per cent in the United States, 10.5 per cent in New Zealand, and 3.7 per cent elsewhere.

Building products had long been Hardies' traditional field, from an unintentional start in 1903, when James Hardie arrived back from a business trip to Britain bearing a case of samples of European-made 'fibro-ciment'.

By 1988, that small start had led to a product list that included fibre cement building materials (cladding, roofing, lining), pipeline systems, a wide range of ceramic and plastic bathroom products, taps, plastic pipeline systems and wall cladding, rangehoods, interior decorating fabrics, wall coverings and floorings, hot water systems (solar, electric, gas), water treatment units, adhesives and sealants, and irrigation equipment (both agricultural and home garden). Building products provided 62.3 per cent of the Group's profits, accounted for 38.7 per cent of its sales, and employed 42.0 per cent of its assets.

The Group was still thrusting forward in fibre cement building products, a field in which it had been Australia's leading manufacturer for seventy years, and virtually sole manufacturer since it had acquired the Wunderlich fibre cement operation in 1977. New products introduced in 1986-1987 included a range of panels for suspended grid ceilings in commercial applications, particularly where products prone to moisture damage were not suitable. Another was Colorbord factory coated planks and eaves sheets, which were winning increasing acceptance in the house re-cladding market. Still another was Rusticated Weatherboard, with a unique concealed jointing system, which had also been well accepted.

A vigorous development program, aimed at providing new lines to extend the range of fibre cement products and replace those that had run their course, was in progress. Group promotion was still based on the composite construction concept, in which fibre cement took its place amongst other building materials in

Computerised drafting systems were among the advanced technological products marketed by the Group as it approached its second century.

house construction. A competition run through the *Australian Women's Weekly* during the year attracted more than 50 000 entries, and resulted in many builders specifying the use of fibre cement products in their home designs.

Recent development of the Group's range of bathroom products included new products from existing Group companies, and acquisitions in Australia and New Zealand. Among them were the Congress range of architectural vitreous china products and the up-market Euro designer vanity cabinets and Heritage taps, all of which had been well received. New Jacuzzi products were also under development. Acquisition of the Crane Plumbers Brassware Manufacturing Division added the Crane range of tapware, bathroom and kitchen accessories and plumbing fittings to the Group's Irwell range. This significantly increased its share of the middle to high quality tap market, and gave it about 30 per cent of the total tap market. Acquisition of McSkimming Industries Limited, the only New Zealand based sanitary ware manufacturer, enabled some trans-Tasman rationalisations. This, and the Closer Economic Relationship arrangements between Australia and New Zealand, led to the sale of New Zealand-produced acrylic spa baths in Australia and of Australian-made Fowler baths in New Zealand.

The Group increased its penetration of the hot water system market in Australia with the acquisition of the Braemar hot water business, and the purchase from the Shell Company of Australia Limited of the half share of S.W. Hart & Co. Pty Limited it did not already own. These moves gave the Group a full range of solar, electric and gas hot water appliances. Solar hot water systems sold well in export markets in the Pacific area, particularly in Japan, where Solahart products were among the few Australian products certified under the Japanese industrial standard.

In paper merchanting, James Hardie Spicers was the largest independent operation of its kind in Australia. Three paper merchanting operations acquired in the United States in the previous three years had given the Group a significant presence in the paper business there. The Group's overseas paper operations also included Alex Cowan, a major envelope maker in New Zealand, where new plant had recently boosted operating efficiency, and Besley & Pike Singapore, a specialist high quality envelope producer.

In paper conversion, the Group made more envelopes than any other Australian company. It also made office and educational stationery that was sold throughout the Pacific basin. Paper merchanting and converting provided 18.7 per cent of the Group's profits, accounted for 32.5 per cent of its sales, and employed 18.9 per cent of its assets.

The Group's technology and services activities included building services in Australia, New Zealand and the United States, health care, technology manufacturing activities, general trading in Australia and New Zealand, and irrigation. Technology and services provided 11.8 per cent of the Group's profits, accounted for 28.8 per cent of its sales, and employed 18.7 per cent of its assets.

Fire protection, air conditioning and security, the three main operations of building services, all turned in good results in the year to 31 March 1987, despite high interest rates that tended to dampen commercial building activity. Government sponsored projects, notably in New South Wales for the forthcoming Bicentennial celebration and works associated with the Darling Harbour project, helped to offset the reduced commercial activity. Major redevelopments of valuable existing

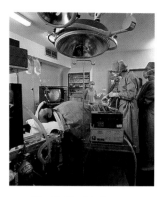

Hardie Health Care supplied the caps, gowns, masks, shoe covers and patient drapes for use in this operation at a Sydney Hospital.

TWO CENTENARY GIFTS

As part of the Group's centenary celebrations, James Hardie interests presented two gifts to the people of Australia: the James Hardie Library of Australian Fine Arts to the State Library of Queensland, and the Thyne Reid Collection of Australian children's books and childhood memorabilia to the National Trust in New South Wales.

The James Hardie Library of Australian Fine Arts was established in 1980, when the Chairman, John B. Reid, learned from publisher Kevin Weldon of the forthcoming sale of the private collection of road transport operator Pat Corrigan, who was an avid collector of books about Australian art, as well as of Australian art itself. With the Group now one of Australia's largest publishers, it seemed appropriate to acquire, preserve and develop the collection in Australia.

The Library has developed into one of the world's most comprehensive collections of source material related to the history of Australian art. Of its 10,000 items, about 60 per cent are classed as 'ephemera', including art exhibition catalogues from 1849 to the present day. Such catalogues are a major source of information about Australian artists and their work.

When it became known that the Group had decided to present the Library to the people of Australia, nineteen state and university libraries lodged submissions on how they would house and manage it. The most enthusiastic and attractive submission was from the State Library of Queensland, which offered to build a special section for the collection within the Arts Centre on the south bank of the Brisbane River. The section would be designed by noted Queensland architect Robin Gibson, who also designed the Arts Centre.

The Thyne Reid Collection of Australian children's books and childhood memorabilia began with the purchase, in 1982, of about 600 books collected by antiquarian book dealer Anne McCormick. The Thyne Reid Trust, established by Thyne Reid to support educational causes in Australia, bought the collection to ensure that it stayed in Australia.

The original collection included the first children's book published in Australia, *A Mother's Offering to Her Children* by Charlotte Barton, published in 1841 by the *Sydney Gazette*. Another item of note was the first edition of *The Way of the Whirlwind* by Mary and Elizabeth Durack, published in 1941 by Consolidated Press.

With John B. Reid's enthusiasm and under Robert Holden's care, this collection has also been built up, from 600 to 4000 items. By the time it was handed over to the National Trust, it included first editions of books illustrated and in some cases also written by May Gibbs, Ida Rentoul Outhwaite, Dorothy Wall, the Lindsays and Pixie O'Harris, and such items as calendars, handkerchiefs, posters, school texts, advertising brochures, greeting cards and posters illustrated by these famous Australian artists.

Among the classics represented in the collection are May Gibbs's *Gumnut Babies* series and *Tales of Snugglepot and Cuddlepie*, Ethel Turner's *Seven Little Australians*, Norman Lindsay's *The Magic Pudding*, Ethel Pedley's *Dot and the Kangaroo* and Mary Grant Bruce's *Billabong* series.

Among items of memorabilia other than books is a collection of board games (including Around the Commonwealth by Air, produced in the 1920s), rocking horses, a toy train big enough to ride on, a tricycle and various other toys.

As Australia's first Museum of Childhood, the collection is on permanent display at the restored Juniper Hall, the Paddington mansion built in 1824 by gin manufacturer Robert Cooper and renovated at a cost of $3 million in 1987.

From the James Hardie Library of Australian Fine Arts is the titlepage to A. B. Paterson's Song of the Wheat, *a hand illumination by Gordon Dalrymple Nicol, Sydney, 1923.*

buildings also generated work. Electrical contracting activities had also made good contributions, and were becoming more and more an integral part of the Building Services Division's overall strategy of offering developers a complete mechanical and electrical package.

Building services were also doing well in New Zealand. Engaged at first only in fire sprinkler systems, the operation there had widened its activities to include all types of fire detection and suppression. It had good prospects for further expansion into building services in the United States with the acquisition in March 1987 of All Points Traders Inc., a marketer of fire systems hardware.

In irrigation, the Group had been moving steadily towards domestic applications since 1983, when it had acquired the Pope garden watering accessory operation, a move reinforced in 1986 with the acquisition of Dawn Plastics, a garden hose manufacturer. The same strategy was being repeated in the international market and was proving to be just as effective. Small irrigation operations in Europe, the Middle East and the Guandong province of China had encouraging potential for the longer term.

General trading and industrial machinery business in Australia, which relied on imports, had been rationalised to adapt to the new market conditions brought about by the twin effects of increased import costs and the withdrawal of the investment allowance, both of which had reduced the demand for machinery. The business was operating satisfactorily on a reduced capital base. In New Zealand, on the other hand, considerable growth had occurred in laundry, textiles and printing equipment supply. Development of a customs clearance and freight forwarding businesses had been a feature of the year just concluded.

As well as the businesses it owned outright, James Hardie Industries Limited had major investments in several companies and a changing portfolio of shares (both ordinary and preference) as well as leveraged leases and zero coupon bonds. The Group's investments employed 20.4 per cent of its assets, and provided 7.2 per cent of its profits. They did, however, have considerable scope for future development.

As James Hardie Industries Limited approached its second century, its 17 822 shareholders enjoyed a dividend increase of two cents per share, bringing it to twenty-four cents, for the year to 31 March 1987. They also enjoyed a two-for-five bonus issue, based on capitalising $66 796 000 of the assets revaluation reserve.

At 31 March 1987, the Group had assets of $1488 million and liabilities of $939 million. If James Hardie had lived to see that, would his nights have been any less hideous for want of sleep than they were in 1908, when the 'overdraft had mounted up to £2800'?

Pipes have long been an important part of Hardies' operations, and in 1984 a new plant was commissioned at Rosehill in New South Wales to make Hobas centrifugally cast, fibreglass-reinforced cement pressure and sewer pipes. The process is carried out under licence from Hobas Engineering AG, a Swiss company. Made in diameters from 450 mm to 2400 mm, Hobas pipes are highly acclaimed in Europe and well accepted in Australia.

APPENDIX 1

James Hardie Industries Limited
Directors and Secretaries
Since incorporation – 23 June 1920

DIRECTORS

Andrew Reid	1920-1939
William Williamson	1920-1920
George Rogers Sutton	1920-1963
Stewart Walter D'Arrietta	1920-1963
R. O. Law	1920-1929
C. P. Truman	1926-1949
Andrew Thyne Reid	1930-1964
Donald Chisholm Cameron	1938-1964
John Thyne Reid	1939-1973
John Thyne Adamson	1950-1971
Frank Ainslie Page	1958-1979
Ashby Arthur William Hooper	1961-1967
Archibald Campbell McDougall	1963-1972
Alan Duncan Woodford	1966-1977
Edward Joseph Heath	1969-1978
Solomon Eric Cohen	1972-1980
Athol Patrick Higgins	1975-1983
John Kevin Roberts	1979-1986
John Alan Napier	1981-1986
John Boyd Reid	1964-
Alexander Thyne Reid	1973-
David Kennedy Macfarlane	1975-
Frederick Desmond Loneragan	1975-
Harry Arnold Hudson	1978-
Keith Hand Davenport	1979-
David Giles Ashworth Say	1980
William Andrew Butterss	1980-
Cyril James Brookes	1981-
Arthur Irwin Trueger	1987-

SECRETARIES

Donald Chisholm Cameron	1920-1955
William Allen Bennett	1955-1962
Donald Cedric Walker	1962-1970
Rex Owen Banks	1970-1980
Richard Walton Hardie	1980-1982
Rodney John Wilson	1982-

APPENDIX 2

James Hardie Industries Limited
Main acquisitions since 23 June 1951, when listed on the stock exchange

1956
Asbestolite Pty Ltd
Asbestos Cement Pty Limited
1959
Better Brakes Holdings Limited
1961
Hardie-Ferodo Pty Limited (60%)
1964
UAC Berhad (interest acquired)
Wunderlich Humes Asbestos Pipes Pty
  Limited
1969
Hardie Holdings Limited
Independent Brokers & Contractors Pty
  Limited
Montpelier Foundry Pty Limited
1970
Hardie Extrusions Pty Limited
Isotex Industries Pty Limited
Utility Castings Limited (NZ)
1976
System-Built Pty Limited
1977
Lee & Wilson Limited (NZ)
Wunderlich Fibre Cement Operations
1978
Reed Consolidated Industries Limited
1979
Besley & Pike Holdings Limited
Fowler Ware Business
Rigby Limited
1980
Don Brake Linings Pty Limited
Hardie-Ferodo Pty Limited (remaining 40%)
1981
Collin Martyn Packaging Pty Limited
Hardie Trading Limited (77.4% not already
  owned)
J. Fielding Holdings Limited
James Hardie Containers Limited
James Hardie Impey Limited (NZ) (71.75%)
K.G.C. Magnetic Tapes Pty Limited
Raybestos – Australian Friction Materials
  Business
Robinhood Industries Pty Limited
1982
Antel Pty Limited
Medical Plastics Pty Limited
Merehurst Limited (UK)
Protopak Pty Limited
Rainspray Sprinklers Pty Limited
Rockware Plastics Pty Limited
1983
Diemoulders Pty Limited

Fire Fighting Enterprises Limited
G.W. Robinson & Co Pty Limited
Irwell Industries Pty Limited
RIS Iberia SA (the 50% remaining after the
  Reed acquisition)
Taft Hardie Group Pty Limited (formed)
Transparent Sheet (A/Asia) Pty Limited
1984
Access Control Systems Limited
Chemline Pty Limited
Colonial Fire Places Pty Limited
Fire & Safety Products A/Asia Pty Limited
Fitek Engineering Pte Limited
Harflex Insurance Pte Limited
HRM Inc (USA)
Jas Robertson Limited (NZ)
Jennings Plastics
Knox Schlapp Pty Limited
Noel Products Limited (NZ)
NSD (Australia) Pty Limited
Pope Irrigation and Garden Products
  Division
Safe-T-Lawn (USA)
S. W. Hart & Co Pty Limited (50%)
1985
Environ Mechanical Services Pty Limited
  (75%)
Finnwad Australia Pty Limited
L.S.E. Manufacturing
Newstate Electrical Pty Limited
Nolex Corporation (USA)
Phoneworld
Weldon-Hardie Pty Limited (formed)
Worldwide Paper Factors Inc (USA)
1986
Airco Service Pty Limited
All Points Trading Inc (Sprink Inc – USA)
Dawn Plastics Pty Limited
Health Care Corporation Pty Limited (50%)
Irridelco (USA)
James Hardie Impey Limited (NZ – remaining
  28.25%)
JHI Berkeley Development Capital Limited
Johns Professional Products
1987
Allibert (Australia) Pty Limited (50%)
Braemar Gas Hot Water Business
Crane Plumbers Brassware Manufacturing
  Business
Gypsum Wallboard Operations of Domtar
  Inc (USA)
La Salle Paper Company (USA)
McSkimming Industries Limited (NZ)
Norwest Gypsum (USA)
S.W. Hart & Co Pty Limited (remaining 50%)
UPEC Plastic Pipe & Fitting Business (NZ)

INDEX